Violent Young Children

Morley D. Glicken

Professor Emeritus
California State University, San Bernardino
and
Executive Director
The Institute for Positive Growth:
A Research, Treatment and Training Cooperative
La Jolla, California

Boston • New York • San Francisco
Mexico City • Montreal • Toronto • London • Madrid • Munich • Paris
Hong Kong • Singapore • Tokyo • Cape Town • Sydney

Series Editor: *Patricia Quinlin*
Editorial Assistant: *Annemarie Kennedy*
Editorial-Production Administrator: *Joe Sweeney*
Editorial-Production Service: *Denise Botelho, Colophon*
Composition Buyer: *Linda Cox*
Manufacturing Buyer: *JoAnne Sweeney*
Cover Administrator: *Kristina Mose-Libon*
Text Composition: *Modern Graphics*

For related titles and support materials, visit our online catalog at www.ablongman.com.

Between the time Website information is gathered and then published, it is not unusual for some sites to have closed. Also, the transcription of URLs can result in typographical errors. The publisher would appreciate notification where these errors occur so that they may be corrected in subsequent editions.

Library of Congress Cataloging-in-Publication Data

Glicken, Morley D.
   Violent young children / by Morley D. Glicken.
     p. cm
   Includes bibliographical references and index.
   ISBN 0-205-38866-3 (alk. paper)
   1. Violence in children.   2. Children and violence.
   3. Conduct disorders in children.   I. Title.

RJ506.V56G56 2004
618.92′8582—dc21

2003050449

Printed in the United States of America

10   9   8   7   6   5   4   3   2   1   RRD-VA   09   08   07   06   05   04   03

This book is dedicated to the wonderful, supportive, and challenging teachers at Belmont Elementary, Central High School, and the University of North Dakota, in Grand Forks. Unlike many children in America who act out their sorrows in the classroom with violent results, my teachers recognized the potential in many of those who seemed troubled and who could have easily become like the children in this book. North Dakota is a model of the positive benefits of public education and an example of the way that dedicated and challenging teachers can positively affect the lives of troubled children. God bless every one of them.

Contents

5 *The Strong Relationship between Child Abuse and Early-Onset Violence* **62**

6 *Sexual Violence by Children* **80**

7 *Treating Violent Children: Clinical Approaches* **98**

11　*Mr. R: An Autobiographical Account of Early Violent Behavior through the Life Cycle*　　**157**

12　*Eliminating Childhood Violence*　　**174**

Preface

Violent young children. Who would have thought it would be necessary to write a book about young children who not only begin committing violent acts before the age of 12, but transition on to very violent behavior as adolescents and young adults? It certainly doesn't please me as a social worker and educator for over 35 years to admit that violent young children represent a serious problem in American life. Violent young children are no longer an anomaly but exist in increasingly large numbers. As this book documents, violent young children commit acts of violence that take a terrible toll on the lives of other children and adults in America. And while some reports suggest that violence has gone down steadily since 1993 and that childhood violence has also decreased, the fact remains that America has far more violent behavior among its children than does any other industrialized country in the world. The homicide rate among preadolescent and adolescent boys in the United States is 10 times higher than in Canada, 15 times higher than in Australia, and 28 times higher than in France or in Germany—data that should impress upon everyone that childhood violence is a terrible problem in the United States.

To complicate matters, there is a huge discrepancy between the number of arrests of violent youth and the actual number of violent crimes committed. According to the U.S. Surgeon General's 2001 Report on Youth Crime, for every crime committed by a youth under the age of 18 resulting in an arrest, nine other violent crimes were committed by juveniles. This dramatic difference between the official arrest rates and the actual amount of crime committed helps give rise to a fear-of-violence index that has gone up 120 percent since 1969. The sad facts are that America is a violent place and young children cause an increasing amount of that violence.

Child crime has not diminished, but our desire to treat child crime as a mental health problem has. Many children under the age of 12 who commit crimes are often not officially involved with juvenile courts. The probability of a child under 12 receiving needed clinical treatment is miniscule. Schools almost never report serious antisocial behavior to the police if the child is age 12 and younger. Bullying, stealing, intimidating, and harassing other children and teachers are behaviors that are all too rampant in U.S schools. So is crime. Most juvenile crime occurs in close proximity to a school.

Because childhood violence is such a serious problem, this book was written to urge helping professionals, school personnel, policy analysts, and, above all, parents to take childhood violence seriously. As is repeatedly noted throughout this book, the younger the onset of violent behavior, the more likely it is to cycle into serious adolescent and adult violence. Half of the children who commit violent acts before the age of 12 go on to commit violence as teenagers and adults. This small cohort is responsible for much of the violent adolescent and adult crime in America. Those of us who work professionally with young children who have committed acts of violence at very young ages should be anxious to provide the best possible diagnostic and treatment assistance to these children. One of the primary reasons that all violent young children don't cycle on to additional violence as adolescents and adults is that they receive needed help, and their behavior modifies and changes. No one should give up on children, and the younger the child, the more hopeful we should be.

Although this is a book about young violent children, it is necessary to discuss children and violence throughout the life cycle. Adolescent and adult violence are discussed as a way of informing the reader that violence may continue on in this young cohort of children if we don't act promptly. And what violence it is: murder, rape, arson, animal mutilation, date and domestic violence, drug- and alcohol-related violence, fire setting, random violence—and one could go on.

For the students and professionals for whom this book is written, the one fact that should prompt all of us to be humane in our thoughts about children who commit violence is that many violent children are the victims of early violence in the form of child abuse. The relationship between child abuse and early-onset violence is so strong, that if we did nothing else to treat violence in the United States, providing children with safe, healthy, and positive environments would go a very long way to reduce violence in America. A child lost to violence because an adult physically, sexually, or emotionally abuses him or her should not happen. As helping professionals, we should make a pledge to end child abuse.

With that in mind, I ask you to read this book, recognizing that although much of it says terrible things about very young children, we need to be mindful that children don't choose to be violent any more than they choose to be disfigured or physically handicapped. Helping professionals can do a great deal to help our violent society become far less violent through early intervention with children who have been the recipients of maltreatment and abuse. A watchful, proactive, and positive approach to young children in need will stop a great deal of violence before it has a chance to rear its ugly head in children who should be enjoying life instead of inflicting pain on others.

This book is written for the hurt, abused, bewildered children of America who need the love and guidance of wise adults to help them through moments of extreme crisis.

Acknowledgments

This book was written because of the concerns I have that violence in young children is increasing. As a social worker, the signs seem clear to me and, as an American, I feel saddened by the violent society in which we live. I approached Allyn and Bacon with the idea for this book and they graciously and quickly agreed to publish it. I want to thank my editor at Allyn and Bacon, Patricia Quinlin, for supporting the publication of this book, and her assistant, Annemarie Kennedy, who has facilitated the processing of everything related to the book. Thanks Pat and Annemarie.

My assistant, Megan Dwyer, has been nothing short of amazing in proofing my chapters and putting my references together, even though my propensity for leaving out vital reference information has not diminished in the three books Megan and I have done together. Thanks also to the fine folks at Central Michigan University who had resources available to authors that make writing a book a good deal easier than it used to be. Thank you to the reviewers for all their suggestions to this book: Rudolph Alexander, Jr., The Ohio State University; Cynthia Crosson-Tower, Harvest Counseling and Consultation; Suman Kukar, Florida International University; and Gerald Landsberg, New York University. Thanks to my daughter, Amy Glicken, for her support, and to her college friend, Renee Bibby, whose work with violent children in Tucson, Arizona gave me the idea for this book. My sister, Gladys Smith, in San Diego, California, is always supportive and our relationship is a good example of how brothers and sisters who fought endlessly with each another as children can become great friends as adults. And finally, I acknowledge my mother and father, Sam and Rose Glicken, who used the dinner table as a forum for every subject imaginable, but particularly for concerns about children. My father was a man ahead of his time, and he predicted a major problem with childhood violence long before it was fashionable to discuss the subject. Unfortunately, he was as right about this issue as he was about many others. Growing up in Russia during the Russian Revolution made him a keen observer of life and gave him the ability to recognize a dramatically changing society. Thanks Mom and Dad. Those long chats at the dinner table had a strong impact on me and influenced this book in many important ways.

About the Author

Dr. Morley Glicken, MSW, MPA, DSW is the former Dean of the Worden School of Social Service in San Antonio, California, the founding director of the Master of Social Work Department at California State University, San Bernardino, the past Director of the Master of Social Work Program at the University of Alabama, and the former Executive Director of Jewish Family Service of Greater Tucson.

Dr. Glicken received his bachelor's degree in Social Work with a minor in Psychology from the University of North Dakota. He holds a master of Social Work degree from the University of Washington, Seattle, and the master of Public Administration and doctor of Social Work degrees from the University of Utah in Salt Lake City, Utah. He is a member of Phi Kappa Phi Honorary Fraternity.

In addition to the two books published with Allyn and Bacon in 2002, *The Role of the Helping Professions in the Treatment of Victims and Perpetrators of Violence* (with Dale Sechrest) and *A Simple Guide to Social Research*, is his forthcoming title, *Using the Strengths Perspective in Social Work Practice: A Positive Approach for the Helping Professions* (Allyn and Bacon, 2004). Dr. Glicken has written over fifty articles for professional journals. He has held clinical social work licenses in Alabama and Kansas and is a member of the Academy of Certified Social Workers. He is currently Professor Emeritus in Social Work at California State University, San Bernardino and Director of the Institute for Positive Growth: A Research, Treatment and Training Cooperative in La Jolla, California. He can be reached online at: mglicken@msn.com.

1

Demographics of Early Violence

This is a book about violence in very young children. It specifically targets children under the age of 12 because so little has been written about this age group. There is strong evidence that many early violence starters are very likely to cycle into serious adolescent and adult perpetrators of violence. Although this population does not commit violence in the almost geometric progression of violence found in adolescents 13 to 20 years of age, the violence they do commit is serious and does damage disproportionate to their numbers. It is all too often the unreported violence of the children who bully and taunt others that so often disrupts learning and creates chaos in the classroom. It is the violence that terrifies us, because it so often appears to be random and pointless.

To help understand the progression of violence through adolescence and into adulthood, the data provided, while focusing on children age 12 and under, also covers adolescents and young adults. Violence among adolescents often begins in childhood as a result of early physical and sexual child abuse and family violence. Many of the children who experience child abuse and family violence have already begun to show the complex signs of future violent behavior, as evidenced in fire setting, sexual abuse, theft, cruelty to animals, and distorted thoughts, which lead to adolescent and adult violence. Although reports of violent crime have gone down from the peak years of 1985 to 1993, the United States is still a very violent society. The beginnings of violence are in childhood, and this book is written with the hope that early detection and treatment of violent behavior will lead to a safer society, one in which all children can grow and prosper.

Violence in Children under Age Eighteen

Trends in juvenile crime are not encouraging. Although overall violent crime decreased after the peak years of 1983 to 1993, the number of juvenile arrests for serious crimes increased (Gramckow & Tompkins, 1999; Bishop, 1997). During this period, juvenile courts experienced disproportionate increases in cases involving violent offenses and weapons. Gramckow and Tompkins (1999) note that cases involving

1

crimes against persons by youth were up almost 100 percent, while the "Violent Crime Index offenses" (a subset of person offenses) were up 98 percent, and weapons law violations were up 156 percent, according to Snyder, Sickmund, and Poe-Yamagata (1996).

Currie (1993) attributes much of the increase in violent juvenile crime to the weakening of traditional socializing institutions of the community—the family, schools, and churches. However, social conditions also have changed. Schools increasingly deal with problems of misbehavior in the classroom. The easy availability of dangerous drugs and guns also has changed the juvenile justice landscape. After a period of relative stability in the rates of violent crime committed by juvenile offenders, the growth in juvenile violence that began in 1985 was accompanied by a steady growth, from 1985 to 1995, in the use of guns by juveniles, "leading to a doubling in the number of juvenile murders committed with guns" (Blumstein, 1995, p. 5). Blumstein attributes the sudden upsurge in juvenile violence to the increased drug trafficking of crack cocaine in the mid-1980s. To service that drug market, "juveniles were recruited, they were armed with guns . . . guns that were diffused into the larger community of juveniles" (p. 6).

Although increases in both adult and juvenile violent crime are cyclical, an overall upward trend occurred during the past 30 years. There is evidence that the intensity of these crimes and their potential for serious injury or death to victims have also increased. Because violent crimes now appear more likely to involve strangers, citizens feel that violent crime is out of their control. These random events occur in schools, at work, and in public places of assembly. Currie (1993) poses the question of what society is to do about this problem, or who should take responsibility. Is it a local, state, or national problem? Who is responsible for prevention efforts? Do solutions go beyond the criminal justice system to the various social agencies that deal with these individuals?

Glicken and Sechrest (2003) note that although only 20 percent of violent crimes are attributed to juveniles, they became noticeably more involved in violent acts in the 1990s. Youth violence is often seen as a problem of youth gangs, which accounted for sharp increases of violence in the late 1990s, but recent random acts of school violence across the country have heightened concern about violence by juveniles in all segments of society. The increased availability of firearms has led to an escalation of physical confrontations, with results ranging from minor injuries to the use of lethal weapons and death. Between 1984 and 1993, the number of juveniles arrested for murder increased 168 percent, and weapons violations rose 126 percent (Fraser, 1996).

Howell and colleagues (1995) report that juvenile violent crime arrests increased by 47 percent from 1988 to 1992, and that juvenile arrests increased by 51 percent for murder, 17 percent for rape, 50 percent for robbery, and 49 percent for aggravated assault (p. 2). Although these rates have decreased since the mid-1990s, they are still 49 percent higher than they were in 1988, and experts predict that youth violence may get worse in the next 10 years because the population of juveniles is projected to increase by 22 percent by 2005 (Fraser, 1996).

It is difficult to predict juvenile violence and crime trends. Part of the problem is the way in which studies that may define violence or crime are differentially conducted, which may confuse comparisons between study findings. Different data collection methods, with variations in the wording of survey questions, may make it difficult to interpret and compare research findings. Methods for the aggregation of survey data and methods of combining crime categories often make it difficult to understand the prevalence of certain types of juvenile crime or violence that are often only applicable to the period of time for which data were gathered.

Specific Violence Data for Children Age Twelve and Under

In data from the Federal Bureau of Investigation's (FBI's) Uniform Crime Reporting Program and the National Juvenile Court Data Archive, Butts and Snyder (1997) show that the 1995 arrest rate for "Violent Crime Index offenses" was 89 per 100,000 for juveniles age 12 and under. For youth ages 13 and 14, the arrest rate was 460 per 100,000, and for older youth, it was an astonishing 979 per 100,000. However, as Butts and Snyder note, arrest rates for juvenile offenders increased disproportionately in recent years. Between 1980 and 1995, the Violent Crime Index rate increased 91 percent for juveniles age 12 and younger, 76 percent for youth ages 13 and 14, and 56 percent for youth age 15 or older. Juvenile court cases involving offenders age 12 or younger increased 32 percent between 1985 and 1994. Juvenile courts in the United States processed 1,555,200 delinquency cases in 1994. This represents a 20 percent increase over the cases processed in 1990 and a 41% increase over the number of cases processed in 1985.

Butts and Snyder (1997) further report that between 1985 and 1994, the number of delinquency cases involving juveniles age 12 or younger grew 32 percent, while delinquency cases (where actual charges were filed) for juveniles ages 13 and 14 increased 49 percent. Cases involving older juveniles grew 39 percent. In all three age groups, offenses against people comprised the most serious increase in charges brought against juvenile offenders between 1985 and 1994. Offenses against people include homicide, rape, robbery, aggravated assault, simple assault, and other violent offenses. In 1994, juveniles age 12 or younger were responsible for 12 percent of all person offense cases, 13 percent of property offense cases, 2 percent of drug law violation cases, 6 percent of public order offense cases (i.e., disorderly conduct, weapons offenses, liquor law violations, etc.), and an astonishing 35 percent of all the arrests for fire setting. The total number of youth arrests grew by 26 percent between 1980 and 1995. Arrests involving children ages 12 or younger grew 24 percent, while those involving juveniles ages 13 and 14 increased by 54 percent (Butts & Snyder, 1997).

Butts and Snyder (1997) also report that there were approximately 148,000 arrests of juveniles for Violent Crime Index offenses in 1995. While Violent Crime Index arrests of older juveniles grew by 47 percent between 1980 and 1995, arrests of juveniles ages 13 and 14 increased by 92 percent, and arrests of juveniles age 12 or younger grew by 102 percent. In 1994, juveniles who were 12 or younger were less likely to have a delinquency petition filed (38 percent) than were youth ages 13 and 14 (52 percent) or older juveniles (59 percent). Although the filing of delinquency petitions increased between 1985 and 1994 for all age groups, the lack of formal filing, particularly among children age 12 and under, suggests serious underreporting of youthful crime and the absence of formal attempts at intervention. Significantly, arrests for weapons possession increased more for children age 12 or younger (206 percent) than for those ages 13 and 14 (167 percent), or older juveniles (93 percent).

Butts and Snyder (1997) conclude their analysis of early childhood violence by noting that it would be inaccurate to suggest that juvenile offenders of today are significantly younger than the offenders of 1983 to 1987. As will be noted throughout this book, other sources suggest just the opposite.

Violent Juvenile Crime Continues to Increase

Commenting on the increase in juvenile crime, Osofsky and Osofsky (2001, p. 287) write,

> Put simply, youth violence in the United States has reached epidemic proportions (Rosenberg and Fenley 1991; Rosenberg, O'Carroll, and Powell 1992). According to the FBI Uniform Crime Reports (Pellegrini, Roundtree, Camagna, and Queirolo 2000), the homicide rate has more than doubled since 1950, with the most recently reported rate being 22 per 100,000 for young people 15–24 years old. To punctuate the meaning of these numbers, it is important to compare this data with that of other similar countries. For example, the homicide rate among males 15–24 years old in the United States is 10 times higher than in Canada, 15 times higher than in Australia, and 28 times higher than in France or Germany (Lester and Yang 1998).

The following data related to the increase in juvenile crime were taken from the FBI's Uniform Crime Reporting Program and the National Juvenile Court Data Archive, which is maintained for the Office of Juvenile Justice and Delinquency Prevention by the National Center for Juvenile Justice, as reported by Butts and Snyder (1997). Findings from their study indicate the following:

- Offenders under age 15 represent the leading edge of the juvenile crime problem, and their numbers have been growing.
- Violent crime arrests grew 94% between 1980 and 1995 for youth under age 15, compared with 47% for older youth.
- The age profile of juvenile offenders has changed somewhat since 1980. Offenders under age 15 accounted for an increased proportion of all juvenile arrests for violent crime in 1995 (30%) compared with 1990 (28%), 1985 (29%), and 1980 (25%), the most significant increases occurring between 1980 and 1985.
- Because offenders under age 15 have a high risk of continued criminal involvement, yet are often more amenable to services and sanctions, juvenile crime

policy should continue to focus on early and effective interventions with these youngest delinquents. (p. 5)

In a postscript to the report, Butts and Synder note that person offenses for children 12 year old and younger have increased from 16 percent to 25 percent. As a result of the increases in all age categories from childhood to young adulthood, delinquency caseloads have doubled nationwide since 1970, and "a judge, prosecutor, or probation officer with 25 years of job experience should expect to see twice as many 12-year-old killers in 1995 as in 1970, simply due to this increased workload" (Butts & Snyder, 1997, p. 10).

Herrenkohl et al. (2001) report that individuals involved in early-onset childhood violence are at a very high risk of committing violent crimes in adolescence and adulthood. The risk for later violent behavior increases the earlier the violence begins. Elliott (1994) found that 45 percent of the children who commit violent offenses by age 11 go on to commit violent offenses in their early 20s. The older the age of onset of violence, the less likely children are to commit violent offenses in adulthood. According to Thornberry, Huizinga, and Loeber (1995), almost twice as many children committing violent acts before the age of 9 commit violent acts in adulthood as compared with children between the ages of 10 and 12.

Kauffman (1997) reports that 80 percent to 90 percent of school-age children and youth, in self-reports, indicate that they have been involved in acts of violence and aggression. A national survey done by Louis Harris for the Harvard University School of Public Health (1993) indicated that 60 percent of the students from sixth through twelfth grade in inner cities, suburbs, and rural areas were easily able to purchase handguns. Thirty-nine percent of the youth who were surveyed said they knew someone who had been killed or wounded by gunfire. In the same poll, over one-third of the students surveyed said that their lives would be shortened because of easy access to guns.

Myles and Simpson (1998) believe that violence among children has increased for the following reasons:

1. There is more violence in society. Children who are exposed to a great degree of violence become desensitized to the meaning and impact of violence.
2. The increased number of violent and seriously disturbed children who are being mainstreamed through regular classrooms has increased school violence at a time when there are decreasing opportunities to place children in residential placements and group homes that might offer a more appropriate experience with less harm to the remaining school-aged children.
3. Many of the violent and emotionally disturbed children currently being mainstreamed in regular classrooms are being taught by teachers who are untrained to work with children who have special social, emotional and educational needs.
4. There are more negative influences in a child's life than ever. This is a result of gang activity, child abuse, family violence, child neglect, and violent neighborhoods that offer few positive role models for children (Kauffman, 1997; Walker, Colvin, & Ramsey, 1995).

Wolfgang (1972, 1987) reports that 6 percent to 7 percent of all boys in a given birth year will become chronic offenders, meaning that they will have five or more arrests before their eighteenth birthdays. He also suggests that these same 6 percent to 7 percent will commit half of all crimes and two-thirds of all violent crimes committed by all the boys born in a given birth year by age 18. Briscoe (1997) notes that Wolfgang's studies have been found accurate by a number of other studies and that increases in the numbers of adolescent males bodes badly, because it increases the number of boys in the 6 to 7 percent category who will become violent perpetrators.

Horowitz (2000) writes that as the number of high profile cases increases,

> so do the thousands of less visible homicides that occur daily in inner cities and in poor, minority neighborhoods. Approximately twenty-three thousand homicides occur each year in the United States, roughly ten percent of which involve a perpetrator who is under eighteen years of age. Between the mid 1980s and the mid 1990s, the number of youths committing homicides had increased by 168%. Juveniles currently account for one in six murder arrests (17%), and the age of those juveniles gets younger and younger every year. For example, in North Carolina in 1997, seventy juveniles under eighteen years of age were arrested on murder charges. Thirty-five were seventeen, twenty-four were sixteen, seven were fifteen, and four were thirteen or fourteen. In 1999, for the first time in North Carolina's history, two eleven-year-old twins were charged with the premeditated murder of their father as well as the attempted murder of their mother and sister. (p. 133)

Horowitz goes on to note that as a result of the increase in violence in America, many Americans are demanding harsher sentences for juveniles. In an opinion poll taken after the 1998 shootings in Jonesboro, Arkansas, in which four students were murdered by two classmates, Horowitz reports that half of the adults in America thought the two killers should receive the death sentence, even though they were only 11 and 13 years of age. Horowitz believes that in this atmosphere of rage against juvenile violence, increasing numbers of states will pass legislation permitting the imposition of the death penalty on progressively younger and younger children, even though the U.S. Supreme Court has held that offenders must be at least 16 years of age before the death penalty can be imposed. Horowitz says that the easy road is to impose the death penalty on child killers but that this approach fails to address the underlying problems in our society that contribute to youth violence. She believes that focusing entirely on punishment will never end youth violence.

Youth Victimization

Hashima and Finkelhor (1999) report the results of the 1994 National Crime Victim Survey, a national evaluation of reported and unreported crime. The overall violent crime victimization rate for youth 12 to 17 years of age in 1994 was 2.7 times higher than the rate for adults. The simple assault rate of youth was 2.9 times higher than the rate for adults, almost 4.0 times as high for simple assault with injury, and 3.0 times as high for simple assault without injury. Boys and girls were almost 3.0 times more likely than their adult counterparts to be victims of assault and violent crime in general. Much of the victimization to youth is done by other youth. In explaining the high rate of youth victimization, Hashima and Finkelhor (1999) note the following:

> The dependent status of youth may make them more vulnerable to victimization. Juveniles have much less choice than adults over whom they associate with, and this can put them into more involuntary contact with high-risk offenders and, thus, at greater jeopardy for victimization (Lynch, 1991). For example, when children live in families that mistreat them, they are not free or able to leave. When they live in dangerous neighborhoods, they cannot choose on their own to move. If they attend a school with many hostile and delinquent peers, they cannot simply change schools or quit. They cannot drive around in private cars, live alone, or work in limited-access offices and factories as can adults. This absence of choice over people and environments may affect juveniles' vulnerability to intimate victimization and street crime. (p. 815)

Overall, the rate of police reporting for juvenile crime victims is lower than for adult crime victims, suggesting that police reports of violent crime, showing a decline since 1993, may not be fully accurate.

Hamburg (1998) considers youth violence to be a public health concern and reports the following data on victimization (pp. 31–54):

- Intentional violence accounts for one-third of all injury deaths in the United States.
- Intentional interpersonal violence disproportionately involves young people as both perpetrators and victims.
- Among minority youth, particularly African Americans, violence has struck with unique force in recent years. Homicide has been the leading cause of death among African American males and females between the ages of 15 and 24 for more than 10 years.
- Firearm-related deaths among African American youth have particularly increased. Between 1984 and 1993, gun-related deaths of young African American males tripled, with the most dramatic rise among those 13 to 18 years old.
- As levels of violence in the general society have risen sharply, it is a disturbing, but not surprising corollary that the levels of violence in and around schools have also increased.
- Research suggests that violence in schools derives mainly from factors external to schools, but may be precipitated or aggravated by the school environment.
- Student assaults on other students are the most frequent type of violence reported in schools.
- In recent years, weapon carrying by students in schools has become a growing source of violence and threat of violence. A study by the Centers for Disease Control and Prevention (1999) found that nearly one-fourth of students nationwide had carried a weapon to school during the month preceding the survey.

- Violent incidents and threats of violence at school negatively affect students, school staff, and the educational process. Fear and feelings of being unsafe cause students to miss school and participate less in class.
- The personal health costs and economic costs to society from the devastation of violence are immense. Nationwide, the average cost of fatal and nonfatal violent injuries was $44,000 in 1992. The total medical cost of all violence that occurred in the United States was estimated at $13.5 billion in 1992.
- Traditionally, youth violence has been addressed by justice or sociological domains and not as a concern for the public health system. In recent years, a proven, effective public health approach has become an increasingly important resource in the effort to prevent youth violence.
- The public health approach emphasizes primary prevention—that is, prevention taking place before the onset of disease or injury. Primary prevention identifies behavioral or environmental risk factors associated with disease and takes steps to educate the community about, or protect it from, these risks.
- Just as application of public health principles and comprehensive strategies reduced the number of deadly traffic accidents and the number of deaths attributed to tobacco use, the public health model can help reduce the extent of injuries and deaths attributed to violence.

Further findings indicate the following:

- The National Summary of Injury Mortality Data for 1981–1997 (unpublished) reports that in 1997, 6,146 young people 15 to 24 years old were victims of homicide, or an average of 17 youth homicide victims per day in the United States.
- Anderson, Kochanek, and Murphy (1997) write that homicide is the second leading cause of death for persons 15 to 24 years of age and the leading cause of death for African Americans. In this age group, homicide is the second leading cause of death for Hispanic youths.
- The National Summary of Injury Mortality Data for 1981 to 1997 (unpublished) notes that since 1988, more than 80 percent of all homicide victims 15 to 19 years of age were killed with a firearm. In 1997, 85 percent of homicide victims 15 to 19 years of age were killed with a firearm.
- Snyder (1997) reports that arrest rates for weapons offenses among youths 10 to 17 years of age doubled between 1987 and 1993 and then dropped 24 percent by 1997. As much as 40 percent of all violent crimes and more than 60 percent of crimes of theft against youth between the ages of 12 and 19 take place in or around schools (Bureau of Justice Statistics, 1991).

The CDC (1999) reports that between July 1992 and June 1994, 105 violent deaths occurred on or near school grounds or at school-associated events. The majority (81 percent) were homicides, and firearms were used in most (77 percent) of the deaths. The violent deaths occurred in communities of all sizes in 25 states. A report sponsored by the U.S. Department of Justice, which was completed after the April 1999 Columbine, Colorado, student massacre is also relevant. The report, which was called *Safe from the Start*, was published in November 2000 (Reno, 2000) and indicates the following:

[O]f the Nation's 22.3 million children between the ages of 12 and 17, approximately 1.8 million have been victims of a serious sexual assault, 3.9 million have been victims of a serious physical assault, and almost 9 million have witnessed serious violence. Every day in 1997, six young people (under the age of 18) were murdered; 56 percent of the victims were killed with a firearm. (p. xii)

A Victim of Violence: A Case Study

Charles is a 10-year-old child who was shot while walking home from school. Charles knows the boys who shot him, but because they're in a gang, Charles won't tell the police their names. He is frightened that they'll try to kill him if he does. He believes the shooting was just a warning. The police have tried to tell Charles that the boys will try to kill him again anyway, but Charles is adamant and says that he's no "snitch."

Charles was targeted by the gang for not respecting their attempts to recruit one of Charles's friends. Charles tried to talk the friend out of joining the gang by telling him how dangerous it would be. When the gang found out about this, Charles knew that he was in trouble. The boys who shot Charles are all under 12 years of age. They were given the assignment of killing Charles as an initiation rite before being offered full membership in the gang. The boys have been told that they had better get Charles *this* time or maybe someone will come looking for *them*. All the boys who tried to shoot him are in Charles's school and are considered violent children who bully and intimidate the other children. One boy had a knife taken from him in a fight on school grounds, while another had been suspended several times for threatening a teacher. Nothing significant has ever happened to any of the boys for dangerous behavior, and they have begun to think that they can get away with anything.

None of the boys has had any experience with guns, and their aim was poor when they tried to shoot Charles. To improve their shooting skills, they've begun shooting at targets in the back of the yard of one of the boy's homes. Everyone knows they're shooting a gun, but nobody reports it. "What's the point?" one of the neighbors says. "The police never come in this neighborhood unless they have a tank. Hell, the postman won't even come here."

The wound Charles sustained shattered his knee and femur. He will never be able to play sports or run again and is in constant pain from the wound. "I was stupid," Charles said, "I shouldn't of said anything to Anthony. I should of let him join that gang. Instead of him getting killed, now it's me who's gonna get it. In this neighborhood, what do you expect? If it ain't at home or on the streets, it's at school or the movies, or the store. There's no place around here where you're safe, and that's a fact."

Discussion

Like all too many children in high-crime areas with gang violence, Charles is at risk. There is no question that Charles will be shot at again by this group of boys or by another group of boys. Rather than working with the police, Charles's cousin Jimmy, a former gang member living in another city and doing well, was asked to come in and intervene for Charles. Jimmy went to the head of the gang and asked that Charles's life be spared. Jimmy argued that Charles had paid dearly with a shattered knee, and the limitations this would place on him during his life were considerable. The gang council, a kind of executive committee

(continued)

Continued

---

composed of the oldest gang members, agreed not to have Charles shot again but wanted Charles to come to them and apologize. Jimmy agreed, and he and Charles went to a gang meeting at which Charles was made to apologize to every one of the members of the gang. Apologizing meant that each member was allowed to hit Charles once. Charles and Jimmy went home after the meeting, and Charles's family nursed his many wounds and bruises. His family is pleased and thanked Jimmy for his help. Charles's mother who has lost two sons to gang violence is also pleased that her son's life has been saved but is angry at Charles for getting himself and the family in trouble with the gang. "What's wrong with you, Charles?" she asked as she was cleaning his wounds. "How many sons do I have to lose before you get the picture? In this neighborhood, there are no good guys and bad guys, just the gang. They run everything. You make them mad and you're dead. But you knew that. Why did you get in their face?" Charles isn't sure, and he's full of anger at what just happened to him. He knows the streets are dangerous and that he'll live, but the experience has made him decide to get his own gun and protect himself. If anyone comes looking for him, he told a friend, it'll be Smith and Wesson they'll answer to. "Those dudes don't take no prisoners," he said.

Like so many other children who live with violence, Charles will buy a cheap gun from someone off the street for, say, $75. It won't shoot straight and it won't look pretty, but sooner or later the gun will kill somebody. That's what guns do, and when you have a child holding one, that's what they often do to other children.

Male versus Female Violence Rates

Scahill (2000) reports that juvenile courts in the United States processed an estimated 1,755,100 delinquency cases in 1997. Delinquency cases involve juveniles who are charged with acts that would constitute a crime (such as aggravated assault or drug offenses) if committed by an adult. Twenty-three percent of the delinquency cases processed in 1997 involved a female offender, as compared with 19 percent in 1988. Between 1988 and 1997, the number of delinquency cases involving females increased 83 percent. The majority (62 percent) of females charged with delinquent acts in 1997 were under age 16. Between 1988 and 1997, the number of delinquency cases involving females under age 16 increased 89 percent, while the number of cases involving females age 16 or older increased 74 percent.

Schahill (2000) goes on to report that for the year 1997, white females accounted for 67 percent of all juvenile delinquency cases, black females accounted for 30 percent, and females of other races accounted for 4 percent. Between 1988 and 1997, the number of cases involving females increased for all racial groups: white, 74 percent; black, 106 percent; and other races, 102 percent. In 1997, the most serious offenses referred in almost half of the juvenile delinquency cases involving females were property offenses, while 25 percent were person offenses, 20 percent were public order offenses, and 7 percent were drug offenses. In 1988, more than half (58 percent) of the delinquency cases involving females were property offenses, 18 percent were person offenses, 19 percent were public order offenses, and 5 percent were drug offenses.

Butts (1996) reports that juvenile courts processed 1.2 million delinquency cases in 1994 involving males, as compared with 324,600 cases involving females. However, the number of delinquency cases involving females increased by 54 percent between 1985 and 1994, while cases involving males increased by 38 percent. The increase in cases involving females reflects a significant increase in offenses against people (up 124 percent for females as opposed to 85 percent for males) and property offense cases (up 40 percent among females, compared with an 18 percent increase among males). Drug violations and public order offense cases increased more among males than among females between 1985 and 1994; however, the percent of growth in cases involving females outpaced males between 1990 and 1994 (Butts, 1996).

Between 1985 and 1994, the delinquency case rate for males increased by 30 percent (from 66.4 to 86.5 cases per 1,000 youth). Among female juveniles, the delinquency case rate grew by 46 percent (from 16.4 to 24.0 cases per 1,000). The person offense case rate for females was 113 percent higher in 1994 than in 1985, while the person offense case rate for males grew by 75 percent. Still, the 1994 person offense case rate was more than three times greater for males than for females (18.2 versus 5.8 cases per 1,000) (Butts, 1996).

Small (2000) notes that from 1963 to 1998, the percentage of female violent arrests increased from 10 percent in 1963, to 17 percent in 1998. In 1963, one out of every 9.7 female arrests were for violent offenses, but by 1998 it had increased to one out of every 6.0 arrests. What Small (2000) calls "remarkable" is that female property arrests increased from one out of every 8.3 arrests in 1963 to a "drastic" one out of every 3.5 arrests in 1998. Female robbery arrests, according to Small, increased from 5 percent in 1963 to 10 percent in 1998. Similarly, females arrested for aggravated assault increased from 14 percent to 20 percent in a 25-year period, while female arrests for burglary increased from 3 percent to 13 percent. Small notes that female auto theft arrests increased from 4 percent to 16 percent and that 35 percent of the larceny arrests in 1998 were young women.

Heimer and De Coster (May 1999) write, "Studies of self-reported delinquency find gender ratios ranging from approximately 1.1 to 5.3, depending on the specific aggressive, assaultive offense measured (Hindelang et al., 1979). These ratios show that although there is a substantial gender gap, girls do engage in a significant amount of violent delinquency" (p. 277).

Peters and Peters (1998) report that in the early 1990s, there was a large increase of young adolescent females, many of color, who were involved in traditionally masculine behaviors, including gang involvement, carrying guns, and fighting. Some researchers, the authors note, suggested an increase in female violence of 125 percent between 1985 and 1994. The *New York Times* (Lee, 1991) reported increases in felony arrests of adolescent females of 48 percent in New York City from 1986 to 1990, 67 percent in New Jersey for the same years and, a 62 percent increase between 1980 and 1990 in Connecticut.

An "Eight Ball Chick": A Case Study

Peters and Peters (1998) use the term "eight ball chicks" to describe young female perpetrators of violence who are as "ruthless and amoral" as their male counterparts (p. 28). Jolene is an example of an eight ball chick. She is tough and violent, uses drugs indiscriminately, has a hair trigger temper, and is a member of very violent gang involved in drug distribution to children. Jolene has been tied to two gang-related killings. The word on the street is that Jolene is a killer for hire. She is 15 years old and has a long juvenile court record dating back to age 8, when she and three other girls badly injured a classmate because the girl was disrespectful and snubbed Jolene in class. Jolene makes it clear to anyone who asks that she doesn't take "shit" from anybody. Jolene has numerous tattoos on her body that she drew herself during one of the many times she was in juvenile detention. The effect is startling and Jolene in full regalia and dressed for the street can be a scary sight.

Jolene comes from a tough family that has socialized her into violence and has taught her to defend herself. In the part of the city Jolene comes from, you have to know how to take care of yourself. Jolene learned early. One of the disarming things about Jolene is a high intelligence, which comes through in many ways. She reads, watches serious films, and has a maturity about her that belies the fact that she's only 15. When the author met with Jolene, they discussed her violent behavior.

"You got to be tough where I come from," she said. "If you're not, someone hurts you. I'd rather do the hurting. I'm not a mean person but I don't want to be a dead person, either. I learned pretty early in my family to take care of myself. My brother tried to rape me when I was 7 and I put a scissor in his eye. He never bothered me again, but he looks like shit (laughs). It makes me happy when I think about it. The girls I run with, they all got treated bad by their families. But what can you do? They're my family and the whole rotten bunch of bastards ain't worth shit, but I still love 'em, ya know? Who else do you have but your family? If I was born with a silver spoon in my mouth like some of them rich bitches I see uptown, I'd be in some fancy private school dating some dude with a stockbroker for a father. But I didn't grow up in a rich family, I grew up on the streets and they're mean, them streets. Some dude made a movie called "Mean Streets." He knew what he was talking about. When I'd get into trouble, my family would lock me out of the house for weeks. What do you do then? You learn to take care of yourself, that's what. You do what you got to do. No one likes to hurt people or steal, but sometimes you get mad and you do things to people. It ain't nice or pretty, but you survive. I figure if I live to be 20, that'll be something. I made a deal with myself that if I'm still around when I'm 20, I'm going to school and learn something. But right now, you gotta stay alive. The girls and the guys, we take care of each other. My family don't give a fuck, so the gang takes over. Most people don't know that gangs ain't all bad. Sure we do some bad stuff, but who would take care of us if it wasn't for the gang? They're family, man, I love 'em. Sometimes people in gangs get mean and you gotta stand up for your rights. I've hurt some people, it's true, but I only done it to protect myself.

"If people don't like chicks like me, they can go fuck themselves. They done this to me . . . put me in a rotten family, in a rotten part of town, with a rotten school. What do they expect? You know how many people get out of this part of town and go to college and become a doctor? None, that's how many. They get killed, or they get strung out on drugs and then get killed, or they end up in jail for life, or they kill themselves. That's the truth. I might die young, but man, I've lived a life already. Kids like me, we're screwed. We won't make it, so why not have some fun? I don't know nobody over 20 from my 'hood who's alive, or not in jail, or who ain't a junkie. When I see them social workers trying to help us, hell, I laugh. It's a joke. You don't help somebody like me. Maybe when I was 4 or 5, but after that, the shit that happens to us? Forget about it. You want to help us, give us a decent life and we'll be fine, you know? Just fine."

Discussion

Jolene is a tough 15-year-old with intelligence and determination but with socialization and life experience that make her a poor candidate for treatment. If she can be kept out of difficulty and alive long enough to reach young adulthood, there are many positives that could be tapped to help her move away from violent crime. She is highly intelligent, tough minded, and highly motivated, and she has leadership qualities that suggest a range of potential attributes for success in adulthood. Possibly the best treatment approach at present is the use of a mentor, a female role model who has gone through what she has and has come out of it, with help. Children like Jolene suffer from an absence of good role models. If a young woman could be found who would appeal to Jolene as a substitute sibling or friend, the intelligence, the desire to know more, the concern for staying alive are all attributes to be used in the process of helping Jolene move from violence to a more productive way of life. Some children don't use counseling well. They're therapy-wise and they know all the therapy ploys, and they use them in reverse to manipulate the clinician.

In Jolene's case, a mentor was found. She is a former street girl who "found" herself in early adulthood, went on to college, and is now a successful businesswoman. She comes from Jolene's neighborhood and Jolene, who will be living in the juvenile facility until she is 18, has begun to relate to her. Little signs of change are noticed by the staff since the mentor has begun seeing Jolene. Jolene appears less contentious and is more cooperative. She's begun working on her high school diploma and takes notice of how she looks. She does well in her schoolwork and has even mentioned college. There are contrary signs as well, and she continues to show indications of aggression and violence if she feels threatened. No one should expect magic, because changing life-long patterns takes time.

Her mentor wrote a short report on her work with Jolene to the juvenile court:

> Jolene is like a lot of street smart kids. She's tough, but tender. It's the tender part of her I see. She loves her family, is loyal to her friends and gang members, is very concerned about her survival, but above all, she has an intelligence that's quick, practical, and needs constant stimulation. She reads and absorbs information quickly and she is very inquisitive. These are the positives, and they should help as she begins to mature into adulthood. The negatives are that she's angry, violent, has a minimal ethical base, and is quite self-centered. Whether the good will outweigh the bad is hard to say. What I do see is a kid who has a chance to improve and to leave street life. But it's a very tough trip to take from the streets to college. I did it, but I had a great mother and a supportive family. I had some good role models who stuck with me when I was in trouble. Jolene has no one except herself and the people like me who take an interest. I'd suggest providing Jolene with all the intellectual stimulation she wants. I'd bring in folks like me to give her another point of view about life. I wouldn't encourage counseling right now since it only antagonizes her. If she wants to take more schooling or more advanced classes, I'd let her. She has low tolerance for frustration but a high amount of drive and desire to make it in life. I'd bet on Jolene. If she can stay out of trouble long enough, I think she'll mature into a decent and productive person. Someone without personal problems? Not on your life. She'll have a ton of them. I do, and most street kids do as well. For life? Maybe, but you have to be hopeful and think that a person who is productive but unhappy is a lot better than a person who is unproductive, unhappy and sitting in prison somewhere. The next 3 to 4 years will tell how Jolene's going to turn out.

Summary

Violent crime rates for all juveniles appear to be going up, despite reports of reduced violence after the peak years of 1983 to 1993. Violence rates among children age 12 and under, while much lower than those of older adolescents, are still very troubling. Early starters of violence, as defined by children below the age of 10, are the children most likely to cycle on to violence in adolescence and young adulthood. As is noted in future chapters, the absolute amount of violence of this small cohort of young children, over the life cycle, is staggering.

Integrative Questions

1. This chapter seems to say that although the amount of violence committed by children under the age of 12 is small compared with that of older children, their level of violence, over the life cycle, is greater. This seems a little difficult to believe, given the incredible amount of violence in children ages 12 to 24. Do you think it's fair to say that a small cohort of young children under the age of 10 is more dangerous than a large cohort of children and young adults ages 12 to 24?

2. Do you think the increase in female crime is a serious concern?

3. Both case studies paint a picture of children living in dangerous neighborhoods. Do you think children in dangerous neighborhoods with involved families do better than children with troubled families, and that the level of danger of the neighborhood is secondary to the degree of support of the family?

4. Which sets of data influence you most: the data that childhood violence is decreasing at present over the peak years of 1983 to 1993, or the data that show that childhood violence in America is 10 to 25 times that of other industrialized countries?

5. If childhood violence is actually decreasing, and there is some question as to whether it is, what do you think is responsible for the decrease?

References

Anderson, R.N., Kochanek, K.D., and Murphy, S.L. (1997). Report of final mortality statistics, 1995. *Monthly Vital Statistics Report, 45,* 11(2 Suppl).

Bishop, D.R. (1997). Juvenile record-handling and practices of the Federal Bureau of Investigation. Paper presented at the Conference on Juvenile Justice Records: Appropriate Criminal and Noncriminal Justice Uses. Washington, DC: Office of Justice Programs, Bureau of Justice Statistics.

Blumstein, A. (1995). Violence by young people: Why the deadly nexus? *National Institute of Justice Journal, 229,* 2–9.

Briscoe, J. (September 1997). Breaking the cycle of violence: A rational approach to at-risk youth. *Federal Probation, 61,* 3–13.

Bureau of Justice Statistics. (1991). *School crime: A national crime victimization survey report.* Washington, DC: U.S. Government Printing Office.

Butts, J.A. (October 1996). Offenders in Juvenile Court, 1994: Gender of Youth. *Juvenile Justice Bulletin (Series OJJDP),* U.S. Department of Justice, Office of Justice Programs, Office of Juvenile Justice and Delinquency Prevention.

Butts, J.A., and Snyder, H.N. (September 1997). *The youngest delinquents: Offenders under age 15*. This bulletin was prepared under Grant Number 95-JN-FX-0008 from the Office of Juvenile Justice and Delinquency Prevention (OJJDP), U.S. Department of Justice.

Centers for Disease Control and Prevention. (1999). *National Summary of Injury Mortality Data, 1981–1997*. Atlanta, Centers for Disease Control and Prevention, National Center for Injury Prevention and Control (unpublished).

Currie, E. (1993). *Reckoning: Drugs, the cities, and the American future*. Washington DC: U.S. Department of Justice, Office of Juvenile Justice Delinquency Prevention.

Elliott, D.S. (1994). Serious violent offenders: Onset, developmental course, and termination: The American Society of Criminology, 1993 Presidential Address. *Criminology*, 32, 1–21.

Fraser, M.W. (1996). Aggressive behavior in childhood and early adolescence: An ecological–developmental perspective on youth violence. *Social Work*, 41, 347–361.

Glicken, M.D., and Sechrest, D.H. (2003). The role of the helping professions in treating and preventing violence. Boston: Allyn & Bacon.

Gramckow, H.P., and Tompkins, E. (1999). *Enhancing prosecutors' ability to combat and prevent juvenile crime in their jurisdictions*. Washington, DC: U.S. Department of Justice, Office of Justice Programs, Office of Juvenile Justice and Delinquency Prevention.

Hamburg, M.A. (1998). Youth Violence is a public health concern. In D.S. Elliott, B. Hamburg, and K.R. Williams (Eds.), *Violence in American schools: A new perspective* (pp. 31–54). New York: Cambridge University Press.

Harris, L. (1993). *Harvard University School of Public Health survey on child and youth violence*. Cambridge, MA: Harvard University School of Public Health.

Hashima, P.Y., and Finkelhor, D. (August 1999). Violent victimization of youth versus adults in the national crime victimization survey. *Journal of Interpersonal Violence*, 14, 799–820.

Heimer, K., and De Coster, S. (May 1999). The gendering of violent delinquency. *Criminology*, 37, 277–317.

Herrenkohl, T.I., Huang, B., Kosterman, R., et al. (February 2001). A comparison of social development processes leading to violent behavior in late adolescence for childhood initiators and adolescent initiators of violence. *Journal of Research in Crime & Delinquency*, 38, 45–63.

Hindelang, M.J., Hirschi, T., and Weiss, J.G. (1979). Correlates of delinquency: The illusion of discrepancy between self-report and official measures. *American Sociological Review*, 44, 955–1014.

Horowitz, M.A. (Summer 2000). Kids who kill: A critique of how the American legal system deals with juveniles who commit homicide. *Law and Contemporary Problems*, 63, 133–177.

Howell, J.C. (Ed.). (1995). *Guide for implementing the comprehensive strategy for serious, violent, and chronic juvenile offenders*. Washington, DC: U.S. Department of Justice, Office of Justice Programs, Office of Juvenile Justice and Delinquency.

Howell, J.C., Krisberg, B., Hawkins, J.D. and Wilson, J.J. (1995). *A sourcebook: Serious violent and chronic juvenile offenders*. Thousand Oaks, CA: Sage.

Kauffman, J.M. (1997). *Characteristics of emotional and behavioral disorders of children and youth*, (6th Ed.). Upper Saddle River, NJ: Merrill.

Lee, F.R. (1991). For gold earrings and protection, more girls take the road to violence. *New York Times*, November 25.

Lester, D. and Yang, B. (1998). *Suicide and homicide in the 20th century: Changes over time*. Hauppauge, NY: Nova Science Publishers.

Lynch, J.P. (1991). Victim behavior and the risk of victimization: Implications of activity specific victimization rates. In G. Kaiser, H. Kury, and H. J. Albrect (Eds.), *Victims and criminal violence* (pp. 543–566). Freiburg, Germany: Eigenverlag Max-Planck-Institute.

Myles, B.S., and Simpson, R.L. (May 1998). Aggression cycle and prevention/intervention strategies. *Intervention in School and Clinic*, 33, 259–264.

Osofsky, H.J., and Osofsky, J.D. (Winter 2001). Violent and aggressive behaviors in youth: A mental health and prevention perspective. *Psychiatry*, vol. 64, 285–295.

Pellegrini, R.J., Roundtree, T., Camagna, T.F., and Queirolo, S.S. (2000). On the epidemiology of violent juvenile crime in America: A total arrest-referenced approach. *Psychological Reports*, 86, 1171–1186.

Peters, S.R., and Peters, S.D. (June 1998). Violent adolescent females. *Corrections Today*, 60, 28–29.

Reno, J. (2000). *Safe from the start: Taking action on children exposed to violence*. Washington, DC: U.S. Department of Justice, Office of Justice Programs, Office of Juvenile Justice and Delinquency Prevention.

Rosenberg, M.L., and Fenley, M.A. (1991). *Violence in America: A public health approach*. New York: Oxford University Press.

Rosenberg, M.L., O'Carroll, P., and Powell, K. (1992). Let's be clear: Violence is a public health problem. *Journal of the American Medical Association*, 267, 3071–3072.

Scahill, M.C. (November 2000). Female delinquency cases, 1997 series: *Fact sheet*, Office of Juvenile Justice and Delinquency Prevention. Available at www.ojjdp.ncjrs.org

Small, K. (2000). Female crime in the United States, 1963–1998: An update. *Gender Issues*, 18, 75–90.

Snyder H.N. (1997). *Juvenile arrest rates for weapons law violations*, 1981–1997. Washington, DC: U.S. Department of Justice, Office of Juvenile Justice and Delinquency Prevention.

Snyder, H., Sickmund, M., and Poe-Yamagata E. (1996). Juvenile offenders and victims: 1996 update on violence. Summary. Washington, DC: U.S. Department of Justice, Office of Juvenile Justice and Delinquency Prevention, U.S. Department of Justice.

Thornberry, T.P., Huizinga, D., and Loeber, R. (1995). The prevention of serious delinquency and violence: Implications from the Program of Research on the Causes and Correlates of Delinquency. In J.C. Howell, B. Krisberg, J.D. Hawkins, and J.J. Wilson (Eds.) *A sourcebook: Serious, violent, and chronic juvenile offenders* (pp. 213–237). Thousand Oaks, CA: Sage.

Walker, H.M., Colvin, G., and Ramsey, E. (1995). *Antisocial behavior in school: Strategies and best practices*. Pacific Grove, CA: Brookes/Cole.

Wolfgang, M.E. (1972). Delinquency in a birth cohort. Chicago: University of Chicago Press.

Wolfgang, M.E. (1987). *From boy to man, from delinquency to crime*. Chicago: University of Chicago Press.

2

Diagnosis: Recognizing the Behaviors Associated with Early-Onset Childhood Violence

In this chapter, the issue of early diagnosis of violent behavior is discussed. It is important to note that although there is evidence that early onset of violent behavior in children is highly correlated with adolescent and adult violence, we are, after all, discussing children whose behavior is not completely formed. Many factors contribute to the continuation or discontinuation of violent behavior in young children. One of the strongest reasons for the discontinuance of violent behavior is early diagnosis and intervention. Further, although profiling children for early signs of violence may lead to needed treatment, we should be cautious about using indications of violent behavior to project into the future. Many things change in a child's life, and the benefits of positive influences, including helping professionals, teachers, mentors, religious affiliations, parents, siblings, and extended family, should not be discounted. Children with early signs of violent behavior should not be categorized but an evaluation should be made to find out why the violent behavior is beginning to show itself so early in life.

There are many reasons for early violent behavior. The helping professions should attempt to use sophisticated and valid diagnostic and assessment approaches that provide clues about the child and his or her behavior. Often violent behavior is a reflection of early childhood physical and sexual abuse and neglect. Early violence may be associated with parental drug and alcohol abuse, learning difficulties, poor peer relationships, and a host of treatable conditions.

If we do not show caution and humanity in working with violent children, we run the risk of so labeling these children that they may have to endure stigma which will exacerbate their anger. In some societies, children with early signs of aggression are killed at ages when they are just beginning to define who they are. Such a fatalistic view of children is hostile to the intent of the helping professions, and it is not the reason this book was written. In civilized societies, early diagnosis leads to treatment and needed support and help. That is the intent of this book and the intent of this chapter on early diagnosis.

Early Signs of Aggression and Antisocial Behavior

According to Sprague and Walker (2000),

> Well-developed antisocial behavior patterns and high levels of aggression evidenced early in a child's life are among the best predictors of delinquent and violent behavior years later (Fagan, 1996; Hawkins & Catalano, 1992). Antisocial patterns that appear early in a child's life and are characterized by high-frequency, intense severity, and occurrence across multiple settings predict a number of ominous outcomes later on, including victimization of others, drug and alcohol use, violence, school failure and dropout, and delinquency (Loeber & Farrington, 1998; Patterson, Reid, & Dishion, 1992). Over the developmental age span, these behavior patterns become more destructive, more aversive, and have much greater social impact as they become elaborated. (p. 369)

Dwyer, Osher, and Warger (1998) believe that we can diagnose potential violence as early as age 5 but that few at-risk youth will commit serious violent acts throughout their life spans. Many at-risk youth with early diagnoses of aggression and violent behaviors, however, will display such major life problems as drug and alcohol abuse, domestic and child abuse, divorce or multiple relationships, employment problems, mental health problems, dependence on social services, and involvement in less serious crimes (Obiakor, Merhing, & Schwenn, 1997).

Wagner and Lane (1998) studied an 8 percent youth cohort ages 10 to 17 that had a youth services referral in 1997 in a large Oregon county whose arrest statistics, according to the authors, were representative of the nation as a whole. Of that 8 percent, 20 percent of the offenders committed 87 percent of all new crime. Sprague and Walker (2000) suggest that there is a small group of juvenile youth who commit almost all serious crimes and that these same youth "are very likely to have begun their careers very early (i.e., before age 12)" (p. 369).

There appears to be a relationship between violence and school disciplinary problems. Disciplinary referrals in elementary and middle schools indicate that 6 percent to 9 percent of the referred children are responsible for more than 50 percent of the total disciplinary referrals and practically all of the serious offenses, including possession of weapons, fighting, assaults on other children, and assaults on teachers (Skiba, Peterson, & Williams, 1997). Early disciplinary problems in school are accurate predictors of future and more serious problems (Walker, Colvin, & Ramsey 1995). According to Walker and colleagues, students with 10 or more disciplinary referrals per year are seriously at risk for school failure and for other more serious life problems. Many of the children who are frequently referred to principals for disciplinary action are defiant and disobedient and may often be involved in bullying and intimidation of other students. They are, according to Sprague and Walker (2000), likely to move on to more serious offenses, including "physical fighting, and then ultimately rape, serious assault, or murder" (p. 370).

Early and Late Starters of Violence

Moffit (1994) believes that children who develop early aggressive tendencies are much more likely to move on to more seriously violent behaviors than are children who show no violent tendencies before adolescence. He calls these two cohorts early and late starters. Late starters show signs of violent behavior in late middle school and even high school. Early starters often show signs of disobedience, bullying, intimidation, and fighting when they begin kindergarten and elementary school.

According to Sprague and Walker (2000), "Early starters are likely to experience antisocial behavior and its toxic effects throughout their lives. Late starters have a far more positive long-term outcome" (p. 370). Walker and Severson (1990) suggest that diagnostic signs of early starters include disobedience, property damage, conduct problems, theft, the need for a great deal of attention, threats, intimidation, and fighting. Although it's wise to remember that diagnostic labels can be misleading and incorrect when applied to children, labels that have been used with children and that correlate with violent behavior include (1) inattention and impulsivity (Lynam, 1996), (2) antisocial personality disorder, (3) conduct disorder, (4) oppositional defiant disorder, and (5) serious emotional disturbance (APA, 1994). Mayer (1995) and Reid (1993) suggest that certain environmental factors may correlate with the potential for violent behavior. The most prominent environmental factors include inconsistent and harsh parenting styles, as well as disorganized or badly functioning schools and the availability of drugs, alcohol, and weapons.

Herrenkohl et al. (2001) note the following:

> Individuals who initiate violent behavior in childhood are at particularly high risk for serious violent offending in adolescence and adulthood. . . . Risk for later violent offending typically diminishes with later ages of initiation (Elliott, 1994; Thornberry, Huizinga, and Loeber, 1995), although initiation of violence at any age into adolescence is associated with an increased probability for violence at subsequent ages (Farrington, 1989). (p. 45)

Elliott (1994) found that 45 percent of the preadolescents who began violent behavior by age 11 went on to commit violent offenses by their early 20s while 25 percent of the children who began violent behavior between the ages of 11 and 12 committed violent offenses through adolescence and into adulthood. Thornberry, Smith, and Rivera et al. (1995) found similar patterns: The later the onset of violence, the less likely the child is to cycle into adult violence. The earlier the violent behavior begins, the more likely it is to continue on into adulthood. In a study of early-onset violence, Herrenkohl, et al. (2001) noted four indicators of future violent behavior in children aged 10: hitting a teacher, having picked fights, the tendency to attack other children, and a report by parents indicating that a child fights a great deal at home or in the neighborhood.

Catalano and Hawkins (1996) suggest that youth violence is the result of socialization into violent behavior that begins in early childhood and continues on through adolescence. Violent behavior in elementary school increases the risk for violence in adolescence and adulthood. By socialization into violence, the authors believe that children have early experiences in antisocial behavior that are reinforced by peers and fail to be extinguished by adults monitoring the behavior. As the antisocial behavior continues, with its particular rewards, the child seeks out others with similar behaviors who may accept, reinforce, and promote new antisocial behaviors, which often lead to violence.

Longitudinal studies by Widom (1999) and McCord (1999) support the concern about aggressive behavior at an early age, particularly its linkages to child abuse and neglect. McCord, whose study of families and child rearing spanned 30 years, found that parental response to aggressive behavior in their sons was related to later aggressive behavior (p. 169). A more recent survey of self-reported delinquency found that one in seven 12-year-olds, or 14 percent, had engaged in assaultive behaviors and that 7 percent reported carrying a handgun (Puzzanchera, 2000).

Recent statistics on juvenile offenders and victims found that the number of children abused, neglected, or endangered more than doubled from 1986 to 1993 (Snyder & Sickmund, 1999, p. 40). In 1993, there were almost 3 million "maltreated or endangered" children, an increase from 1.4 million in 1986. Abuse and neglect were classified as physical, sexual, or emotional. Most of these youths entered the child welfare system through child protective services. In 1997, 14.1 million juveniles, or one-fifth of all juveniles, lived in poverty.

Thornberry, Smith, Rivera, Huizina, et al. (1999) reported on the impact of family disruption and its relationship to delinquency. They reported that from 1970 to 1997, the proportion of U.S. households having children who live with both parents declined by 64 percent to 35 percent for African Americans, and from 90 percent to 74 percent for whites. They concluded that, "Overall, the data reported here indicate a consistent relationship between a greater number of family transitions and a higher level of delinquency and drug abuse" (p. 4). The authors indicated that adolescents who experienced family stress were more likely to have difficulty managing anger and other negative emotions, although further research was needed.

Another factor related to the increase in delinquent behavior is the relative isolation of some neighborhoods from their larger communities. This is particularly true in the case of inner-city youth who are often insulated from outside influences. Poor schools and weak social institutions can lead to a lack of achievement and lower motivation. Economic and social discrimination and poor employment prospects can lead to participation in gangs and criminal activity that may ultimately result in violent crimes. The *1999 National Report Series* of the Office of Juvenile Justice and Delinquency Prevention (Bilchik, 1999) describes minority involvement in the juvenile justice system:

> The most recent statistics available reveal significant racial and ethnic disparity in the confinement of juvenile offenders. In 1997, minorities made up one-third of the

juvenile population nationwide but accounted for nearly two-thirds of the detained and committed population in secure juvenile facilities. For black juveniles, the disparities were most evident. (p. 1)

Juveniles ages 16 to 17 accounted for 48 percent of all juvenile arrests and 51 percent of the violent crimes. Black youth comprised 15 percent of the juvenile population in 1997 but accounted for 26 percent of all arrests and 44 percent of all juvenile arrests for violent offenses. Minorities accounted for 7 in 10 youths held in custody for a violent offense (Bilchik, 1999, p. 11). The report calls for an effort to provide "all youth with an equal opportunity to learn, thrive, and achieve at every stage of their lives" (p. 1).

Exposure to Violence

Hagan and Foster (2001) report that as many as 25 percent of all adolescents have witnessed a shooting or killing. Exposure to violence is strongly related to violent behaviors (DuRant et al., 1994), hostile and aggressive behavior and bullying (Moses, 1999), childhood and adolescent depression (Schwab-Stone et al., 1995), and suicidal thoughts and attempts (Pastore, Fisher, & Friedman, 1996). Schwab-Stone et al. (1999) considered a range of outcomes and found a relationship between neighborhood violence, reduced school performance, and lowered expectations for future success.

Many professionals believe there is a strong connection between child abuse and neglect and childhood, adolescent, and adult antisocial behavior and violence. Widom (1992) followed 1,575 cases from childhood through young adulthood, comparing the arrest records of children with reported and verified child abuse and neglect with children who had no recorded evidence of child abuse or neglect. The two groups were matched by age, race, sex, and approximate family socioeconomic status. The findings indicated the following: (1) The children who had been abused or neglected were 53 percent more likely to be arrested as juveniles; (2) the abused children were 38 percent more likely to be arrested as adults; (3) the abused children were 38 percent more likely to be arrested for a violent crime; (4) the abused children were 77 percent more likely to be arrested if they were females (5) the children who had suffered abuse and neglect were arrested 1 year younger for their first arrest; and (6) when compared with nonabused children, abused children committed twice as many offenses and were arrested 89 percent more frequently than the children who were not abused. In follow-up interviews, Widom (1992) found serious problems in other areas of the child's life, including depression and suicide, poor cognitive skills, extremely low IQs, poor reading skills, alcohol and drug problems, and unemployment and underemployment.

Drug and Fetal Alcohol Syndrome

In 1992–1993, of the 4 million women who gave birth during that period, 221,000 used illegal drugs during their pregnancies and 757,000 used alcohol during and after their pregnancies (National Institutes of Health, 2001). Although Hilton (1991) stated that drinking rates for women have remained fairly constant since the 1960s, drinking during pregnancy has increased significantly. The Centers for Disease Control and Prevention (1997) report that drinking among pregnant women increased from 12.4 percent in 1991 to 16.3 percent in 1995. The rate of frequent drinking was four times higher in 1995 than it was in 1991, with an increase from 0.8 percent in 1991 to 3.5 percent in 1995 (CDC, 1997).

May and Gossage (2001) believe that fetal alcohol syndrome (FAS) may be as high as 9.1 per 1,000 live births, or 1 percent of the children born, but as low as 0.26 per 1,000 for certain low-risk groups. High-risk groups for FAS include Native and African American children, and mothers who are alcohol addicted. Abel and Sokol (1987) estimated that about 6 percent of the children born to alcoholic women have FAS, although for children born after an FAS sibling, Abel (1988) found the risk of FAS to be 70 percent. Majewski (1978a, 1978b) and Olegard et al. (1979) reported that even if a child does not have all of the symptoms of full-blown FAS, babies of alcoholic women have a higher rate of many of the individual characteristics of FAS. Children with FAS commonly exhibit behavioral problems. Majewski (1978a, 1978b) and Streissguth et al. (1991) found that children and adults with FAS often show signs of behavioral problems, including poor concentration and attention, stubbornness, social withdrawal, and higher rates of conduct problems (e.g., lying, cheating, and stealing). Streissguth (1993) noted that adults with FAS often experience alcohol and drug abuse and antisocial behavior.

Children of alcoholic mothers but not born with FAS often experience behavioral problems. Brown et al. (1991) indicated that children who have been exposed to alcohol throughout pregnancy show attention deficit problems and behavioral problems in school. Larkby and Day (1997) noted that even though the child might not be born with FAS, the alcoholic mother's lifestyle may seriously affect the functioning of the developing child. Landesman-Dwyer (1982) reported that 4-year-old children whose mothers drank one to five drinks per day during pregnancy were less attentive and more active when compared with children of mothers who drank less.

Bullying

Natvig, Albrektsen, and Quarnstrom (2001) found that the prevalence of bullying was about 10 percent in a population of youth ages 13 to 15. The authors defined *bullying* as repeated aggressive behavior carried out over time (Olweus, 1997). The authors also noted that bullies are often considered to be stronger than their victims. Pulkkinen and Tremblay (1992) reported that bullies are typically aggressive, nonsocial, and hyperactive, but Olweus (1997) suggested that some bullies are insecure and anxious. Interestingly, on measures of self-esteem and self-views, Baumeister, Smart, and Boden (1996) found that youths with violent behavior often hold unrealistically positive self-views that are not supported by feedback from teachers, classmates, and parents. Lazarus and Folkman (1984) suggested that bullying may be a function of adjusting to new and often unclear demands of school and may indicate discomfort and confusion rather than antisocial tendencies.

Peterson and Skiba (2001) defined *bullying* as repeated and intentional injury or discomfort inflicted by one or more other students. Bullying may include physical and verbal assaults, obscene gestures, and intentional exclusion. Whitney and Smith (1993) reported that bullying takes place where there is little adult supervision, in such likely places as playgrounds and hallways. Bullies are often larger than their victims and believe that the use of violence is acceptable. Victims may be friendless in class, tend to be more anxious and insecure than other students, and may respond to bullying by crying and avoidance when attacked. These reactions may be reinforcing to bullies. Borg (1998) reported that bullied children feel vengeful, angry, and full of self-pity after being bullied. If untreated, bullied children may develop depression or physical illness, and even become suicidal. Borg (1998) noted that students who are bullies in elementary school may become involved in criminal and aggressive conduct during and after adolescence. Craig and Pepler (1997) believe that bullying is often tolerated by teachers and estimate that teachers intervene in only 4 percent of all incidents involving bullying behavior.

Natvig, Albrektsen, and Quarnstrom (2001) reported a significant relationship between bullying and increased feelings of alienation from school. The authors defined *alienation* as the degree to which children who bully experience school as "meaningless and unchallenging." The authors suggested that one way to deal with bullying is to find school activities that are more meaningful and challenging to these children. As an example, Ames (1992) suggested that one way to make school more meaningful is to find ways of providing learning experiences that are less focused on memorizing and repeating knowledge, the activities many students find boring and frustrating. These activities, which may not suit the learning style of children prone to bullying, may also increase stress because memorizing and repeating information are skills these children often lack. Consequently, the child who does poorly in school may take his or her failure out on other children in the form of hostile and aggressive behaviors. There are, of course, other less enlightened views of bullying which suggest that bullies enjoy their position of power and superiority over weaker and less violence prone classmates, and that their behavior is intended to allow the bully to get his or her way with little concern for the pain the behavior may cause others.

Cruelty to Animals

Clifton (2000) suggests a relationship between cruelty to animals and early onset of violence in children. He writes that cruelty to animals is a symptom of the inability to "empathize with others and may lead to treating others in a manner consistent with the symptoms of conduct disorder—with callous disregard, and without feelings of regret or remorse" (p. 87).

Tapia (1971) found that in ten of eighteen case histories of children who were cruel and abusive to animals, bullying, fighting, fire setting, and stealing were also commonly associated behaviors. Tapia (1971) further noted that cruelty to animals suggests children with problems of "aggression with poor control of impulses" (p. 76). Tingle et al. (1986) found that nearly half of the rapists and over one-fourth of the pedophiles they studied had been cruel to animals as children. In a study of serial killers, Lockwood and Church (1998), noted that 36 percent of the serial killers reported killing and torturing animals in childhood. Miller and Knutson (1997) found a relationship between physical abuse in childhood and animal cruelty among two populations—criminals and college students. In both groups, there was a positive correlation between harsh physical punishment of children by parents and animal cruelty. The authors noted that the term *childhood physical abuse* includes such parental behaviors as severe spankings, punching, kicking, and choking.

Ascione (1998) found that 71 percent of the battered women living in a shelter reported that their partners had harmed or killed at least one of their pets. One-fifth of the women in Ascione's study delayed leaving their abusive partners because of their concern for the welfare of their pets. Clifton (2000) suggested a relationship between early childhood onset of cruelty to animals and later-life family violence, and Arkow (1996), Ascione, (1993), and Boat (1995) saw a connection between early childhood cruelty to animals and abuse of intimates in later life.

Fire Setting

The National Fire Protection Association (1999) reports that each year, fires set by juveniles account for a large amount of the property damage and deaths related to all fires in the United States. More than any other population, the fires set by children and adolescents are more likely to result in death (National Fire Protection Association, 1999). In 1998 alone, fires set by children and adolescents in the United States resulted in 6,215 deaths, another 30,800 injuries, and billions of dollars in property damage (National Fire Protection Association, 1999). A 1997 *Juvenile Justice Bulletin* (OJJPD, 1997) reported that juveniles under the age of 12 accounted for 35 percent of the arrests for arson in youths under the age of 18.

Fire setting is one of the serious violent activities that young children are believed to commit. In a study of 186 juvenile fire setters, Showers and Pickrell (1987) found that 86 percent were males with an average age of 10. The authors noted that juvenile fire setters often come from families whose parents abuse drugs or alcohol and that the children are likely to have experienced emotional neglect and physical abuse. Juvenile fire setters, according to Showers and Pickrell (1987), are also more likely to display poor academic performance. Kolko and Kazdin (1991) found that fire setters tend to have poorer social skills than non-fire setters and that they are more secretive, significantly more aggressive, but less assertive than non-fire setters. Raines and Foy (1994) noted that typical juvenile fire setters have often experienced emotional neglect and/or physical abuse, have poor academic performance, and express more anger and aggressiveness than non-fire setters. In a sample of male arsonists ages 15 to 21, Repo and Virkkunen (1997) found that 65 percent of the offenders had a history of *conduct disorders* with aggressive features and alcohol dependence. The authors noted that fire setting and criminal recidivism among young adult male fire setters is usually associated with childhood-onset conduct disorders.

Sakheim and Osborn (1999) indicate that fire setting by children and adolescents is a dangerous act with often grave consequences. Kolko (1985) believes that one in every four fire setters may be a recidivist. One obvious way to distinguish serious from less serious fire setters, according to Sakheim and Osborn (1999), is to distinguish between the severe group of fire setters whose intent is to do damage and the minor-risk group which has curiosity about fire. The authors believe that minor-risk fire setters can be treated in the community with fire safety education and child and family counseling, while severe fire setters may require residential treatment. According to the authors, juveniles in the high-risk group set an average of 5.3 fires with deliberate intent to harm or to punish people by destroying their property. The authors also found that high-risk fire setters derived sexual gratification from setting fires and often had fantasies about revenge and retaliation. A high number of serious fire setters had histories of acting in a sadistic way toward other children and to animals. Few of the serious fire setters (27 percent) felt remorse or shame for the consequences of their fire setting, according to the authors.

Preoccupation with Violence in the Media

In Chapters 3 and 4, on the topic of school violence, a set of personal characteristics is noted that cumulatively tends to suggest increased potential for violence. O'Toole (1999) developed these characteristics for use in identifying violent children. They include such behaviors as low tolerance for frustration, the inability to deal with criticism, poor social skills, rigid and opinionated behavior, and a fascination with sensational violence and violence-filled entertainment. A great deal of concern has been raised about the relationship between early-onset violence and a violent mass culture. The American Psychological Association, on its national Website (2002), reported the following:

> Children who watched many hours of TV violence when they were in elementary school tended to also show a higher level of aggressive behavior when they became teenagers. By observing these youngsters until they were 30 years old, researchers found that the ones who'd watched a lot of TV when they were eight years old were more likely to be arrested and prosecuted for criminal acts as adults. (p. 2)

Huston et al. (1992) noted that children who watch violent shows are more likely to hit their playmates, be noncompliant with class rules, fail to finish tasks, and have poor frustration tolerance. Bandura, Ross, and Ross (1963), Cannon (1989), and Wilson and Hunter (1983) all found that children constantly exposed to violence in the media are likely to incorporate it in their behaviors. Javier, Herron, and Primavera (1998) believe that it's unfair to blame the media for violence. Violence, they suggest, is prompted by other factors, including parents and other adults who tolerate and even glorify violence, adults who abuse substances, poorly supervised children whose behavior and preoccupation with violence is not adequately monitored by adult caretakers, and peers who reinforce violent tendencies. The authors write,

> As parents, we need to monitor what our children watch on television and watch with them. . . . As educators, we need to teach children how to understand what they watch on television. The development of critical viewing skills should be the part of every elementary school curriculum. . . . As citizens, we need to be concerned about the quality of life in our society. Our concerns about violence should not only include the need to monitor the kinds of programs our children watch but to advocate an understanding of the personal, family and societal issues which cause violence and determine what role television can play in reaching that understanding. (p. 352)

Simons (2001) notes that by the time a child completes elementary school, he or she has seen 8,000 murders on television. And while others may argue that if the home environment is right and if the child is healthy, TV violence doesn't greatly affect children, Simons believes that it does. She notes that when the aggressor in violent entertainment is admired by the child, the child begins to believe that violence will go unpunished if the reasons for violent behavior are considered fair and correct by the child. She gives the example of her own child, who was sent home from school for fighting. Her son proudly told her that the other child didn't respect him and he had to be in charge. When the mother gave a disapproving look, the child shouted at his mother, "You don't understand! All the boys fight, Mom" (p. 12). Simons (2001) also cautions that children are not yet socialized to understand nuances of violent behavior. They don't understand transitions, subtle changes in behavior, or irony. They're very concrete in their understanding of character development. What may be admirable to a child in a character may be reprehensible to an adult. Furthermore, Simons argues that as children become desensitized to violence and their fear response becomes "muted," they may seek more gruesome shows and sights "to get the same thrill response and excitement, all in an attempt to master their fear" (p. 13). Finally, Simons notes that children believe that those who are victimized in the media deserve to be victimized, because they are bad or should be punished. Simons observes, "This increases the likelihood that children will act on aggressive impulses, with the confidence that they are right and that their actions are the way to resolve the conflict" (p. 15).

Simons (p. 17) gives some practical guidelines for ways of handling TV violence at home. She suggests limiting total television for the family to two hours and watching TV with a child to see what he or she is viewing. She also suggests introducing children to different programming and monitoring the level of violence, even in cartoon shows. Discussing with the child different ways in which a situation can be dealt with nonviolently can be helpful. Providing other alternatives to violent entertainment, such as outdoor activities, libraries, and sports, may be another alternative to a child watching violence in the media. Observe the adult TV viewing habits, she suggests. Children will often watch what the adult watches. Keep TVs out of the child's room and turn off the TV during meals. If children fight, unplug the TV.

Childhood-Onset Conduct Disorder: A Case Study

John is a 7-year-old child who has been "acting out" in his first-grade class. He hits, kicks, pulls hair, bullies, and steals from the other children. The problem has been escalating over the past year. John has been tested for hyperactivity, minimal organic brain damage, low intelligence, learning disorders, and physical problems that might trigger violent reactions, and he has been given a battery of tests to rule out medical problems that might be consistent with highly aggressive behavior. All the tests have come back negative for any particular problem. Johnny's parents are mortified by his behavior. They have two older children who do very well in school and are considered model students. The parents report that Johnny showed signs of aggression very early in life. By age 1, he was terrorizing their dog. They had to give the dog away to friends because John would not leave it alone. At age 3, John walked across the street and killed the fish in a neighbor's tank. When caught emptying the tank on the floor, he calmly denied that he done anything. John lies easily, and by 5 years of age was accomplished at covering up any aggressive and antisocial acts he committed. He has set two fires in the past year that the parents know about and was caught by his father trying to burn down a garden shed in the back of the house. John tends to blame others for everything. He needs a great deal of attention. When it isn't forthcoming, he physically attacks his classmates and his teachers, all of whom are frightened of him. Enough parents have complained so that John has been taken out of school and is being seen in therapy for the first time.

The clinician gave John a battery of psychological tests, including several projective tests developed for children. His conclusion was that if John were an adult, he would have many of the diagnostic characteristics of a *Personality Disorder, AntiSocial Type* (301.7) (APA, 1994, p. 649). Because of John's age, the clinician was tempted to give John a diagnosis of *Oppositional Defiant Disorder* (313.81) (APA, 1994, p. 93). This is a less severe diagnosis and involves loss of temper, arguing, and defiant and spiteful behavior. After eight hours of testing and interviewing, however, the clinician diagnosed John with a *Conduct Disorder, Childhood-Onset Type* (312.81) (APA, 1994, p. 86). The *DSM–IV* defines a Childhood-Onset Type Conduct Disorder in children who have at least one characteristic of a conduct disorder before the age of 10. Children with Child-Onset Conduct Disorders "frequently display physical aggression toward others, have disturbed peer relationships, may have had oppositional defiant disorder during early childhood, and usually have symptoms that meet full criteria for Conduct Disorder before puberty. These individuals are more likely to have persistent Conduct Disorder and Adult Anti-social Personality Disorder than are those with Adolescent Onset Type Conduct Disorders" (APA, 1994, p. 86).

The *DSM–IV* goes on to say that a diagnosis of a Conduct Disorder can be given when persistent antisocial behavior exists over the prior 12 months in which the child has met three or more of the following criteria with at least one criterion present in the past six months:

1) Aggression to People and Animals: a) The child bullies, threatens and initiates fights; b) has used a weapon; c) is physically cruel to people and/or animals; d) has stolen while confronting others; e) has forced someone into sexual activity. 2) Destruction of Property: a) The child deliberately sets fires and/or deliberately destroys property. 3) Deceitfulness or Theft: a) The child has broken into someone else's property, lies or cons others, and/or

(continued)

Continued

---

is involved in shoplifting. 4) Serious Violation of Rules: a) The child often stays out at night without parental permission before age 13; b) has runaway at least twice; and c) is often truant before the age of 13. (APA, 1994, p. 90)

The clinician believes that John has almost all of the characteristics of a Childhood-Onset-Type Conduct Disorder and that the problem is "severe" in nature. In a severe form of a childhood Conduct Disorder, "Many conduct problems [exist] in excess of those required to make the diagnosis **or** the conduct problems cause considerable harm to others" (APA, 1994, p. 91). The clinician believes that John is developing highly dangerous behaviors that will very likely cycle on through childhood, into adolescence, and on to adulthood. In boys under age 18, the diagnosis of Conduct Disorder appears to be increasingly used, and rates of Conduct Disorder for boys under age 18 are estimated at 6 percent to 16 percent, while rates for girls are estimated as 2 percent to 9 percent (APA, 1994, p. 88). Murray and Myers (1998) describe conduct disorders as chronic, severe, antisocial behaviors that typically begin in early childhood and extend into adulthood. The authors believe that symptoms of a conduct disorder are consistently present at home, at school, with peers, and in the community. However, the invisible children who make up a cohort of those who commit school violence (Shubert, et al., 1999) may not exhibit these exact behavioral problems and are often diagnosed as severely depressed or emotionally labile.

In describing John, the clinician, goes on to note,

Johnny is a robust and severely Conduct Disordered child. He acts out whenever he feels like it, has no sense of right or wrong, is driven by impulses, doesn't respect authority, is manipulative, and is able to get his way much of the time. When he doesn't get his way, he uses high levels of violent aggression with children, adolescents, and adults. Most people are frightened by his naked aggression and see in Johnny a very dangerous child capable of doing great harm. Just as there are people who are born with birth defects, mental retardation, and other infirmities, Johnny seems to have been aggressive and impulse driven from an early age. There is nothing to suggest parental neglect or abuse. The parents are appalled by his behavior, unable to control it, and believe that Johnny needs very intensive professional help. For these reasons, I am recommending that Johnny be placed in a facility for young emotionally disturbed children. There have been some very positive results from early residential placements for children with severe Childhood-Onset Conduct Disorders. Perhaps placing him as early as age 7 will have a positive preventive impact.

Discussion

The diagnosis of a Conduct Disorder so early in a child's life may be seen by some as overly harsh, pejorative, and even leading to a life-long label, implying that John will be a dangerous person throughout his life. Clinicians sometimes use a diagnosis that is more severe than might be called for by the child's behavior to get needed help for the child before the symptoms worsen and the child does something that causes severe harm to others. In John's case, the diagnosis seems correct. John needs residential help. He needs to live in an environment in which he can learn restraint, impulse control, right from wrong, and the other developmental behaviors he should have mastered at an earlier age. Although it is true that almost half of the children with early-onset behavioral problems move into more aggressive behavior during adolescence and adulthood, treatment is certainly worth a try.

More than a few early-onset, behaviorally troubled children like John have reduced or even eliminated their aggressive, antisocial behavior as a result of positive intervention. In John's case, he was transferred to a private facility that deals exclusively with children very much like himself. It is a highly regimented facility with strict rules and a token economy. The better children do in obeying the rules of the facility and in their individual and group therapy, school work, and personal conduct, the more benefits and privileges they receive. John, as it turns out, likes the military structure of the facility. He likes knowing what is acceptable and unacceptable. He appreciates it when people know he's lying and trying to con them, and confront him about his behavior. It is an exhilarating experience to be around others who know more about him than he does. The staff is highly professional and fair. If there are disagreements among the residents, the problems are worked out quickly, equitably, and, in John's view, in a way that allows everyone to save face. John is thriving in the facility. His initial score on an IQ test in the low-normal range has been replaced by a score in the high-normal range because he wasn't trying on the initial test. His social behavior has improved, and he has begun to think about becoming a soldier. The transformation in his behavior is startling. He sees his family often and has gone home on vacations without incident.

John was reevaluated by a clinician a year after being sent to the private facility. The clinician wrote:

> John is still an impulse driven, amoral, and potentially dangerous child. The initial diagnosis was correct. The benefit of the early intervention has been to provide external controls that are fair and reasonable and that act to inhibit his more anti-social impulses. With children like John who enjoy the paramilitary structure of the facility and the tightly enforced rules, they do well as long as the facility stays within their narrow definition of what they consider a healthy environment. As staff changes or as the child matures, age and maturation might find the child influenced by other more powerful role models among the residents. When this happens, children like John who have such good initial gain, often take a turn for the worse. A number of our residents have become participants in hate groups that utilize paramilitary organizational structures. Others have entered gang life that is, in a way, a paramilitary structure. We always hope that children like John will develop a moral compass because of the treatment they receive, but robust and severe childhood onset Conduct Disorders have a poor track record and tend to cycle on to other more serious offenses once they leave the facility. John will need long-term outpatient help when he returns home.

John is age 12 now and lives at home. He is a mediocre but compliant student who has begun entering chat rooms with adolescents who have strong feelings of hatred for certain ethnic, religious, and racial groups. John believes that if these groups were eliminated, the world would be a "cleaner" place. He has begun attending meetings of a domestic hate group organized along paramilitary lines and is learning military discipline. He has promised the group leader to stay out of trouble at school so he can help the group when it begins to rid the world of Blacks, Jews, immigrants with dark skin, and Arabs. John is also developing strong fantasies of raping young girls and finds among his peers in the hate group, others with similar fantasies. John thinks he has finally come home and is happy now. He thinks his special skills will be used and that he will make a contribution to the world, something his parents preach to him every day.

Summary

Once again, the reader is cautioned to remember that the early signs of violence in children noted in this chapter are overall signs to consider in evaluating children. They are to be used to diagnose and treat, not to label or predict long-term problems with violence. Changes in the child's life, as is noted throughout this book, can bring with them some startling changes in the child's potential for violence. This chapter suggested a strong relationship between early-life child abuse and violence. Violent children may show potential for violence through bullying, fire setting, cruelty to animals, school misconduct and poor performance, and compulsive attraction to mass media violence.

Integrative Questions _____

1. The question of early diagnosis of violent behavior is fraught with moral issues. If we label too early and if the label is incorrect, children may be stigmatized for life. Can you think of alternatives to using *DSM-IV* labels with children?

2. There appears to be a fairly strong relationship between child abuse and neglect and early-onset childhood violence. Shouldn't we be putting our energies into reducing the amount of child abuse and neglect rather than punishing young children for the acts of their parents?

3. Older adolescents commit the most violent behavior. Do you accept the labels noted in this chapter of early and late violence starters and the belief that late violence starters are ultimately less dangerous over the life span?

4. What might be some reasons why many fire starters are very young children?

5. The idea that a very small number of violent children do most of the violent crime throughout the life cycle suggests that we focus on that cohort of young children by preventing their violent behavior through early and, perhaps, long-term residential treatment. Do you agree?

References _____

Abel, E.L. (1988). Fetal alcohol syndrome in families. *Neurotoxicology and Teratology*, 10(1), 1–2.

Abel, E.L., and Sokol, R.J. (1987). Incidence of fetal alcohol syndrome and economic impact of FAS-related anomalies. *Drug and Alcohol Dependence*, 19(1), 51–70.

American Psychiatric Association. (1994). *Diagnostic and statistical manual of mental disorders* (4th ed.). Washington, DC: American Psychiatric Association.

American Psychological Association National Website (June 2002). Is youth violence just another fact of life? Available online at: www.apa.org/ppo/issues/pbviolence.html.

Ames, C. (1992). Classrooms: Goals, structures, and student motivation. *Journal of Educational Psychology*, 84(3), 261–271.

Arkow, P. (1996). The relationships between animal abuse and other forms of family violence. Family *Violence and Sexual Assault Bulletin*, 12, 29–34.

Ascione, E.R. (1993). Children who are cruel to animals: A review of research and implications for developmental psychology. *Anthrozoos*. 6, 226–247.

Ascione, E.R. (1998). Battered women's reports of their partner's and their children's cruelty to animals. *Journal of Emotional Abuse*, 1, 119–133.

Bandura, A., Ross, D., and Ross, S.A. (1963). Vicarious learning and imitative learning. *Psychological Bulletin*, 67, 601–607.

Baumeister, R.F., Smart, L., and Boden, J.M. (1996). Relation of threatened egotism to violence and aggression: The dark side of high self-esteem. *Psychological Review*, 103(1), 5–33.

Bilchik, S. (1999). Minorities in the juvenile justice system. *1999 National Report Series*. Washington, DC: Office of Juvenile Justice and Delinquency Prevention, U.S. Department of Justice.

Boat, B.W. (1995). The relationship between violence to children and violence to animals: An ignored link. *Journal of Interpersonal Violence*, 10, 229–235.

Borg, M.G. (1998). The emotional reactions of school bullies and their victims. *Educational Psychology*, 18, 433–444.

Brown, R.T., Coles, C.D., Smith, I.E., Platzman, K.A., Silverstein, J., Erikson, S., and Falek, A. (1991). Effects of prenatal alcohol exposure at school age. *Neurotoxicology and Teratology*, 13(4), 369–376.

Cannon, C. (1989). Children's advocates pressuring lawmakers. *Miami Herald*, May 28, p. D2.

Catalano, R.F., and Hawkins, J.D. (1996). The social development model: A theory of antisocial behavior." In J.D. Hawkins, (ed.). *Delinquency and Crime: Current Theories* (pp. 149–197). New York: Cambridge University Press.

Centers for Disease Control and Prevention. (1997). Alcohol consumption among pregnant and childbearing-aged women—United States, 1991 and 1995. *Morbidity and Mortality Weekly Report*, 46 (16), 346–350.

Craig, W.M., and Pepler, D.J. (1997). Observations of bullying and victimization in the schoolyard. *Canadian Journal of School Psychology*, 13, 41–60.

DuRant, Robert H., Cadenhead, C., Pendergrast, R.A., Slavens, G., and Linder, C.W. (1994). Factors associated with the use of violence among urban black adolescents. *American Journal of Public Health*, 84, 612–617.

Dwyer, K.P., Osher, D., and Warger, W. (1998). *Early warning, timely response: A guide to safe schools*. Washington, DC: U.S. Department of Education. (ERIC Document Reproduction Service No. ED. 418 372).

Elliott, D.S. (1994). "Serious violent offenders: Onset, developmental course, and termination: The American Society of Criminology 1993 Presidential Address." *Criminology*, 32.

Elliott, D.S., Hamburg, B., and Williams, K.R. (1998). *Violence in American schools: A new perspective*. Boulder, CO: Center for the Study and Prevention of Violence.

Fagan, J. (June 1996). Recent perspectives on youth violence. Paper presented at the Northwest Conference on Youth Violence, Seattle, Washington.

Farrington, D.P. (1989). Early predictors of adolescent aggression and adult violence. *Violence and Victims*, 4, 79–100.

Flynn, C.P. (January 2000). Why family professionals can no longer ignore violence toward animals. *Family Relations*, 49, 87–95.

Hagen, J., and Foster, H. (2001). Youth violence and the end of adolescence. *American Sociological Review*, December 874–899.

Hawkins, D., and Catalano, R. (1992). *Communities that care*. San Francisco: Jossey-Bass.

Herrenkohl, T., Huang, I., Kosterman, B. et al. (February 2001). A comparison of social development processes leading to violent behavior in late adolescence for childhood initiators and adolescent initiators of violence. *Journal of Research in Crime and Delinquency*, 38, 45–63.

Hilton, M.E. (1991). The demographic distribution of drinking patterns in 1984. In W.B. Clark and M.E. Hilton (Eds.), *Alcohol in America: Drinking practices and problems* (pp. 73–86). Albany: State University of New York Press.

Huston, A.C., Donnerstein, E., Fairchild, H., Feshbach, N.D., Katz, P.A., Murray, J.P., Rubinstein, E.A., Wilcox, B., and Zuckerman, D. (1992). *Big world, small screen: The role of television in American society*. Lincoln: University of Nebraska Press.

Javier, R.A., Herron, W.G., and Primavera, L.H. (1998). Violence and the media: A psychological analysis. *International Journal of Instructional Media*, 25, 339–355.

Kolko, D.J. (1985). Juvenile fire setting: A review and methodological critique. *Clinical Psychology Review*, 31, 345–376.

Kolko, D.J. and Kazdin, A.E. (1991). Aggression and psychopathology in match playing and fire setting children: A replication and extension. *Journal of Clinical Child Psychology*, 20, 191–201.

Landesman-Dwyer, S. (1992). The relationship of children's behavior to maternal alcohol consumption. In E.L. Abel (Ed.), *Fetal alcohol syndrome: Volume II, Human Studies* (pp. 127–148). Boca Raton, FL: CRC Press.

Larkby, C., and Day, N. (1997). The effects of prenatal alcohol exposure. *Alcohol Health and Research World*, 21, 192–198.

Lazarus, R.S., and Folkman, S. (1984). *Stress, Appraisal and Coping*. New York: Springer.

Lockwood, R., and Church, A. (1998). Deadly serious: An FBI perspective on animal cruelty. In R. Lockwood and F. R. Ascione (Eds.), *Cruelty to animals and interpersonal violence: Readings in research and application* (pp. 241–245). West Lafayette, IN: Purdue University Press.

Loeber, R., and Farrington, D.P. (1998). *Serious and violent juvenile offenders: Risk factors and successful interventions*. Thousand Oaks, CA: Sage.

Lynam, D. (1996). Early identification of chronic offenders: Who is the fledgling psychopath? *Psychological Bulletin*, 120, 209–234.

Majewski, F. (1978a). Alcoholic embryopathy. *Fortschrifte der Medizin*, 96(43), 2207–2213.

Majewski, F. (1978b). The damaging effect of alcohol on offspring. *Nervenarzt*, 49(7), 410–416.

May, P.A., and Gossage, J.P. (2001). Estimating the prevalence of fetal alcohol syndrome: A summary. *Alcohol Research and Health*, 25, 159–167.

Mayer, G.R. (1995). Preventing antisocial behavior in the schools. *Journal of Applied Behavior Analysis*, 28, 467–478.

McCord, J. (1999). Family relationships, juvenile delinquency, and adult criminality. In F.R. Scarpitti and A.L. Nielson (Eds.), *Crime and criminals: Contemporary and classic readings* (pp. 167–176). Los Angeles: Roxbury.

Miller, K.S., and Knutson, J.F. (1997). Reports of severe physical punishment and exposure to animal cruelty by inmates convicted of felonies and by university students. *Child Abuse and Neglect*, 21, 59–82.

Moffitt, T.E. (1994). Adolescence-limited and life-course persistent antisocial behavior: A developmental taxonomy. *Psychological Review*, 100, 674–701.

Moses, A. (1999). Exposure to violence, depression, and hostility in a sample of inner city high school youth. *Journal of Adolescence*, 22, 21–32.

Murray, B.A., and Myers, M.A. (1998). Conduct disorders and the special-education trap. *The Education Digest*, 63, 48–53.

National Fire Protection Association. (1999). Statistics on the national fire problem. Available online at: www.fema.gov/nfpa/

National Institutes of Health. (September 28, 2001). Pregnancy and Drug Use, # 13568, Bethesda, MD: Retrieved June 26, 2002 from the World Wide Web: www.nida.nih.gov/infofax/pregnancy/ternds.html

Natvig, G.K., Albrektsen, G., and Qvarnstrom, U. (2001). School-related stress experience as a risk factor for bullying behavior. *Journal of Youth & Adolescence*, 30, 561–575.

Obiakor, F.E., Merhing, T.A., and Schwenn, J.O. (1997). *Disruption, disaster, and death: Helping students deal with crises*. Reston, VA: The Council for Exceptional Children. (ERIC Document Reproduction Service No. ED 403 709).

Office of Juvenile Justice and Delinqency Prevention. *The Juvenile Bulletin*, September 1997.

Olegard, R., Sabel, K.G., Aronsson, M., Sandin, B., Johansson, P.R., Carlsson, C., Kyllerman, M., Iverson, K., and Hrbek, A. (1979). Effects on the child of alcohol abuse during pregnancy: Retrospective and prospective studies. *Acta Paediatrica Scandinavica*, 275 (Suppl), 112–121.

Olweus, D. (1997). Bully/victim problems in school: Facts and intervention. *European Journal Psychology and Education*, XII(4), 495–510.

O'Toole, M.E. (1999). *The school shooter: A threat assessment perspective*. Quantico, VA: National Center for the Analysis of Violent Crime.

Pastore, D.R., Fisher, M., and Friedman, S. (1996). Violence and mental health problems among urban high school students. *Journal of Adolescent Health*, 18, 320–324.

Patterson, G.R., Reid, J.B., and Dishion, T.J. (1992). *A social interactional approach: Antisocial boys.* Eugene, OR: Castalia Press.

Peterson, R.L., and Skiba, R. (Jan./Feb. 2001). Creating school climates that prevent school violence. *The Clearing House*, 74, 155–163.

Pulkkinen, L., and Tremblay, R.E. (1992). Patterns of boys' social adjustment in two cultures and at different ages: A longitudinal perspective. *International Journal of Behavior*, 15(4), 527–553.

Puzzanchera, C. (February 2000). *Self-reported delinquency by 12-year-olds, 1997.* Washington, DC: Office of Juvenile Justice and Delinquency Prevention, U.S. Department of Justice.

Raines, J.C., and Foy, C.W. (December 1994). Extinguishing the fires within: Treating juvenile fire setters. *Families in Society: The Journal of Contemporary Human Services*, 75, 596–607.

Reid, J. (1993). Prevention of conduct disorder before and after school entry: Relating interventions to developmental findings. *Development and Psychopathology*, 5(1/2): 243-262.

Repo, E., and Virkkunen, M. (1997). Young arsonists: History of conduct disorder, psychiatric diagnoses and criminal recidivism. *Journal of Forensic Psychiatry*, 8(2), 311–320.

Sakheim, G.A., Osborn, E. (1999). Severe vs. nonsevere fire setters revisited. *Child Welfare*, 78, 411–434.

Schwab-Stone, M., Ayers, T.S., Kasprow, W., Voyce, C., Barone, C., Shriver, T., and Weissberg, R. (1995). No safe haven: A study of violence exposure in an urban community. *Journal of the American Academy of Child and Adolescent Psychiatry*, 38, 1343–1352.

Schwab-Stone, M., Chuansheng, C., Greenberger, E., Silver, D., Lichtman, J., and Voyce, C. (1999). No safe haven II: The effects of violence exposure on youth. *Journal of the American Academy of Child and Adolescent Psychiatry*, 38, 359–367.

Showers, J., and Pickrell, E. (1987). Child fire setters: A study of three populations. *Hospital and Community Psychiatry*, 38, 495–501.

Shubert, T. H., Bressette, S., Deeken, J., and Bender, W. N. (1999). Analysis of random school shootings. In W. N. Bender, G. Clinton, and R. L. Bender (Eds.), *Violence prevention and reduction in schools* (pp. 97–101). Austin, TX: PROED

Simons, L.E. (2001). Media violence. *Offspring*, Spring 1(1): 12–16.

Skiba, R.J., Peterson, R.L., and Williams, T. (1997). Office referrals and suspensions: Disciplinary intervention in middle schools. *Education and Treatment of Children*, 20, 295–315.

Snyder, H.N., and Sickmund, M. (1999). *Juvenile offenders and victims: 1999 national report.* Washington, DC: Office of Juvenile Justice and Delinquency Prevention, U.S. Department of Justice.

Sprague, J.R., and Walker, H.M. (Spring 2000). Early identification and intervention for youth with antisocial and violent behavior. *Exceptional Children*, 66, 367–379.

Streissguth, A.P. (1993). Fetal alcohol syndrome in older patients. *Alcohol and Alcoholism* 2(Suppl), 209–212.

Streissguth, A.P., Aase, J.M., Clarren, S.K., Randels, S.P., Ladue, R.A., and Smith, D.F. (1991). Fetal alcohol syndrome in adolescents and adults. *Journal of the American Medical Association*, 265(15), 1961–1967.

Tapia, E.H. (1971). Children who are cruel to animals. *Child Psychiatry and Human Development*, 2, 70–77.

Thornberry, T.P., Huizinga, D., and Loeber, R. (1995). The prevention of serious delinquency and violence: Implications from the program of research on the causes and correlates of delinquency. In J.C. Howell, B. Krisberg, J.D. Hawkins, and J.J. Wilson (Eds.) *A sourcebook: Serious, violent, and chronic juvenile offenders* (pp. 213–237). Thousand Oaks, CA: Sage.

Thornberry, T.P., Smith, C.A., Rivera, C., Huizinga, D., and Stouthamer-Loeber, M. (September, 1999). *Family disruption and delinquency.* Washington, DC: Office of Juvenile Justice and Delinquency Prevention, U.S. Department of Justice.

Tingle, D., Barnard. G.W., Robbins, G., Newman, G., and Hutchinson, D. (1986). Childhood and adolescent characteristics of pedophiles and rapists. *International Journal of Law and Psychiatry*, 9 (Suppl), 103–116.

Wagner, L., and Lane, L. (1998). *Juvenile justice services: 1997 report.* Eugene, OR: Lane County Department of Youth Services.

Walker, H.M., and Severson, H.H. (1990). *Systematic screening for behavior disorders*. Longmont, CO: Sopris West.

Walker, H.M., Colvin, G., and Ramsey, E. (1995). Antisocial behavior in school: Strategies and best practices. Pacific Grove, CA: Brooks/Cole.

Whitney, L., and Smith, P. (1993). A survey of the nature and extent of bully/victim problems in junior/middle and secondary schools. *Educational Research*, 35, 3–25.

Widom, C.S. (October 1992). *The cycle of violence*. Washington, DC: National Institute of Justice Research in Brief.

Widom, C.S. (1999). The cycle of violence. In F.R. Scarpitti and A.L. Nielson (Eds.), *Crime and criminals: Contemporary and classic readings* (pp. 332–334). Los Angeles: Roxbury.

Wilson, W., and Hunter, R. (1983). Movie-inspired violence. *Psychological Reports*, 53, 435–441.

3

School Violence

With several high-profile shootings in the past few years, we have become aware of the high level of violence in American schools. Although *school violence* usually makes us think of school shootings, in this chapter the term has expanded meaning and includes bullying, intimidation, threats, theft, sexual harassment, and violence near schools grounds. As we will see in the following discussion, school violence is a serious problem in American schools. Further, the profiles that define the children most likely to commit school violence may not adequately include the "invisible children," who are often the recipients of bullying and intimidation by schoolmates, and who harbor resentments that sometimes resolve themselves in school shootings and other acts of violent retribution.

Amount of School Violence

Sprague and Walker (2000) report that more than 100,000 students bring weapons to school each day and that more than forty students are killed or wounded with these weapons annually. They note that many students experience bullying and other behaviors that have a negative impact on their school-related functioning. The authors report that over 6,000 teachers are threatened each year and that over 200 teachers each year are assaulted by students on school grounds. Schools are often used by gangs to recruit new gang members, and gang activities often disrupt normal classroom functioning and give students a sense of danger (Committee for Children, 1997; National School Safety Center, 1996; Walker, Colvin, & Ramsey, 1995). Crowe (1991) notes that a National Institute of Education study revealed that 40 percent of the robberies and 36 percent of the assaults against urban youth took place on or near school grounds. Of the students who admit to bringing weapons to school, half say the weapons are for protection against other youth with weapons.

The 1999 Youth Risk Behavior Survey (National Center for Injury Prevention and Control, 2001), summarized school-related violence by noting that

- 35.7% of high school students reported being in a physical fight in the past 12 months and 4% of students were injured in a physical fight seriously enough to require treatment by a doctor or nurse.
- 17.3% of high school students carried a weapon (e.g., gun, knife, or club) during the 30 days preceding the survey.
- 4.9% of high school students carried a gun during the 30 days preceding the survey.
- 14.2% of high school students had been in a physical fight on school property one or more times in the past 12 months.
- 7.7% of high school students were threatened or injured with a weapon on school property during the 12 months preceding the survey.
- 6.9% of high school students carried a weapon on school property during the 30 days preceding the survey.
- 5.2% of students had missed 1 or more days of school during the 30 days preceding the survey because they had felt too unsafe to go to school.

In a study by Peterson et al. (1998), 202 teachers, building administrators, and district administrators in 15 school districts of varying sizes from 12 states, representing all geographical regions of the United States, participated in a study of school violence. The authors reported that most respondents had experienced some level of violence at least one or more times in the past two years. Sixty-three percent of the respondents said they had been verbally threatened or intimidated, 28 percent had been physically threatened or intimidated, 11 percent had been sexually threatened or intimidated, 68 percent had been verbally attacked, 9 percent had been physically attacked, and 55 percent indicated that their room, their personal property, or the school in which they worked had been seriously vandalized. Twenty-six percent of the respondents said that violence was increasing or greatly increasing at the preschool level and 53 percent said that violence was increasing or greatly increasing at the elementary level. Almost 65 percent of the respondents said that violence was increasing at the middle school, junior high, and at senior high levels.

Stevens (1995) reports that almost 3 million crimes are committed on or near a school campus each year, constituting 11 percent of all reported crimes in America (Sautter, 1995). Kauffman (1997) notes that 80 percent to 90 percent of all school-age children and youth, in reports to others, indicate that they have been involved in acts of violence and aggression. Siegel and Senna (1994) report that a large proportion of these violent acts occur in school. Murray and Myers (1998) indicate that only 9 percent of the juvenile violent crimes committed in schools are reported to criminal justice authorities, compared with a 37 percent report rate for similar juvenile street crime. The authors believe these data suggest that schools are avoiding involvement in the juvenile justice system.

Fitzpatrick (1999) reports that even as violence has declined in the United States, violence among children and adolescents remains a very problematic area of concern. Although national homicide rates have been fairly stable in the past two decades, homicides by youth under the age of 25 have more than doubled in the past 20 years. Since the early 1980s, youth under the age of 18 were victims of violence at a rate five to six times that of adults (Bureau of Justice Statistics, 1997). Much of this violence happens near schools and may have its origins in the interactions children have with other schoolmates. Of the children victimized by violence, males, particularly black males, were victims of violence at twice the rate of white males. Children from households earning less than $15,000 a year were two to three times more likely to be victims of violence compared with their higher income counterparts (Bureau of Justice Statistics, 1997). Clearly, there are conditions of gender, income, and neighborhoods that increase the probability of school violence.

Reasons for Increased School Violence

In a study by Peterson et al. (1998), the primary reasons for the increase in school violence, as suggested by the authors, are:

> lack of rules or family structure, 94%; lack of involvement or parental supervision, 94%; violence acted out by parents, 93%; parental drug use, 90%; student drug/alcohol use, 90%; violent movies, 85%; student poor self-concept/emotional disturbance, 85%; violence in television programs, 84%; nontraditional family/family structure, 83%; and gang activities, 80%. (p. 348)

Fitzpatrick (1999) believes that another reason for increased school violence is the unwillingness of large numbers of youth to walk away from fights. Youth, at all age ranges, who believe that it isn't possible to walk away from a fight are at significant risk of violence, either during the confrontation or later, through acts of revenge. Fitzpatrick goes on to suggest that once a child is challenged, he or she must fight or lose the respect of peers. This reaction often leads nonviolent children into violent acts and victimization. Fitzpatrick also reports that boys in elementary and middle schools have a greater chance of being involved in violence than will girls, but that girls tend to become involved in fighting and aggressive behavior later in their teenage years. Myles and Simpson (1998) believe there are three major reasons for increased school violence in America:

1. There is a significant increase in aggression and violence in America (Kauffman, 1997; Walker, Colvin, & Ramsey, 1995). Frequent exposure to acts of violence make violence socially acceptable and serves to desensitize children from their significance.

2. Increasing numbers of seriously disturbed, violent, and socially maladjusted children in the classroom increase school aggression and violence. This comes at a time when there are fewer resources available to refer children with potential for school violence.

3. There is a lack of teachers trained to work with violent children in the general classroom. Appropriate support systems to help teachers cope with violent children are lacking.

In his study of school violence, Fitzpatrick (1999) came to the interesting conclusion that a major predictor of school victimization was how safe students assessed their school environments to be. He found that students in elementary schools and middle schools who had more negative views of the safety of their school environments were also victimized more often. Fitzpatrick (1999) believes that children who perceive dangerous environments often find themselves in the midst of those very environments and, as a result, experience a higher degree of violence. This is particularly true for elementary-age children who may know that certain children in the school are dangerous but are unable to avoid them.

Gang Influences on School Violence

The influence of gangs on younger children is significant and has a particular impact on schools. Young people join gangs for a variety of reasons: a search for love; structure and discipline; a sense of belonging and commitment; the need for recognition and power; companionship, training, excitement, and activities; a sense of self-worth and status; a place of acceptance; the need for physical safety and protection; and part of a family tradition (Glicken and Sechrest, 2003).

Not all children who are at risk for gang affiliation actually join gangs. According to Sechrest (2001), some common characteristics among children living in poverty and adverse situations who seem to be stress-resistant and avoid gang affiliation are as follows:

1. The children are well liked by peers and adults and have well-developed social and interpersonal skills.
2. They were reflective rather than impulsive about their behavior.
3. They have a high sense of self-esteem, self-efficacy, and personal responsibility.
4. They have an internal locus of control and believe they are able to influence their environment in a positive manner.
5. They demonstrate an ability to be flexible in their coping strategies.
6. They have well-developed problem-solving skills and intellectual abilities.
7. They have positive role models and have been exposed to more positive than negative experiences.
8. They have a sense of hope for the future and a belief in their own abilities.
9. They have an ability to cope with the crises and problems that arise in their lives.

Reasons for gang membership continue to be studied in considerable detail, but there is relatively little information on the process of transitioning from gang life. Hughes (1997) studied ex-gang members who successfully made the transition from gang life to other more socially acceptable activities. She reported four reasons for the transition from gang involvement: (1) concern for the well-being of young children, often their own; (2) fear of physical harm, incarceration, or both; (3) time to contemplate their lives, often done in prisons; and (4) support and modeling by helping professionals and indigenous community helpers.

The most promising reason for the transition from gang life, according to Hughes (1997), appears to be respect and concern for the safety of young children. Many gang members have fathered children. As their children begin to grow, these fathers experience concern for the welfare of the children. Additionally, ex-gang members have begun to share similar concerns with at-risk youth in their communities and mentor them away from gang involvement. Using the notion of concern for young children as a reason for transitioning from gang life, it would be very useful to find out when that concern for the safety of children begins and how social service organizations can use this information to facilitate the transition from gang involvement. It also might be useful to find out whether the transition from gang involvement occurs early enough to discourage the young children related to gang members from involvement in gang-related activities. One of the major reasons for gang involvement, according to Sechrest (2001) is the family tradition of being in the same gang as a parent or sibling. Sometimes, family tradition is used in the form of a "legacy" for early recruitment into gangs and may occur during elementary school, when young recruits are given assignments to test their mettle as potential gang members. Such assignments may involve school violence and/or random violence including the use of weapons. As dangerous as gang activity can be in schools, Schwartz (1996) writes,

> Gang activity at school is particularly susceptible to "the Ostrich syndrome," as administrators may ignore the problem. An unfortunate consequence of such denial is that opportunities to reduce violence are lost. This creates a situation where teachers do not feel supported when they impose discipline, students do not feel protected, and the violence-prone think they will not be punished. (p. 1)

Although Chapter 4 deals entirely with school programs to reduce violence, Schwartz (1996) offers some general violence-reduction approaches that seem specific to reducing potential gang activity in schools:

> 1. An accurate assessment of the existence of violence and, especially, gang activity. 2. Use all the resources in the community, including social services and law enforcement, and not just rely on school officials to deal with the problem. 3. Incorporate family services into both community and school programs. 4. Intervene early in a child's life. 5. Include not only anti-violence strategies but also positive experiences. 6. Create and communicate clearly defined behavior codes, and enforce them strictly and uniformly. 7. Prepare to engage in a long-term effort. (p. 5)

Another potential remedy for gang violence in schools is a program called Father to Father, a national initiative supported by former Vice President Al Gore for the purpose of strengthening the bond between fathers and sons. Nationally, numerous agencies have joined this initiative and have developed specific programs focused on fatherhood, an idea that could help gang members use their concern for the safety of children to leave gang life. Although these programs have promising anecdotal rates of success, none has been studied with any degree of objectivity.

Gang Violence

Regarding the number of youth involved in gangs, one estimate is that more than 3,875 youth gangs exist, with a total of more than 200,000 gang members in the 79 largest U.S. cities (Spergel, 1995). Research suggests that there is a significant connection between gang involvement, gang violence, and firearms. Quinn and Downs (1995, p. 15) studied 835 male inmates in six juvenile correctional facilities in four states. The authors found that movement from non-gang membership to gang membership brought increases in most forms of gun-involved conduct. Forty-five percent of the sample described gun theft as a regular gang activity. Sixty-eight percent said their gang regularly bought and sold guns, and 61 percent described "driving around and shooting at people you don't like" as a regular gang activity involving children as young as age 10.

Johnson (1999) noted that during the past two decades, the United States has seen the youth gang problem grow at an alarming rate, with gang members increasingly under the age of 12. Johnson (1999) reported that the number of cities with youth gang problems increased from an estimated 286 cities with more than 2,000 gangs and nearly 100,000 gang members in 1980 to about 2,000 cities with more than 25,000 gangs and 650,000 members in 1995, data that are almost three times higher than Spergel's (1995) estimates. Youth gangs are present and active in nearly every state, as well as in Puerto Rico and other territories. Few large cities are gang-free, and many cities and towns with populations of less than 25,000 are reporting gang problems. Thus, the issue of youth gangs is now affecting new localities, such as small towns and rural areas.

James, A Victim of School Violence: A Case Study

James is a sixth grader in a low-income area of an eastern city of moderate size. There is a great deal of bullying and intimidation of students by classmates in James's school. Most of the children are too frightened to report the harassment and just accept it as part of the price they pay for being poor. Many of the children believe that the schools they go to are little more than warehouses, places to keep them off the streets and out of trouble. Little actual learning takes place as a parade of new teachers present themselves weekly and then mysteriously disappear. Most of each day is spent disciplining boys who act out in class. Hardly anyone studies or takes school seriously. By age 12, many of the children believe their life path has been set and that nothing positive will happen to them. Their teachers reinforce this feeling of pessimism through attitudes that suggest to students that the teachers wished they were somewhere else.

James is a serious boy with serious aspirations. His parents, although desperately poor, have strong hopes for James. He thinks if he does well in life, he can help his family leave the poverty and the high crime in a neighborhood he has begun to despise and fear. There is a classmate of James by the name of Ronald who is in the midst of being initiated into a gang. Ronald hates James because James represents everything that Ronald feels he can't be. Ronald has decided to hurt James and has asked his gang friends to help out. One afternoon in school, the boys found James alone in the bathroom and severely beat him. James lay semiconscious in the bathroom for hours until he was found by a janitor, who called 911. The police wondered why no one had gone looking for James or why the bathroom was unsupervised, but in a school as poorly functioning as James's, these are daily occurrences and people have begun going to the restrooms in packs. The major criticism of James by his classmates was that he shouldn't have gone to the bathroom alone.

Ronald and his friends were sent to juvenile hall and were held until a hearing sent them to a juvenile facility in a different part of the state.

James feels no comfort in this because he believes he is marked for further violence by Ronald's gang friends. He feels so unsafe at school that he can hardly function, and his grades have begun to slip. Because the school district is experiencing a severe financial crisis, there are no crisis counselors for him to see at school and little in his area of the community to offer him the supportive help he needs after such a serious trauma. His parents have taken matters into their own hands and have decided to leave the community and move to a safer school for James. This was a difficult move but one that turned out to have a very positive impact on James. The actions of his parents touched him deeply and he has recommitted himself to school work and has returned to some of his prior feelings of optimism. Like too many victims of violence, however, a core of James has been changed and he is hypervigilant and less trustful than he used to be. He knows he'll make it in life and help his family, but he will never view the world as either safe or fair. Cynicism in someone so young can go a long way to creating unhappiness, even in the face of achievement, and James knows that he has changed and that he has to be tough and unsentimental about life.

Discussion

It's shameful that the children most at risk of violence are often the same children who have the least protection from violence. It's easy enough to blame the school district, but schools like James's former school are badly underfunded, and good teachers can't be forced to teach in schools in which they feel unsafe. Many of the schools that are failing to provide either a safe environment or a sound educational experience are taken over by counties or states with little positive benefit. Like the inner cities of many urban areas of America, inner-city schools are violence prone. Getting a sound education for the children who most need it is difficult when much of the day is spent dealing with serious acting-out behavior in the classroom.

As is noted throughout this book, the solutions to school violence are varied and complex, but as a national effort, children should not be in unsafe schools. Children showing early signs of violence need to be identified and provided services. Sometimes statistics fail to describe situations fully for children like James who grow up in high-poverty areas. In a book entitled *Kids Count Data Book* (State Profiles of Child Well-Being), published by the Annie E. Casey Foundation (2002), some figures help describe the plight of children like James whose parents lack financial resources and whose lives are very much at risk as a result. In the United States in 1999, there were 12,844 violent deaths of children age 1 to 14; 10,396 deaths from homicide and suicide in children age 15 to 19; 1,514,000 teens who dropped out of school; 1,291,000 teens who dropped out of school and were not working; 18,000,000 children living with parents where no parent had full-time year-round work; 13,500,000 children living in homes below the poverty level; and over 9,000,000 families headed by a single parent (Annie E. Casey Foundation, 2002, p. 179). These are data that beg for solutions, and until we can do a great deal better for children like James and his family, we can expect continued high levels of school violence in high-poverty, high-crime areas of the country.

Profiling Children with Potential for School Violence

The FBI, in a 1999 report entitled *The School Shooter: A Threat Assessment Perspective* (O'Toole 1999), developed a profile of characteristics consistent with children who have potential to kill others at school (1999, pp. 17–21). It should be noted that this list of characteristics is meant to provide a cumulative picture of many disparate characteristics. Children may have some of these characteristics and not be considered dangerous. When a child has many of these characteristics, however, the potential for violence increases.

1. **Low Frustration Tolerance:** The student is easily insulted, angered and hurt by real or perceived injuries done to him by others and has difficulty tolerating frustration.
2. **Poor Coping Skills:** The student consistently shows little if any ability to deal with frustration, criticism, disappointment, failure, rejection, or humiliation. His or her response is typically inappropriate, exaggerated, immature or disproportionate.
3. **Lack of Resiliency:** The student is unable to bounce back even when some time has elapsed since a frustrating or disappointing setback or putdown.
4. **Failed Love Relationship:** The student feels rejected and humiliated after the end of a love relationship and cannot accept or come to terms with the rejection.
5. **Injustice Collector:** The student will not forgive or forget the wrongs [others have done] or the people they believe responsible. The student may keep a "hit list" with the names of people he feels have wronged him.
6. **Signs of Depression:** The student shows lethargy, physical fatigue, a morose or dark outlook on life, a sense of malaise, and a loss of interest in activities that he once enjoyed.
7. **Narcissism:** The student is self-centered, lacks insight into the needs of others, and blames others for failures and disappointments. He or she may display signs of paranoia and assumes an attitude of self-importance or grandiosity that masks feelings of unworthiness (Malmquist, 1996).
8. **Alienation:** The student consistently feels different or estranged from others. It is more than being a loner and involves feelings of isolation, sadness, loneliness, not belonging, and not fitting in.
9. **Dehumanizes Others:** The student views other people as "non-persons" or objects to be thwarted. This attitude may appear in the student's artwork, writing, or conversations with others.
10. **Lack of Empathy:** The student shows an inability to understand the feelings of others. When others show emotion, the student may ridicule them.
11. **Exaggerated Sense of Entitlement:** The student expects special treatment and reacts negatively when he doesn't receive it.
12. **Attitude of Superiority:** The student has a sense of being superior and presents himself as smarter, more creative, more talented, more experienced, and worldlier than others.

13. **Exaggerated Need for Attention:** The student shows a pathological need for attention, positive or negative.

14. **Externalizes Blame:** The student fails to take responsibility for his actions. Often the student seems impervious to rational arguments or to common sense.

15. **Masks Low Self-Esteem:** Though appearing arrogant, the student's conduct veils underlying low self-esteem.

16. **Anger Management Problems:** The student is unable to express anger appropriately and has temper tantrums and outbursts that may be directed at people who had nothing to do with the original incident.

17. **Intolerance:** The student expresses racial or religious intolerance and displays symbols, jewelry or tattoos to express that intolerance.

18. **Inappropriate Humor:** The student's humor is insulting, macabre, belittling, or mean.

19. **Manipulative:** The student constantly tries to con others and win the trust of others so that they will excuse away threatening or aberrant behavior.

20. **Lack of Trust:** The lack of trust may approach a clinically paranoid state.

21. **Closed Social Group:** The student appears introverted or only associates with a small group and excludes others.

22. **Dramatic Changes in Behavior:** The student may show reckless disregard for school rules, dress codes, schedules, and other regulations.

23. **Rigid and Opinionated:** The student appears rigid, judgmental, and cynical and voices strong opinions about subjects they know little about, often disregarding logic and facts.

24. **Unusual Interest in Sensational Violence:** The student demonstrates an unusual interest in school shootings and other acts of violence. He may even admire the killers or express a desire to carry out similar acts.

25. **Fascination with Violence-Filled Entertainment:** The student shows an unusual fascination with movies, TV shows, computer games, music videos or printed material that focus intensively on themes of violence, hatred, control, power, death and destruction.

26. **Negative Role Models:** The student may be drawn to inappropriate role models such as Hitler, Satan or others associated with violence and destruction.

27. **Behavior Appears Relevant to Carrying out a Threat:** The student may spend inordinate amounts of time practicing with firearms, at the expense of other activities. The behavior appears to be related to possible threats to others.

An Alternative Profile: Invisible Children

Shubert et al. (1999) studied the random school shootings that took place from October 1997 to May 1998, in Pearl, Mississippi; West Paducah, Kentucky; Jonesboro, Arkansas; Edinboro, Pennsylvania; and Springfield, Oregon. The authors used various source materials from multiple press reports to develop primary reasons for the shootings. The data Shubert et al. (1999, p. 105) collected suggest the following:

1. Peers thought the shooters had serious emotional problems and a disregard for human life.
2. The shooters were almost completely estranged from family and friends.
3. All of the shooters had discussed violence and the killing of others in advance of the shootings. These discussions of violence and killings were ignored.
4. All the shooters had average or above-average intelligence.
5. On the days of the shootings, all of the perpetrators acted in organized and deliberate ways, suggesting that they had a plan and that the plan had been practiced in advance.

The authors also examined two subsequent shootings at Columbine High School in Littleton, Colorado, and Heritage High School in Conyers, Georgia. In the Georgia shootings, the student was being treated medically for depression (Skeesis, 2000), and one of the Columbine killers was described as troubled and suffering from depression and obsessive thinking. Fellow students at Columbine High School said that prior to the killings the shooters would "walk with their heads down, because if they looked up they'd get thrown into lockers and get called a 'fag'" (Bender 1999, p. 106). The shooters at Columbine High School made a videotape before the killings that showed the two boys acting out feelings of anger and revenge (Skeesis, 2000). Pressley (1999) reported that just before the killings in Georgia, the shooter had broken up with his girlfriend and had spoken of suicide and of bringing a gun to school. Only a day before the killings, the student told classmates that he would "blow up the classroom" (Cloud, 1999). Skeesis (2000) reported that all of the shooters involved in the Columbine and Georgia killings had access to many weapons and had built up arsenals of guns and ammunition that they had bought at gun shows. Barnard (1999) reported that the two Columbine killers had an increasing disregard for life and had bragged to friends about mutilating animals.

Bender, Shubert, and McLaughlin (2001) suggest that the FBI profile we usually associate with violent children didn't fit the young adolescent children involved in the aforementioned incidents of school killings. Instead,

> it becomes increasingly clear that the perpetrators are not the children who, traditionally, have been associated with violent acts within the schools; that is, they are not the school bullies or kids who have been previously identified as aggressive. A different group of students is committing these random shooting acts. [They are] the students who are easiest to ignore and they are using violence to offset and counteract their anonymity. They have internalized their aggression to such an extent that an explosion of violence is the result. Bender (1999) initially used the term "invisible kids" to identify the group of kids who were the perpetrators in the random shootings in schools. This term was selected to underscore the fact that these students were generally unknown by many school personnel prior to the shooting incidents because they were not noted for overt behavior problems. On the other hand, because these perpetrators seem to be frequently identified as "nerds" or "geeks," other students may bully and pick on them rather than ignore them. Emotionally wounded because of being shunned by other students, these students are essentially invisible to the adults in the school. Through an overtly violent act, these invisible kids seem to be demonstrating that they do have power in the school environment and that they will no longer accept a peer-imposed label of "nerd" or "geek." (p. 108)

Jack: A Case Study of School Violence

Jack is an 11-year-old fifth grader in a public elementary school in an affluent suburb of a southwestern city. Jack has violent fantasies about killing his classmates and teachers. Jack's fantasies of killing began early in his school career, and he can remember wanting to hurt other children as early as kindergarten. Jack is a very quiet, polite, and withdrawn child who keeps his fantasies hidden from others. While cleaning out his desk during a vacation break, his fifth-grade teacher found an Internet article that described ways of making simple bombs. The teacher immediately contacted the principal. Because of the school's no-violence policy, Jack was suspended and required to go for counseling.

Jack denied that the article belonged to him and claimed that someone else put the article in his desk. However, a search of his home computer by the police found a number of saved Internet articles related to bomb construction and the purchase of weapons. Jack had also been in a chat room composed of children and adolescents who assume other identities, many of them violent. Jack calls himself the "Death Giver" and describes himself as someone who plans revenge on the kids at school who "think that I'm a geek and treat me like crap. They don't know how much I hate them." A further search of his room found some equipment for constructing a bomb and a small arsenal of ammunition. One of Jack's friends, who worried about him, told his father that Jack had a gun and that he had been shooting it at targets with names of classmates, "someplace out in the country." The father told the authorities. Again, Jack denied that he had a gun.

Jack is hostile and uncommunicative in counseling. He thinks the counselor is "a dork" and refuses to cooperate. The parents haven't helped and urge Jack not to say anything that might incriminate him, or them. They hired a lawyer who brought suit against the school district for suspending Jack and the counseling was discontinued. A week after Jack was reinstated in school, a small bomb blast, set off during the weekend, destroyed Jack's homeroom. Jack was arrested and remanded to Juvenile Hall where he awaited a hearing and a presentence investigation. His lawyer instructed Jack not to talk to the authorities, and because of his age, his parents and the attorney had to be present when he was questioned. Because juvenile court has broader latitude in the way it handles cases, the juvenile judge permitted Jack to return home under close supervision by his parents. He also ordered Jack to undergo a psychological evaluation.

Discussion

A court-appointed clinical psychologist saw Jack for six hours. Jack was also given a battery of psychological tests, including an IQ test and tests to screen for serious behavioral problems. The following is a summary of his report:

> Jack is an 11-year-old male Caucasian child with high intellectual functioning. He is introverted, very angry, highly suspicious, and resentful of authority. He believes that other children have mistreated him for as long as he can remember and feels a deep and abiding anger at his schoolmates and teachers, whom he thinks have rejected and ridiculed him. Jack is an only child of professional parents who have ignored him while pursuing their careers. To placate him and to make up for their inattention, they have provided Jack with every material object he desires. They leave him unsupervised most of the time and have no real interest in his life. They reject the notion that Jack is violent and instead, see him as a highly intelligent child who likes to be alone. The father says that Jack is quite a bit

(continued)

Continued

like he was when the father was 11 and the father turned out just fine. The parents don't find his preoccupation with killing unusual and note that many boys his age are preoccupied with war, killing, and revenge. "Just look at the video games those kids watch," they told me. Jack has many violent video games and finds a kindred spirit in the anti-heroes who kill and maraud their way through life. The parents believe that Jack is going through a "stage" and that he will grow out of it. They point out that Jack won a science award last year for his work on explosives and say that the school is confusing a scientific interest with an emotional problem. They don't believe that Jack needs help and have decided to send him to a private school where he can pursue his science interests."

The psychologist continued,

In my view, Jack needs long term treatment in a confined and supervised setting. He is unremorseful about the bombing, denies culpability, and says that whomever set the bomb off was "cool." He wishes the bomb would have done more damage and that someone was present when the bomb went off. Jack is a violent young man and without treatment and supervision to provide a moral and emotional base, Jack is a time bomb waiting to go off. If Jack were an adult, he would be diagnosed as a Paranoid Personality Disorder: 301.0 (American Psychiatric Association, 1994, p. 634).

Jack's parents and attorney were able to convince the juvenile court judge to allow Jack to go away to school. The judge stipulated that, as a condition of allowing him to go away to school, Jack was to attend counseling sessions. Because the school is out of the court's jurisdiction, Jack and his parents ultimately declined treatment and Jack was left in the hands of a private school that knew nothing about Jack's emotional problems or his fantasies about killing. Two years later, Jack set off a bomb in the lunchroom of his school cafeteria, seriously injuring five students. Jack is currently in a treatment facility for violent youth, but his prognosis is very poor.

The staff member assigned to Jack notes,

Jack lives in a fantasy world where he believes that others are out to get him. He constantly thinks about paying others back for the harm he believes they've done to him. He has no close relationships with the other children, is a loner, and is avoided by the other residents who feel that his disturbed behavior makes him more dangerous than they are. They view him as a sort of mad scientist, a description Jack likes. Some of the children call him "Dr. Dementia" and laugh at him behind his back. Jack thinks up elaborate ways of paying them back. We have already found several small, ingeniously made bombs in his room. Jack's parents never come to visit and seldom call. He is full of loathing for his parents and refuses to take their occasional calls or read their letters and cards. He is, in our view, far too disturbed to attend the local middle school and is being taught by a tutor. He is required to come to group and individual therapy but uses the time to make fun of the therapist or to share his fantasies with the other children. We believe that Jack will try to kill someone in the facility and we make continual checks on his room."

Summary

School violence is a serious American problem, plaguing schools systems all over the country. The increase in rates of violence and the fact that many victims of school violence may start becoming perpetrators should give us pause as we consider the many intelligent children who are treated badly by lower functioning classmates and who consider acts of violence as ways of payback for the humiliation they've suffered. An FBI profile was presented that gives a number of characteristics of violence-prone youth in schools, but several writers advanced the notion that children who have been bullied and harassed by school mates may form a core of "invisible children" who outwardly seem nonviolent but inwardly harbor strong feelings of anger that sometimes lead to violence.

Integrative Questions

1. In your experiences in school, did you feel that teachers and administrators ignored the bullying and harassing behavior of certain students?

2. In your school experiences, did you encounter gang activities? What were they, how young were the gang members, and how dangerous did you perceive those activities to be?

3. Although school shootings have resulted in few lost lives, they do underscore school violence. In your school experiences, what students behaviors did you find the most disruptive, potentially dangerous, and in need of prevention?

4. Do you feel that dress codes, no tolerance for violence policies, and stricter codes of conduct will reduce school violence?

5. In the discussion of invisible children who end up commiting violent activities in school, why do you think the students assess them as violent but teachers and administrators don't?

References

American Psychiatric Association. (1994). *Diagnostic and statistical manual of mental disorders* (4th ed.). Washington, DC: American Psychiatric Association.

Annie E. Casey Foundation. (2002). *2002 Kids Count Data Book*. Baltimore: Annie E. Casey Foundation.

Barnard, N.D. (November 1999). The psychology of abuse. Retrieved November 1999 from Physicians Committee for Responsible Medicine (PCRM) web site: www.perm.org

Bender, W.N. (April 1999). *Violence prevention in the school*. An invited workshop presented at the Doylestown Public School Board of Education, Doylestown, PA.

Bender, W.N. (November 2001). Invisible kids: Preventing school violence by identifying kids in trouble. *Intervention in School and Clinic*, 37, 105–111.

Bender, W.N., Shubert, T. H., and McLaughlin, P.J. (November 2001). Invisible kids: Preventing school violence by identifying kids in trouble. *Intervention in School and Clinic*, 37, 105–111.

Bureau of Justice Statistics. (1997). *Criminal victimization, 1973-95.* Washington, DC: U.S. Government Printing Office.

Cloud, J. (May 1999). *Just a routine school shooting. Time.* Retrieved October 1999 from the World Wide Web: http://www.time.com: Just a routine school shooting.

Committee for Children. (1997). *Second step: Violence prevention curriculum.* Seattle: Committee for Children.

Critical Incident Response Group. (1999). *The school shooter: A threat assessment perspective.* National Center for the Analysis of Violent Crime. Quantico, VA: FBI Academy.

Crowe, T. (1991). *Habitual offenders: Guidelines for citizen action and public responses.* Washington, DC: Office of Juvenile Justice and Delinquency Prevention, U.S. Department of Justice.

Fitzpatrick, K.M. (October 1999). Violent victimization among America's school children. *Journal of Interpersonal Violence,* 14, 1055–1069.

Glicken, M., and Sechrest, D. (2003). *The role of the helping professions in treating and preventing violence.* Boston: Allyn & Bacon.

Hughes, M.J. (1997 June). An exploratory study of young adult black and Latino males and the factors facilitating their decisions to make positive behavioral changes. *Smith College Studies in Social Work,* 67, 401–414.

Johnson, L. (August 1999). Understanding and responding to youth violence: A juvenile corrections approach. *Corrections Today,* 61(5), 62–64.

Kauffman, J.M. (1997). *Characteristics of emotional and behavioral disorders of children and youth* (6th ed.). Upper Saddle River, NJ: Merrill.

Malmquist, C.P. (1996). *Homicide: A psychiatric perspective.* Washington, DC: American Psychiatric Press.

Murray, B.A., and Myers, M.A. (April 1998). Conduct disorders and the special-education trap. *The Education Digest,* 63, 48–53.

Myles, B.S., and Simpson, R.L. (May 1998). Aggression and violence by school-age children and youth: Understanding the aggression cycle and prevention/intervention strategies. *Intervention in School and Clinic,* 33, 259–264.

National Center for Injury Prevention and Control. (2001). Facts about violence among youth and violence in schools, NCIPC, Atlanta, Georgia. Available at www.cdc.gov/ncipc/cmpfact.htm

National School Safety Center. (March 1996). *National School Safety Center Newsletter.* Malibu, CA: National School Safety Center.

O'Toole, M.E. (1999). *The school shooter: A threat assessment perspective.* Quantico, VA: National Center for the Analysis of Violent Crime.

Petersen, G.J., Pietrzak, D. Speaker, D., and Kathryne, M. (September 1998). The enemy within: A national study on school violence and prevention. *Urban Education,* 33, 331–359.

Pressley, S.A. (May 1999). Six wounded in Georgia school shooting. *Washington Post.* Retrieved October 1999 from www.washingtonpost.com: Wounded in GA. School Shooting.

Quinn, J.F., and Downs, B. (1995). Predictors of gang violence: The impact of drugs and guns on police perceptions in nine States. *Journal of Gang Research,* 2(3), 15–27.

Sautter, R. (January 1995). Standing up to violence [Special report]. *Phi Delta Kappan,* 76, kl–k2.

Schwartz, W. (October 1996). An overview of strategies to reduce school violence. *ERIC Clearing House on Urban Education,* No. 115, EDO-UD-96-4.

Sechrest, D. (2001). *Juvenile crime: A predictive study.* Unpublished document.

Shubert, T.H., Bressette, S., Deeken, J., and Bender, W.N. (1999). Analysis of random school shootings. In W.N. Bender, G. Clinton, and R.L. Bender (Eds.), *Violence prevention and reduction in schools* (pp. 97–101). Austin: PRO-ED.

Siegel, L.J., and Senna, J.J. (1994). *Juvenile delinquency: Theory, practice, and law* (5th ed.). St. Paul, MN: West.

Skeesis, A. (January 2000). Monsters among us. . . . The tragedy at Columbine high; The victims/the heroes, Could it have been prevented? Columbine High School Tragedy Web Ring, Retrieved June 2002 from www.angelfire.com

Spergel, I. (1995). *The youth gang problem: A community approach.* New York: Oxford University Press.

Sprague, J.R., and Walker, H.M. (Spring 2000). Early identification and intervention for youth with antisocial and violent behavior. *Exceptional Children, 66,* 367–379.

Stevens, R. (April 26, 1995). Increasing violence in schools. In W.N. Bender & R.L. Bender (Eds.), *Teachers' safety.* (Teleconference produced by the Teacher's Workshop, Bishop, GA).

Walker, H.M., Colvin, G., and Ramsey, E. (1995). *Antisocial behavior in school: Strategies and best practices.* Pacific Grove, CA: Brooks/Cole.

4

Programs to Treat and Prevent School Violence

This chapter considers ways of reducing school violence through school-based programs and initiatives. Several case studies also are presented that focus on school violence and explain what other communities have done to help resolve the problem. Finally, the chapter ends with a discussion of rural school violence, an understudied and certainly underdocumented problem. Many of the most recent school shootings have occurred in rural communities, and not writing about the special problems of rural schools allows an incomplete discussion of the subject.

School-Based Violence Programs

Peterson and Skiba (2001, p. 155) suggest four ways to decrease school violence from an institutional point of view: (1) parent and community involvement, (2) character education, (3) violence prevention and conflict resolution curricula, and (4) bullying prevention.

Parent and Community Involvement

Christenson (1995) and Weiss and Edwards (1992) indicate that parent involvement encourages a more constructive learning environment by creating goals for parents in the home and teachers in the school that work to enhance both environments and are consistent in their objectives. With home and school working together, the impact on the community is positive, and goals for all three environments are consistent. Peterson and Skiba (2001) believe that increasing the involvement of parents can result in home environments that enhance student learning and increase cooperation with schools. High levels of parent–school cooperation can lead to less violent schools that respond to the potential for violence in more creative and effective ways. Epstein (1992) believes that schools can become involved in teaching parents better skills for managing and enforcing discipline in the home. One school, for example, requires parents of students who are at risk of being expelled to attend meetings to work on solutions for their child's acting-out behavior (Peterson & Skiba, 2001). Tasks that need to be done at home by children can be shared with parents so they are involved. By encouraging parents to become involved with schools, a cooperative spirit emerges that leads to faster and more effective responses to issues of violence. Parent involvement has been positively associated with student success, higher attendance rates, and lower suspension rates (Kube & Ratigan, 1991). Increased involvement by parents has been shown to provide better teacher satisfaction, improved parent understanding of school policies, better parent–child communication, and more successful and effective school programs, according to Peterson and Skiba (2001).

Character Education

Character education is the notion that schools have to take a direct role in teaching values to children. This should be done across the curriculum. London (1987) believes that character education focuses on civic involvement, the rules of citizenship in a just society, and in a child's personal commitment to becoming a productive and dependable citizen. According to Lickona (1988), character education in elementary school should achieve three objectives:

> 1) To promote development away from egocentrism and excessive individualism and toward cooperative relationships and mutual respect; 2) to foster the growth of moral agency—the capacity to think, feel, and act morally; and, 3) to develop in the classroom and in the school a moral community based on fairness, caring, and participation— such a community being a moral end in itself as well as a support system for the character development of each individual student. (p. 420)

To achieve these goals, Lickona proposed four processes in the classroom: (1) building self-esteem and a sense of community, (2) learning to work together and to help others, (3) thinking about the outcomes of one's behavior and its impact on others, and (4) learning to make decisions that reflect group input and are participatory.

Violence Prevention and Conflict Resolution Curricula

These approaches teach children to use alternatives to violence when resolving interpersonal conflicts. These curricula may include programs that teach children conflict resolution strategies; actual conflict resolution teams headed up by students who patrol the school grounds and can provide conflict resolution as a way of reducing tension before the conflict is reported to the school authorities; and programs to teach children ways of avoiding situations in which violence might occur. Films, role-plays, and simulations may be used. Parents might also become involved and conflict resolution might be extended to problems in the home. Topics covered in conflict resolution curricula include anger management; learning to identify and express feelings about others; discussing issues related to racial, ethnic, and gender differences; and learning to cope with stress.

Bullying Prevention Programs

Bullying prevention programs are schoolwide zero-tolerance polices. The components of a successful bullying prevention program include improved adult supervision; classroom rules against bullying; positive and negative consequences for following and violating rules, respectively, interventions with the bullies and the victims; meetings with parents of bullies and victims; and regular classroom meetings to discuss ways of dealing with bullying. In elementary level schools, worksheets, role-plays, and related literature (stories about bullies and victims, for example) may be incorporated into the curricula. These comprehensive programs for dealing with bullying have been used in the curricula of many schools in many different countries and cultures, according to Olweus and Limber (1999). Olewus (1993) reported that one program using school, classroom, and individual and family interventions reduced bullying by 50 percent. Other programs, reported by Peterson and Skiba (2001, p. 155), have been shown to reduce fighting, vandalism, and truancy, while also increasing overall student satisfaction with school. However, as a number of authors remind us, most bullying goes undetected or ignored and leads to very negative impacts on victims, bullies, and on the entire school system. Well-developed programs teach all students that bullying is not acceptable behavior. Effective programs have significantly reduced the rate of bullying and have lead to much better school climates.

Additional Approaches to Decreasing School Violence

Schwartz (1996) suggests a variety of antiviolence programs for use in the schools. Among those programs is a no-tolerance policy for any sort of a dangerous weapon, with frequent searches for weapons in lockers and weapons detection at the school entryway. Schwartz also believes that helping children find suitable activities after school, and until their parents are home, is another highly effective way of reducing school violence after school lets out. She strongly supports a program to give children and adolescents an opportunity to stay after school under supervision to improve their scholastic performance, and for older children to find work in the community through help from the school. Schwartz encourages school systems to initiate antigang programs and to maintain dress codes that forbid the use of gang paraphernalia. The security of schools can be enhanced by monitoring halls at all time and by helping students and parents understand, through cooperative meetings, the dangers of violence. She also believes that antiviolence programs, with their focus on a safe school environment for everyone, require a very high degree of cooperation among teachers, who must commit to such programs because the teachers have the majority of the responsibility for enforcing the programs. Schools with violence problems should also provide self-esteem programs for children who suffer from low self-esteem, a condition that can lead to learning delays. Finally, Schwartz believes that most school violence originates with violence in the home and urges schools to initiate programs to provide services to children from violent homes and their families. She rightly notes that violence in families has a way of filtering back to the school in the form of school violence.

Several factors related to the school environment have been linked with aggression in youth, including strict and inflexible classroom rules, teacher hostility, and the lack of classroom management. In addition, youth in overcrowded schools are more aggressive toward peers than are adolescents attending uncrowded schools. Within the classroom, aggressive children have been observed to be more disruptive and off-task than their nonaggressive peers. Furthermore, low academic achievement, academic failure, lack of commitment to school, and school drop-outs have been associated with delinquent and aggressive behavior (Glicken & Sechrest, 2003).

Official school disciplinary or expulsion statistics may not accurately capture the true level of criminality, violent behavior, or gun possession problems at schools. Because most school-based crimes are customarily resolved as disciplinary offenses rather than matters to be resolved by the authorities outside of the school, rates of violence and weapon possessions at schools may greatly underestimate such behavior because official tracking mechanisms are often inadequate. For example, students and teachers may not report violent incidents or weapon possessions because they are afraid of reprisals or because they might feel that they will incur official criticism. Schools are relatively safe places when compared with estimates of aggregate juvenile crime and violence numbers; nevertheless, school-based levels of crime and violence are underestimated. School environments today are places where too much violence, crime, and weapon carrying occur, and student fears concerning violence and crime are real and have an adverse impact on student school attendance and learning. To reinforce the concerns students have about the safety of their schools, the National Center for Education Statistics (1995) estimates that about 160,000 students are absent from school every day because they do not want to become victims of violence.

Studer (1996) suggests the use of assertiveness training to teach children that they can be assertive without being aggressive, and writes,

> Aggression is an action that enhances the aggressor while it minimizes and violates the rights of others. The intent of the aggressive behavior is to humiliate and dominate. This behavior is in contrast to passive behaviors that are self-denying and inhibiting, as a person's own rights are disregarded and he or she gives in to demands of others. Instead, Baer (1976) defined assertiveness as "win-win" behavior in which an individual can stand up for his or her own rights in such a way that the rights of others are not disregarded. (p. 188)

Huey and Rank (1984) found assertiveness training to be very helpful with disruptive, low-achieving children who were referred for counseling because of their aggressive, acting-out behavior. The authors noted that after being given eight hours of assertiveness training, these children were less aggressive but were more assertive in the classroom. Mathias (1992) reported that the "DeBug" System, a training program to teach children assertiveness, showed overwhelmingly positive results in the classroom and substantially reduced aggressive behavior.

An Innovative School District Deals with School Violence: A Case Study

The school district in this case study asked that its name not be used because it is in the midst of a study to test the effectiveness of the approach described here. It felt that undue attention might create changes in the data, which would affect the findings. For this reason, the district is given a fictitious name of the Petofsky School District, an urban inner-city school district with very high rates of school violence and gang activity.

After the beating and rape of a sixth-grade teacher by one of her 12-year-old students, one of a series of violent crimes to plague the school district, the Petofsky School Board voted to adopt an innovative approach to the prevention and treatment of school violence. The district initiated a no-tolerance policy on violence, but one with a heart. All incidents of violence, either committed or prevented, were to be assessed and, if possible, treated. This policy was adopted as threats were called in daily of school bombings that effectively closed down all of the schools in the district, including the grade K-6 elementary schools. A chance break helped authorities find the caller of the bomb threats—an 11-year-old male white youth with an unremarkable school record and no history of acting-out behavior. The child, whose name is Robert, is one of the invisible children who act out against classmates because they perceive themselves as being disliked and picked on by their classmates. This was certainly the case with Robert, who has been the object of ridicule since kindergarten because of a severe cleft palate and speech problems. Many of the children have been unmerciful in their bullying and taunting of Robert, who has a deep sense of rage at the hurtful behavior he has had to endure. Robert has had his clothes taken away in the boys shower, his picture posted all over the school with derogatory statements, his hair forcibly cut Marine fashion, and an endless number of hurtful, ego-deflating, and damaging acts of violence. He is full of anger and seeks to take it out by disrupting the school and frightening his classmates. Robert is a very intelligent child and has been able to computer-enhance his voice so that his bomb threats have a robot-like quality that frightens the secretaries and the school-aged helpers who answer the phones.

Robert's parents are very angry at the school for not controlling the teasing and bullying he has had to endure. They have done everything to protect their child but without any help from the school, which sympathizes with Robert's plight but says that it is too understaffed to do much about it. When the School Board discovered the reason for the bomb threats, it created a policy that makes taunts and humiliating statements as serious as actual violence. Three boys and a girl in Robert's fifth-grade class, responsible for Robert's harassment, were suspended with mandatory treatment. Robert was also suspended for a semester, but he was provided very high level treatment and then transferred to a charter school with a good reputation for controlling mean-spirited behavior among its students.

Since instituting the no-taunting or bullying policy, Petofsky has experienced a sharp decline in school violence. As the violence has been reduced, the level of achievement of the children has risen significantly. Petofsky recognizes that children do badly in violent environments and has made a concerted effort to prevent violence at all costs. When violence occurs, the district tries to find out the cause, provide expert treatment, and recognizes that children who act out in school do so for reasons that may be preventable and treatable. The suspended children are all in empathy-training classes and continue in treatment. Children who force other children to the brink of violence are dangerous and need the same help as the offenders they taunt and abuse into violence.

The Relationship between Family Deterioration and School Violence

An entire chapter (Chapter 5) is devoted to the relationship between family violence and childhood violence. However, in this chapter on treatment programs to reduce school violence, a short introduction to the impact of family violence and family deterioration is offered as an introduction to treatment programs within schools.

Studer (1996) writes that the family is thought to be the most violent institution in our society (Myers, 1993). Problems within the family, Studer notes, are often solved using aggression. Myers (1993) reports that 17 percent of all homicides in the United States occur within a family situation. Studer (1996) believes that when parents use harsh physical means to discipline their children, children learn that battering and physical aggression are normal ways of expressing frustration and resolving problems. Aggressive problem-solving techniques may often be practiced in the school setting and are reinforced when the child successfully resolves conflict through the use of aggression and intimidation. Griffin (1987) found that children who demonstrate physically aggressive and antisocial behaviors and have developmental and academic problems before age 9 display more aggressive tendencies as adults than do individuals who do not demonstrate early behavioral and educational problems.

Herrenkohl and Russo (2001) suggest that child abuse and neglect reinforce a sense of distrust in children that may lead to aggressive interactions with peers and adults. The authors believe that abuse and neglect by parents model the way a child is likely to interact with others. Erikson's (1963) "stages" of psychosocial development include the development of trust. If a child experiences harsh physical punishment and neglect by a parent, it's possible that the child's subsequent distrust related to hostile feelings toward the parents might then define the child's interactions with others. Rutter (1987) believes that abuse and neglect by parents often leads to a sense of vulnerability in children that may cycle into aggression. Rutter also believes that vulnerable children sometimes use aggression as a way of coping with feelings of vulnerability and fear. Schools are one of the earliest social situations in which children may feel vulnerable, inadequate, angry, less intelligent, ignored, and a host of other emotions that may result in early aggression.

In a study of teacher ratings of the causes of school violence, Petersen, Pietrzak, and Speaker (1998) found that the top four rated causes were lack of rules or family structure, a lack of involvement or parental supervision, violence acted out by parents, and parental drug use. Commenting on the changing structure of American families and what they consider to be the increasing deterioration of family life, the authors write,

> As the basic structure of the family disintegrates, violence among family members increases, and this domestic violence spills into the classroom (Lystad, 1985). A new picture of the school must emerge to provide the variety of services that are needed by families to alleviate incidents of school violence. Home, school, and community must come together in a central location (i.e., the school campus) to make possible this reorganization of schools. Schools should strive to become part of any positive commu-

nity effort (Hranitz & Eddowes, 1990). The successful combination of administrators, faculty, health care practitioners, counselors, social workers, childcare workers, technological support, and community agency availability and funding is an essential component of the proactive elementary model. The family must be committed to the educational process, whereas the educational structure must be committed to the family. Because the data indicate that schools need to take on roles previously played by family members, the roles of teacher and administrator must also evolve. It may be that schools will need to fill the gap in these areas for families who are unable or unwilling to become involved. (p. 353)

The idea that schools may need to fill the gap left by violent and/or deteriorating families is one frequently expressed in the literature but often criticized by educators. Educators complain that not enough training, time, and resources are available to teach academic subjects, let alone make up for deteriorating families. However, Bender, Shubert, and McLaughlin (2001), in their study of school violence, write, "Educators must be proactive and demand that some of the funds spent on school safety efforts be allocated to support educators' time to reflect on the emotional well-being of each student in an effort to identify the children who need some significant adult to reach out to them" (p. 109).

Rather than doing as Bender and colleagues (2001) suggest, however, Murray and Myers (1998) noted that, all too often, children who begin to act out in the classroom are placed in special education classes and are classified as "Severely Emotionally Disturbed, following a serious offense, as the path of least resistance" (p. 48). Often, these children have conduct disorders and are neither severely emotionally disturbed nor in need of special education classes, which are, Murray and Myers noted, for truly disabled children: "Mislabeling a child to obtain services, to prevent a child from being expelled, or to remove the student to a special classroom is both inappropriate and unethical" (p. 48). The authors believe that children who act out do not fare well in special education classes and can disrupt a truly disabled population of students. Schools that support inappropriate diagnoses and placements "may be creating incubators for future antisocial or even criminal behavior" (p. 48). To emphasize their point, they give an example of misdiagnosis by a group of teachers: "At the end of the exercise, teacher groups were embarrassed to learn they had recommended Severely Emotionally Disturbed special-education placement and little if any success for each of the fictitious students—Abraham Lincoln, Eleanor Roosevelt, Thomas Edison, Albert Einstein, and Will Rogers" (p. 53).

Petersen, Pietrzak, and Speaker (1998), call for a new definition of schools as "town centers" that offer a variety of services needed by deteriorating and dysfunctional families to reduce school violence. Because family life is chaotic for many violence-prone children, the authors argue that schools must assume many of the roles previously played by family members and that the function of teachers and administrators must also change. The authors argue that family disintegration requires schools to take responsibility for teaching moral conduct. Education, they note, is more than "simply teaching the cognitive attributes of character development; it must also include the emotional attributes of moral maturity, such as conscience, self-respect, empathy, and self-control" (p. 350).

A Program for Violent Families

Because family violence is so often related to school violence, the Rose Elementary School, in a moderately sized industrial city in the northeastern industrial belt of the United States, believed that reducing the amount of bullying and intimidation of children and the hidden violence that resulted would require work with children and their families wherever family violence was known or suspected. The school board passed a policy that all bullying, intimidation, threats, harassment, theft, or any form of physical abuse used against another child, teacher, or staff member would result in mandatory counseling for the child and for his or her parents. Eighty percent of the children and parents in this cohort were involved in family violence. Another 10 percent of the parents were abusing substances, while the remaining 10 percent had problems in discipline and establishing consistent rules for the child to follow. All were brought together for counseling sessions with school social workers on a weekly basis. There were also required parenting classes. To make the point abundantly clear, a police officer was present at the meetings in case an adult became abusive. Many of the children from families known to be involved in domestic violence were being seen professionally, but the extra attention was welcomed by the children. Prior to the start of this program, the parents were seen in treatment on a hit-and-miss basis, and many of the fathers had never been involved in treatment or parenting classes because of work schedules or an unwillingness to cooperate.

Some of the parents were openly hostile to the need to attend the program and frequently voiced their objections. It was made clear to parents that early signs of violence in school were intolerable behaviors in this era of school shootings. Schools should be safe havens for children and teachers, and the learning environment should be stress-free. Children who intimidated and bullied, frightened the other children and made learning difficult. Much of the reason for a child's behavior came from home situations in which there was considerable violence. Violence at home was deemed intolerable, and the continued violence by children in school would be taken as a sign of the parents' inability to resolve their problems in nonviolent ways. Parents would be charged with child endangerment if family violence didn't stop immediately. The purpose of the classes the parents were attending was to teach parents the new skills needed to control their anger and to eliminate violence. If parents failed to attend, the matter would be turned over to the police. School violence had become an epidemic, and it would stop, *now.*

Parents were provided individual and group therapy on Saturday mornings from 8 to 11 A.M. From 11 A.M. to 2 P.M., they sat in anger-management classes and parent effectiveness training classes. From 2 to 4 P.M., they provided feedback, told stories of success and failure, shared concerns about their children, discussed their lack of awareness of the harm the parental fighting was having on their kids, and other topics that evolved as the sessions continued. There were 40 sets of parents at the beginning of the program. Three sets dropped out and were reported to the police. Eight fathers dropped out, but their wives stayed on. The fathers were reported to the police, and six returned as a result. The program was planned for 12 weeks but went on for almost a year as families began to experience the giddy feeling of functioning well. The bullying behavior ceased among the children of the parents being treated. The Rose School believes that bullying is a very serious sign of dangerous aggression, one that is preventable and treatable. As bullying rates declined, the school blossomed and Rose became a model school for the district and attracted many of the district's most promising children. Rose is a strict, no-nonsense school. Rules are taken seriously. It's not everyone's cup of tea. But as far as violence prevention goes, Rose is a safe school with increased state achievement scores, which have placed it in the upper 5 percent of all schools in the state. Before the violence prevention program, the school was in the 50th percentile. Stopping violence makes a difference, and the children and parents at Rose are the beneficiaries of a tough stance taken by the local school board members.

School Violence in Rural Communities

While this book was being written, the author was living in a rural community of about 25,000 people, located in a sparsely populated area of Michigan. Like many rural communities, this one was not immune from school violence. The local high school and middle schools have an unusually high number of bomb threats, and the local university had a number of bomb threats after the September 11, 2001, bombings of the World Trade Centers. The local paper seemed to be reporting more serious violence in the community including the rape and mutilation stabbing of a young woman my student assistant knew well. In March 2002, a distraught ex-husband killed his ex-wife and two members of her family in the parking lot of the local courthouse, a place I walked by everyday. A woman who was killed was my landlady's niece. When I expressed my sympathies to my landlord, he told me he was certain that the reason that nothing had been done to prevent the killings, after many restraining orders had been violated by the shooter, was that the niece's ex-husband was a "snitch" for the local police on drug manufacturing and distribution in the community.

The community feels like a safe town, but these isolated behaviors suggest that it may not be as safe as one would like to think. In a sense, this community represents many other small communities in America, where violence is greater than one might anticipate. We often think that *rural* means *nonviolent* and that violence only takes place in the urban schools and communities with large inner cities, but the reality is that many school killings have taken place in small, reasonably affluent communities with well-regarded schools. For this reason, it is important to remember that many of the same dynamics that cause violence in urban schools exist in rural schools. In rural communities, one finds alcoholism, family violence, drug dealing, poorly functioning families with little ability to discipline children, rural poverty, and every variation of cruelty and abuse one can imagine. What is often different in rural communities, however, is the lack of resources to provide needed services or trained mental health workers to help schools cope when violence takes place. To obtain needed help for violence-related issues in a rural community, one might need to drive 70 miles or more to the nearest larger community, a time commitment many people cannot make.

We think of poverty as an urban plight, but rural schools often suffer from extreme underfunding by poor rural counties that hope to provide more but lack the tax base to do so.

In rural communities, people often know one another over a lifetime. Forcing neighbors and friends to attend parent effectiveness treatment programs, or programs to decrease violence, can cause long-term animosities among neighbors and friends. When the person you want to attend these programs lives down the street from you, and his or her family is prominent in the community, it makes many school personnel reluctant to be overly assertive. Similarly, courts can be lenient to a fault because the judge may know a child and his family, or they may attend the same church. The author was told of a case in which a child struck a principal but was allowed back in the school after only a brief suspension. Rural communities, sad to say, have problems with school violence and often have a more difficult time dealing with those problems than do urban schools.

As a final sad commentary on the problems of rural schools, the author's former community has a Native American tribe living in the area surrounding the community. Members of the tribe have lived there for many hundreds of years, and for many of those years, children from the tribe attending local schools did poorly academically, had high drop-out rates, and were discriminated against in ways that should make all of us feel ashamed. The problem of rural discrimination against diverse populations is one of the shameful by-products of the homogeneity of rural life. My daughter went to elementary school and high school in Dubuque, Iowa, a beautiful rural community on the banks of the Mississippi River and only 17 miles from Galena, Illinois, where Ulysses S. Grant worked for his brother and father after being cashiered out of the army for alcoholism. The Dubuque School Superintendent urged the School Board to welcome diverse families and their children to the community. It was, she said, not good for children to grow up and have virtually no experience with diversity when the world was quickly becoming such a diverse place. A handful of non-white families accepted the challenge and moved to Dubuque, only to be met with overt racism that ended in days of racially motivated fighting in the Dubuque schools. Rural communities are often ill equipped for the changes in the composition of a community as new industries bring in groups of people who have different cultures, religious beliefs, languages, and strong ideas about the seriousness and importance of education.

The issue of rural schools and their problems requires the most serious consideration. Many of the same programs suggested for other schools must be implemented. New ways of funding schools must be devised so that rural schools are not resource-poor schools. And discrimination needs to be dealt with. When the author was growing up in Grand Forks, North Dakota, shortly after news about the Holocaust reached us, there were *more* episodes of anti-Semitism to Jewish children, our families, and to me personally than I can recount here. It stung then and it stings now to be called names, and to be fought with just because of your ethnicity, or to have people make assumptions about you that are entirely stereotypic. You never completely get over the discrimination you experience as a child. What I experienced in the 1940s makes me very concerned about the amount of discrimination in rural schools, which I think has become problematic throughout the country. Rural schools have a long way to go to develop programs to reduce racial, ethnic, religious, and gender intolerance. They can't begin to make those changes soon enough.

Summary

A number of programs to deal with school violence are discussed in this chapter. Among those programs are prevention of bullying, treatment of family violence, programs to build self-esteem, policies of no tolerance for violence, schools with cooperative arrangements with parents, and schools that support community efforts to reduce violence. The discussion of the role of educators to make up for deteriorating families centered on the need to help children develop a moral base that might lead to more socially responsible behavior.

Integrative Questions

1. Giving so much responsibility to educators to make up for the decline in family functioning seems absurd given declining academic scores and the difficulty children in many districts have in passing state achievement tests. Do you think it's wise to give added responsibilities to schools to socialize children whose families cannot do it?

2. School violence seems to exist without the involvement of the juvenile justice system, according to data presented in Chapters 2, 3, and 4. Do you feel that schools must be obligated to report violence in all of its manifestations if our violence problem is to be resolved?

3. Although children who act out should not be placed in special education classes, according to Murray and Myers, and they probably should not be mainstreamed because they're disruptive, where should they be placed?

4. Much has been made of the deteriorating nature of American families. Do you think family life in America is as dysfunctional as some authors think it is, and if so, why do you think it is so bad?

5. Programs to increase self-esteem in acting-out children seem wrong-headed. Many of these children have very high self-esteem and believe that they are special people who have the right to act out and to get their way. What do you think of self-esteem programs and their effectiveness in reducing aggression in schools?

References

Baer, J. (1976). *How to be an assertive (not aggressive) woman in life, in love, and on the job: A total guide to self-assertiveness*. New York: New American Library.

Bender, W.N., Shubert, T.H., and McLaughlin, P.J. (2001). Invisible kids: preventing school violence by identifying kids in trouble. *Intervention in School and Clinic*, 37, 105–111.

Christenson, S.L. (1995). Families and schools: What is the role of the school psychologist? *School Psychology Quarterly*, 10(2), 118–132.

Epstein, J.L. (1992). School and family partnerships: Leadership roles for school psychologists. In S.L. Christenson and J.C. Conoley (Eds.), *Home–school collaboration* (pp. 215–243). Silver Spring, MD: The National Association of School Psychologists.

Erikson, E. (1963). *Childhood and society*. New York: Norton.

Glicken, M.D., and Sechrest, D. (2003). *The role of the helping profession in treating and preventing violence*. Boston: Allyn & Bacon.

Griffin, G. (1987). Childhood predictive characteristics of aggressive adolescents. *Exceptional Children*, 54, 246–252.

Herrenkohl, R.C. and Russo, M.J. (February 2001). Abusive early child rearing and early childhood aggression. *Child Maltreatment*, 1, 3–16.

Hranitz, J.R., and Eddowes, E.A. (Fall 1990). Violence: A crisis in homes and schools. *Childhood Education*, 67, 4–7.

Huey, W.C., and Rank, R.C. (1984). Effects of counselor and peer-led groups' assertive training on black adolescent aggression. *Journal of Counseling Psychology*, 31, 95–98.

Kube, B.A., and Ratigan, G. (1991). All present and accounted for: A no-nonsense policy on student attendance keeps kids showing up for class—and learning. *The American School Board Journal*, 22–23.

Lickona, T. (February 1988). Four strategies for fostering character development in children. *Phi Delta Kappan*, 419–423.

London, P. (May 1987). Character education and clinical intervention: A paradigm shift for US schools. *Phi Delta Kappan*, 667–673.

Lystad, M. (1985). Innovative mental health services for child disaster victims. *Children Today*, 14, 13–17.

Mathias, C.E. (1992). Touching the lives of children: Consultative interventions that work. *Elementary School Guidance and Counseling*, 26, 190–201.

Murray, B.A., and Myers, M.A. (1998). Conduct disorders and the special-education trap. *Education Digest*, 63, 48–53.

Myers, J. (1993). *Social psychology* (3rd Ed.). New York: McGraw-Hill.

National Center for Education Statistics. (1995). *Annual Report 1995*. Washington, DC: U.S. Department of Education.

Olweus, D. (1993). *Bullying at school: What we know and what we can do*. Malden, MA: Blackwell.

Olweus, D., and Limber, S. (1999). Bullying prevention program. In D.S. Elliot (Ed.), *Blueprints for violence prevention*. Denver, CO: C and M Press.

Petersen, G.J., Pietrzak, D., and Speaker, K.M. (1998). The enemy within: A national study on school violence and prevention. *Urban Education*, 33, 331–359.

Peterson, R.L., and Skiba, R. January/February 2001). Creating school climates that prevent school violence. *The Clearing House*, 74, 155–163.

Rutter, M. (1987). Psychological resilience and protective mechanisms. *American Journal of Orthopsychiatry*, 57, 316–331.

Schwartz, W. (October 1996). An overview of strategies to reduce school violence. *ERIC Clearing House on Urban Education*, No. 115, EDO-UD-96-4. New York: Columbia University.

Studer, J. (1996). Understanding and preventing aggressive responses in youth. *Elementary School Guidance and Counseling*, 30, 194–203.

Weiss, H.M., and Edwards, M.E. (1992). The family–school collaboration project: Systemic interventions for school improvement. In S.L. Christenson, and J.C. Conoley (Eds.), *Home–school collaboration* (pp. 215–243). Silver Spring, MD: The National Association of School Psychologists.

5

The Strong Relationship between Child Abuse and Early-Onset Violence

Throughout, this book notes the considerable relationship between child abuse and early-onset violence in victims. The relationship is so compelling that we would be remiss not to offer a separate chapter on the diagnosis and treatment of child abuse. Some of the material in this chapter was also reported by Glicken and Sechrest (2003).

The Impact of Child Abuse

The Children's Bureau, a division of the Department of Health and Human Services (DHHS) collected data submitted by all of the states on child abuse and neglect in the United States for the year 2000 (The Children's Bureau, 2002). The data they collected are as follows:

1. In 2000, 3 million referrals regarding the welfare of approximately 5 million children were made to child protective service agencies in the United States. Sixty-two percent of the referrals were screened in and about one-third of the referrals (38 percent) were screened out. Screened-in referrals received investigations or assessments to determine whether maltreatment could be proven. Screened-out reports were sometimes referred to other appropriate health and social service agencies. Sedlack (1997) notes that there were 2.1 million reports of abused and neglected children in a 1986 study by the AAPC indicating that the number of reports had increased by almost 1 million in less than 15 years.

2. Approximately 879,000 children were found to be victims of child maltreatment (neglect, medical neglect, physical abuse, sexual abuse, and psychological maltreatment). Almost two-thirds of the child victims suffered neglect (including medical neglect); 19 percent were physically abused; 10 percent were sexually abused; and 8 percent were psychologically maltreated.

3. The rate of child victims per 1,000 children has been declining from 15.3 victims per 1,000 children in the population in 1993 to 11.8 victims per 1,000 children in the population in 1999. The victimization rate for 2000 rose slightly to 12.2 per 1,000 children in 2000. The rate of victimization for children at birth to 3 years old was 15.7 victims per 1,000 children of the same age. The victimization rate for children ages 16 and 17 was 5.7 victims per 1,000 children of the same age.

4. Victimization rates were almost the same for male and female victims (11.2 and 12.8 per 1,000 children, respectively). However, the sexual abuse rate was 1.7 victims per 1,000 female children compared to 0.4 victims per 1,000 male children. Fifty-one percent of all victims of child maltreatment were white; a quarter were African American; 15 percent were Hispanic; 2 percent were American Indian/Alaska Natives, and 1 percent were Asian/Pacific Islanders.

5. Almost 1,200 children died of abuse or neglect in 2000. Children less than a year old accounted for 44 percent of child fatalities. Almost 85 percent of all child fatalities were younger than 6 years of age.

6. Eighty-four percent of the victims were abused by a parent or by parents. Mothers acting alone were responsible for 47 percent of the neglect victims and 32 percent of physical abuse victims. Nonrelatives, fathers acting alone, and other relatives were responsible for 29 percent, 22 percent and 19 percent, respectively, of sexual abuse victims.

7. More than half of the child victims (478,000) received services. One-fifth of all victims were removed from their homes and placed in foster care. Nineteen percent of the children who were not found to be victims of maltreatment also received services.

In the National Family Violence Survey conducted by Straus and Gelles (1990), it was estimated that 110 out of every 1,000 children in the general population experience severe violence by their parents and that 23 in 1,000 experienced very severe or life threatening violence. Severe violence was defined as kicking, biting, punching, hitting, beating up, threatening with a weapon, or using a knife or gun (Sedlak, 1997, p. 178). Very severe violence resulted in serious bodily damage to a child. Since lower income families are much more likely to have abuse reported by an outside party than are more affluent families, it was estimated by Straus and Gelles (1990) that inclusion of potential abuse by more affluent families could raise the actual amount of abuse by 50 percent.

When the home situation becomes extremely dysfunctional and abusive, children may run away. A 1988 study reported by Finkelhor, Hotaling, and Sedlak (2000) indicates that about 133,000 children run away from home each year and while away, stay in insecure and unfamiliar places. The same study reports that almost 60,000 children were thrown out of their homes. Almost 140,000 abused and neglected children were reported missing to the police. Approximately 163,000 children were abducted by one parent in an attempt to permanently conceal the whereabouts of the child from the other parent. These additional data suggest that the impact of abuse and neglect often lead to children being abandoned or running away to other unsafe environments where they may experience additional harm (Finkelhor, Hotaling, and Sedlak, 2000).

The available data from multiple sources indicate that much of the reported abuse and neglect is committed against children under the age of 4. The probability that child abuse and neglect is a leading cause of childhood deaths seems to be generally accepted. However, official statistics identify causes of death from abuse and neglect mainly in medical terms (per "International Classification of Diseases" listings). A child whose death is officially recorded as pneumonia may, in fact, have contracted the illness as a result of being poorly clothed, fed, housed, or neglected medically. Many child abuse experts feel that abuse or neglect could be the underlying reason for death in many cases in which the cause is attributed to medical reasons.

Although child abuse is frequently reported against young children, the problem of adolescent abuse is often underestimated. Unfortunately, child protective agencies frequently bypass adolescents because they are considered to be less "at risk" than are younger children, and because adolescents are seen as having more options than younger children. Because it is believed that adolescents are able to leave the house until the parent or caretaker "calms down," they are not considered as helpless as younger children. However, many of the child prostitutes or the children involved in alcohol and drug abuse are victims of physical or sexual abuse and neglect at home. Adolescents may have more options than younger children, but they are not necessarily positive options. Adolescent abuse remains a serious problem that deserves attention and action.

In her study of the factors that influence the multiple forms of child abuse and neglect, Sedlack (1997) reported that family income is a strong factor. She notes that,

> compared to children whose families had incomes of $30,000 a year or more, children from families with incomes below $15,000 per year were found to have:
>
> 1. Twenty-one times greater risk of physical abuse.
> 2. More than 24 times the risk of sexual abuse.
> 3. Between 20 and 162 times the risk of physical neglect (depending on the children's other characteristics).
> 4. More than 13 times greater risk of emotional maltreatment.
> 5. Sixteen times greater risk of multiple maltreatment, and
> 6. Between 78 and 97 times greater risk of educational neglect. (Sedlack, in Brown & Brown, 1997, p. 171)

Gathering accurate information and statistics is recognized as a problem at most levels of government. Efforts are being made, however, to develop systems that will more accurately reflect the scope and degree of child abuse and neglect. The number of suspected child abuse cases reported and investigated in the United States has steadily risen over the years as a result of better laws and increased attention paid to the problem by professionals and the public.

Another aspect of child abuse is the children who witness domestic violence between adults. There is a very high probability that children who watch domestic abuse, or are themselves victims of abuse, will abuse their children and spouses. Dodge, Bates, and Petit (1990) suggest that the experience of physical abuse in early childhood is a risk marker for the development of aggressive behavior patterns. The authors report a threefold increase in this risk in children who have witnessed abuse in their own families and a significant increase in the way in which these children incorrectly view the hostile intent of others. Van Hasselt, et al. (1988) note that the literature is "replete with descriptions of the severely damaging impact of family on the social and physical functioning of their victims" (p. 3).

Abusers socialize those whom they abuse. Children of abusive parents often abuse others or enter into abusive relationships in which they are the victims of abuse. These patterns, although dysfunctional, often feel normal to victims. Frequently, abusers encourage grown children to use abuse with their own spouses, and abused children, in adulthood, may reinforce the cycle of abuse. Lacking the skills to contain rage, a single angry man or woman may perpetuate generations of violence (Glicken & Sechrest, 2003).

Dodge and Richard (1986) report that aggressive children have a greater tendency to see hostile intentions from the vague aggressive acts of others than will non-aggressive children. Consequently, aggressive children are more likely to attack misperceived aggressors. This finding suggests that children who experience early abuse develop an attribution toward violent behavior and that abusive role models are likely to encourage the use of violence by children at a very early age.

Diagnosing Child Abuse

In determining when child abuse and neglect exist, child protective agency workers frequently use the following federal and state mandated guidelines (Feller, 1992; DePanfilis & Salus, 1992; Brokenburr, 1994).

1. *The Age of the Child:* State laws provide upper age limits of children protected by mandated reporting of health and education professionals; however, it is important to recognize that abuse and neglect can have more harmful effects on younger children. If a parent has slapped an infant and believes that slapping and shaking a child are appropriate disciplinary measures, the infant could be in danger, but an older child might not be.

2. *The Location of the Injury:* Physical injuries to the face and head are more likely to cause severe or permanent damage than are injuries to other parts of the body. Accidental injuries commonly leave bruises on the shins, knees, elbows, and

forehead. Bruises will not have any uniform pattern if they are accidentally caused, for example, by a fall from a bicycle. Injuries inflicted on purpose often have some discernible patterns and may, for example, appear on both buttocks, both sides of the neck, and both hands or both ears.

3. *The Use of an Object:* Objects such as coat hangers, sandals, straps, belts, kitchen utensils, electric cords, pipes, or fists are more likely to cause serious injuries than an is open-handed spanking. Often, the instrument used can be recognized by the distinctive shape of the injuries it inflicts. Electrical cords often leave a long loop-shaped bruise. Teeth marks are easily recognized in bite injuries.

4. *When Corporal Punishment Becomes Physical Abuse:* Parents often try to excuse the marks on their child by saying that the child deserved punishment for misbehavior. However, an injury to a child cannot be condoned. The worker may understand the provocation that triggered the abuse, and this will be helpful in working with the parents. Sometimes the punishment doesn't leave marks but it is still abusive, for example, when a child is locked in a closet or chained in the yard.

5. *Examples of Physical Neglect: Neglect* can be defined as a failure to provide a proper level of care, including food, clothing, shelter, hygiene, medical attention, and supervision. If a child has an ear infection and the parents do not use the medical options available to them, then the caseworker might need a court order to ensure that the child gets immediate care. Shelter that is unheated in the winter or is bug-infested is a reason for the worker to intervene. Malnutrition and failure to thrive are clear grounds for intervention. Inadequate clothing for the season, or clothing that isn't washed also requires intervention. When money is used for illegal drugs or alcohol by the parents and the children subsequently are deprived of basic needs such as food, shelter, clothing, or medical care, most states would consider this neglectful.

6. *Educational Neglect:* Poor school attendance is another form of parental neglect that is considered a reason for intervention by child protective services. The child may be missing school because of poor health, or a parent may require an older child to stay home and care for younger siblings. Often, children may not be attending school because of chaos, domestic violence, child abuse, or other forms of crisis in the home.

7. *Insufficient Supervision:* There are many aspects to consider when determining that a lack of parental supervision constitutes neglect. The ages of the children, the time of day or night they are left unsupervised, and the length of time they are alone are all important factors. Whether the parents left a phone number and food for the children are also considerations. Abandonment is an extreme form of neglect. *Throwaways* is a term used for children whose parents kick them out of the home or move away, leaving the children to fend for themselves.

8. *Moral Neglect:* Children who are allowed or encouraged to steal or prostitute themselves suffer from moral neglect. Sometimes parents will use children to make pornography. Runaways have often been victims of moral neglect, as well as physical neglect, and abuse.

9. *Emotional Abuse and Neglect:* Emotional abuse is parental behavior that causes psychological harm to the child. Abusive threats to lock up the child, have them arrested by the police, or send them away thoroughly frighten and immobilize children and are examples of emotional abuse. When a parent or caretaker fails to provide adequate love and caring or intellectual stimulation, the child may often suffer from emotional neglect. Children with emotional abuse problems may exhibit developmental lags, withdrawal, or attachment problems that make it difficult for them to bond with others. They also may appear apathetic and have difficulty developing intimate relationships.

10. *Sexual Abuse:* When a parent or any caretaker responsible for a child commits or allows any sexual act to be committed on a child, it is considered sexual abuse. Sexual abuse occurs most often within a family. The sexual activity between a family member and child is called incest, with the most common form of incest being father–daughter sexual abuse. Another form of sexual abuse is sexual contact between the child and a non-relative known to the child. This form of sexual abuse is considered "sexual assault." Sexual assault also includes sexual activity initiated by a stranger. Sexual assault and incest are extremely traumatic and frightening to the child because force or threats are often used. Incest is also very damaging to the victim because the person responsible is usually in a position that would normally engender trust and should have protected rather than exploited the child. There is no question of degree or definition in the case of sexual abuse. Any sexual activity between a child and an adult or someone significantly further along in their physical and emotional development is considered sexual abuse.

11. *Resilience:* The literature is beginning to suggest that some children are resilient and may be able to cope with child abuse and neglect in ways that are much more functional and successful than other children. Many researchers (Masten, 1989; Okum et al., 1994; Radke-Yarrow and Brown, 1993; Werner, 1993) think this may be true, but we caution the reader that there is little evidence that child abuse and neglect fail to have subtle and more serious negative effects on psychosocial functioning as children develop into adulthood. However, to be certain that resilience is factored into the clinicians' diagnostic impression of children who are abused and neglected, the following summary of work by Tiet, Bird, and Davies (1998) on resilient youth who have experienced serious life traumas, including maltreatment, is added:

> In conclusion, resilient youth tend to live in higher-functioning families and receive more guidance and supervision by their parents and other adults in the family. Other adults in the family may complement the parents in providing guidance and support to the youth and in enhancing youth adjustment. Higher educational aspiration may also provide high-risk youth with a sense of direction and hope. Although IQ had no impact in youth at low risk, youth at high risk who have a higher IQ may cope better and therefore avert the harmful effects of adverse life events. (p. 1198)

John, Child Abuse and Early-Onset Violence: A Case Study

John is an 8-year-old child who abuses animals. John was sexually molested by his father from age 3 to age 7. His father also tortured the child, and John has burn marks over much of his upper torso from cigarettes and boiling hot liquids. John's mother claims she didn't know that he was being abused, but reports from other members of the family confirm that she knew all along, but did nothing. The father is currently in jail for seven years for child abuse, while the mother is on probation for child endangerment.

John hates women and has begun to have fantasies about hurting them. Thus far, his violence has been limited to animals. While he tortures them, he fantasizes about hurting women. He would like to kill his mother and blames her for the abuse because she did nothing to prevent it. John is withdrawn and inarticulate. He has a difficult time explaining feelings and generally loses his temper when he tries to explain his feelings and thoughts. His language skills are very limited, but in drawings he's made for the psychologist doing John's evaluation for Juvenile Court, his pictures show death and mutilation to women. All of his drawings have death and mutilation as a constant theme and are drawn primarily in reds and blacks. When the psychologist asked him to draw a house, a tree, and a person and then tell him a story about the drawing, John drew a house without windows. The only person standing next to a scrawny shrub (his drawing of a tree) was John. In telling the story about the house, the tree, and the person, John said the following:

"Everybody in the house is dead. The little boy killed them. They were mean to him. He's alone." The therapist asked what happened to his family? John replied, "The daddy had his head cut off and the mom had her 'tits' cut off. The mom got burned up. Someone poured stuff on her. She burned. She yelled a lot. It sounded good." The therapist asked John what the little boy intended to do now that he was all alone. "The little boy is happy. He wants to hurt dogs and cats and nobody will stop him." Why does the little boy want to hurt dogs and cats? "The little boy isn't strong enough to hurt big people." Who would the little boy hurt if he could? "Women with big tits." Is there anyone the little boy knows who is like that? "No." Why do the women have to have big breasts? "Big men like women with big tits. They like to fuck them. I'm not big and I'd like to fuck them too." Does that mean hurting them, John? "Yeah. Fucking is hurting them." Did anyone do that to the little boy? "I don't know. The little boy doesn't care about that. He wants to hurt dogs and cats and women with big tits." Why is the little boy so mad at women? "They don't take care of you. They should be moms, but they don't want to be. They should be punished." Didn't the little boy's mom take care of him? "She didn't. He cried and asked her to but she just wanted to drink and watch T.V." Did the dad hurt the little boy? "Yeah." Did the mom hurt the little boy? "Yeah." What did she do to him? "She put his wee wee in her mouth sometimes." Did he tell the dad? "The dad put his wee wee in his mouth, too." That must have been terrible for the little boy. "Yeah. He told his teacher but she didn't believe him." Why not? "She's just like the mom with big tits. She hates little boys." Do all women hate little boys? "Yeah." Doesn't the little boy know any nice women? "No." Not one? "No." Why is the little boy more angry with the mom than the dad? "I don't know. Moms take care of kids, dad's don't." Do you know a mom who takes care of her kids? "Joey's mom, but she doesn't have big tits like a big woman." So the little boy is only mad at women with large breasts? "Yeah, not little girls, just women with big tits." Was the dad mad at his wife? "Yeah. That's why he fucked the little boy."

Discussion

It may seem odd that the object of John's rage is his mother and women who look like her, but many children who have been physically and sexually abused take their rage out on the passive parent whom they believe should have cared for them and protected them. That John is also suggesting that his mother sexually abused him adds weight to his rage. Can we take a story John is telling us about a child in a drawing and conclude that he is talking about himself? Not always, and it would be important to gather more information before we reach any conclusions. Yet, the house, tree, person drawing and the story told by a child are very useful diagnostically. Often the child talking about another child will lapse into talking about himself or herself. At the very least, the drawings and story test are useful in determining the child's fantasies. John's fantasies are disturbing and violent. He is going to hurt someone soon if he isn't offered help. What can we do for John? An 8-year-year-old child is not completely shaped. There is still time to help John deal with his rage against his mother. The following services are recommended immediately to help John:

1. Assign him a caring and nurturing female therapist with none of the physical or emotional characteristics of his mother. Let him work through his anger at women with someone who will accept his anger and work with it in a positive and supportive way. Don't shy away from having him discuss what was done to him, because it's an important part of his healing.

2. Help him develop the facility of using language to express his feelings. People who can use language are less likely to use violence when they feel frustrated. Don't let him continue to use derogatory slang words for sex or for body parts. The use of derogatory words tells you that he feels that sex is dirty. Using more appropriate language might help him develop a more positive feeling about his own sexuality.

3. Help him understand that what was done to him was horrible and should never have happened, but that he's not responsible. It wasn't his fault. Sometimes the people who are supposed to love us do unloving things, but that's not his fault.

4. Help him realize that hurting others will not make him feel better. Get a promise from him that he won't hurt animals anymore, and point out logically that animals never hurt him. Hurting animals is not a way to get back at the people who did harm to him.

5. Help him confront his mother and father for what they did to him either in a letter or in a role-play. Some therapists would actually have John confront his parents directly, but that's asking a lot of a child. If it goes badly, he may feel even more powerless and angry.

6. Provide him with moral grounding so that he can internalize a moral code of conduct. He'll do that if he trusts the worker and wants to please her. Working on trust and consistency in the relationship is vital.

7. Let him share his feelings in their rawest form. Don't act shocked or repulsed by what he says. Let him talk, even if what he says is disturbing. Point out that he has lots of reasons for feeling angry. Explain to him that the best way to make up for what was done to him is to have a happy and successful life. Focus on his positive accomplishments and praise him for positive changes.

(continued)

Continued

8. Let him meet other children who have been abused and have become successful in their lives. Let them help him understand the nature of his rage, how common it is, and how other children have successfully worked it through.

9. Be prepared for a great deal of manipulation and attempts to find out if you are trustworthy. John has no reason to trust anyone and will do a great deal of testing before he decides he can trust you, even a little. Keep in mind what was done to him, and don't lose your temper at some of his behavior. If he breaks rules of treatment, however, be firm and consistent without attacking him personally. Remind him of the rules and the consequences he has agreed to if the rules are broken.

10. Present a positive view of family life so that he can have a model in his mind of what a healthier family might be like. Try to find a suitable foster family when he is ready for placement. This may not be possible for a while, but ultimately, if he is to reintegrate, he needs a caring and kind family life so that he can recognize that he actually feels good about himself in the presence of supportive adult caretakers.

11. Be prepared for more acting-out behavior before he gets better. There is no reason yet for him to stop harming animals or having violent fantasies. If and when treatment begins to have a positive effect, there may be a period of regression in which he hides his anger from everyone but still feels angry.

12. Be prepared, but don't dwell on the possibility that the harm done to him may be too great for him to benefit from treatment. Be ready to consider a long-term placement in a supervised treatment setting to ensure the safety of others.

The Impact of Physical Child Abuse and Neglect

General Indicators

Laurence Miller (1999) suggests that the following are indicators of Post Traumatic Stress Disorder in Child Victims of Abuse who have been traumatized:

> High levels of anxiety and hyper-vigilance causing the child's nervous system to constantly be on alert, irritability, denial, intrusive thoughts which create panic attacks, nightmares with similar themes of violence, impaired concentration and memory lapses, withdrawal and isolation, acting-out, repetitive play, self-blame, foreshortened future (where the abused child believes that they will live a short length of time), regression, periods of amnesia and somatizing the trauma into physical illnesses including headaches, dizziness, heart palpitations, breathing problems, and stomach aches are among a large number of complaints noted in children who have been physically abused. (p. 32)

There are considerable data to show that child abuse has a particularly negative impact on children that may continue into adulthood. That impact, both physical and emotional, may include the following: a very high probability that children who witness domestic abuse or, are themselves victims of abuse, will abuse their children and spouses. As mentioned previously, Dodge, Bates, and Petit (1990) offer evidence that the experience of physical abuse in early childhood is a risk marker for the development of aggressive behavioral patterns. The authors report a threefold increase in the risk to become abusive in children who have witnessed abuse in their families and a significant increase in the way in which these children incorrectly view the hostile intent of others. Children who have been abused suffer from an inability to solve personal problems (Dodge, Bates, & Petit, 1990). Widom (1989) notes that individuals who have been identified by juvenile courts as abuse victims as children are 42 percent more likely than controls to perpetuate the cycle of violence by committing violent acts as adults.

Glicken (1995) notes that victims of physical abuse are far more likely to enter into relationships with people who have themselves been abused, or who will abuse them. This tendency to enter into relationships with abuse victims often assures the continuation of violence in relationships. Physical abuse of adults and children frequently moves into sexual abuse, particularly when substances are used and impulse control is poor.

This change in the focus of the abuse from adults to children may be explained by the perpetrators' increasing rage at situations that unconsciously remind them of the early abuse in their own lives. Abusive men and women may experience sadistic joy in abusing animals or in taking treasured personal items from others in the home. Abuse also may include destruction of property, delight in ridiculing, and special pleasure in making others feel as helpless and as powerless as the abusers felt as children when they were being abused (Glicken, 1995).

There is strong evidence that child abuse is one of the leading causes of death and disfigurement of children in the United States. However, because men are stronger physically, the damage done to children by men is often much greater than that done by women. Battered children often suffer from serious physical problems that may include the loss of sight, brain damage, severe disfigurement, burns that leave scars, loss of the use of limbs, paralysis, and deafness (ears and eyes are special targets of abusers) (Glicken, 1995).

The emotional harm to children who have witnessed domestic violence or who have themselves been victims of abuse includes severe life-long depression, rages that translate into panic and anxiety disorders, substance abuse, underemployment or difficulty working, sexual disorders, low self-esteem, prostitution (85 percent of the prostitutes who have been interviewed report having been physically and/or sexually abused as children [Utah Public Television, 1991]), and difficulty controlling anger.

Recognizing Sexual Abuse

Some specific behavioral indicators in young children who have been sexually abused include the following (Kessler & Hyden, 1991; DePanfilis & Salus, 1992): age-inappropriate understanding of sexual terms and overtly inappropriate, unusual, seductive, or aggressive sexual behavior with peers and adults; compulsive curiosity about sexual matters or sexual areas of the body in self and others; repeated concerns about homosexuality (particularly in boys who have been molested by a male perpetrator); fear of the child's parents or caretakers as well as fear of going home; eating disorders (overeating, eating too little, aversion to certain foods); school problems or significant changes in school performance (attitudes in class and/or grades); false maturity or age-inappropriate behaviors, including bed wetting and thumb sucking; sleep problems, including nightmares, fear of falling asleep, fretful sleep patterns, or sleeping very long hours; enuresis (bed wetting), which may be a defense against the perpetrator molesting the child at night; significant behavioral changes that seem new and abrupt; an inability to concentrate; withdrawal from activities and friends; and a preoccupation with death.

The guilt and shame of the child victim and the frequent involvement of parents, stepparents, friends, or other persons caring for the child make it very difficult for children to come forward to report sexual abuse. Despite these problems, as public awareness develops and as children are taught more about sexual abuse in school, reports of sexual abuse made to child protective agencies continue to increase.

A child who does seek help often is accused of fabricating the story because people frequently cannot believe that a well-liked or respected member of the community is capable of sexual abuse. Because it is the word of the child against that of the adult, the child may give in to pressure from parents or caretakers and take back the accusation of sexual abuse. This happens because the child may feel guilty and frightened about "turning in" the abuser or breaking up the family. This process of recanting a sexual abuse complaint leads many child protective workers and law enforcement officers to be skeptical about a child's complaint of sexual abuse, particularly in children who may appear manipulative or who have had prior disagreements with parents. Recanting an accusation of sexual abuse may leave the child feeling helpless and guilty about causing so much trouble for the family. The reality of sexual abuse is that without third-party confirmation or someone else reporting the abuse, the child often feels committed to keep the abuse secret. To reinforce the desire to keep the abuse secret, the abuser may use shame, fear, and actual threats with the child. If the abuser is a parent, the child may worry that reporting the parent will result in foster care and the abusing parent being sent to jail. These and other concerns are often repeatedly told to the victim by the perpetrator until the child victim is more concerned about the results of reporting the abuse than the abuse itself.

Physical and Behavioral Problems in Older Children and Adolescents Who Have Been Sexually Abused

The following behavioral problems might be related to older children and adolescents who have been sexually abused: poor hygiene or excessive bathing; poor relations with friends and peers and poor interpersonal skills; isolation, loneliness, withdrawn behavior, and depression; and acting out, running away, and displaying aggressive, antisocial, or delinquent behavior. Children who have been sexually abused often have school problems that might include frequent absences, behavioral problems in the classroom, falling asleep in class, and drawings and stories told by the child that might suggest severe inner turmoil. Additional school-related problems might include a sudden and unusual decline in academic performance, the unwillingness to undress and shower in public for gym classes, or an unwillingness to be involved in sports or other activities requiring close physical contact with others. Prostitution or sexual acting out may also suggest sexual abuse. Children who have been sexually abused often suffer from "school phobias" and are afraid of going to school for fear that the family may break up because of the abuse and, on coming home from school, that he or she will be alone in the world. Care must be taken not to assume sexual abuse just because any of the symptoms listed here are noted in the child's behavior. Any of these symptoms may be indicative of other problems unrelated to sexual abuse (Brokenburr, 1994; Kessler & Hyden, 1991).

Children who have been sexually abused may also be overly seductive or sexual with others, or they may feel great discomfort with those of the opposite sex. They may have gifts given to them by the abuser that are extravagant or suggest secrets between the child and the abuser. Often, when asked where the gift came from, the child will have no logical or acceptable answer. Children who have been sexually abused often suffer from depression and chronic fatigue. Suicide attempts, even by very young children, are not uncommon in sexual abuse cases. One of the new areas of interest in the understanding of depression in children under the age of 6 is our tendency to confuse a suicide attempt with an accident. Children who run out into the street or who drink poisonous liquids, and who know better or who have never exhibited a tendency to use bad judgment before, may be depressed and suicidal. Further symptoms related to child sexual abuse might include drug and alcohol use at a very early age, fire setting, frequent bouts of crying, anorexia and other eating disorders, and chronic unhappiness. Care must be taken to collect sufficient data before making a diagnosis of child sexual abuse (Brokenburr, 1994; Kessler & Hyden, 1991).

The following physical symptoms may be found in younger children, as well as older children and adolescents: physical trauma or irritations to the anal/genital area (pain, itching, swelling, bruising, bleeding, lacerations, especially if unexplained or inconsistent); difficulty in walking or sitting because of genital or anal pain; sexually transmitted diseases; and pain on urination or defecation (Brokenburr, 1994; Kessler & Hyden, 1991).

Kim, A Physically Abused and Neglected Child: A Case Study

Kim is an 11-year-old girl who was physically abused and neglected by her schizophrenic mother and her alcoholic father since she was age 4. Kim's parents believe that she is possessed by evil spirits and beat her and chained her to walls much of the time she was growing up. A neighbor's complaint led to the discovery of unspeakable conditions in the home and to Kim's being placed in a foster home when she was age 9. While in the foster home, Kim tried to smother the foster parents' baby and put rat poison in the parents' food. She tried, on a number of occasions, to have sex with the foster father. As these episodes grew more serious, the foster parents were unable to care for Kim and she was returned to the state and placed in a more secure group home.

Kim is nearly completely nonverbal. She looks like a 5-year-old and has stunted growth. She has little understanding of table manners or cleanliness and often grabs food and eats it raw. She has suffered severe malnutrition. After a year in the group home,

(continued)

Continued

Kim's language skills and social interactions have improved considerably. She is able to verbalize feelings and feels comfortable in the group home. An IQ test shows very low functioning (in the range of 70), caused, more than likely, by severe malnutrition. She never wants to see her parents again and will not have to, because parental rights have been permanently terminated. The case was a high-profile case in the media, not only because of the severe abuse, but because the situation had been called to the attention of child protective services on 15 separate occasions with nothing done to investigate it. It also became public knowledge that the director of the child welfare agency in Kim's community was a member of a pedophile organization, and the serious malfunctioning of the agency led to his being fired from his job.

Kim is becoming a sweet young lady. Her potential seems unlimited, and the staff of the group home and her therapist believe that her IQ will increase as she develops additional language skills and confidence in herself. Kim never went to school; she was kept at home by her parents because they thought she would bring evil to other children. Both parents are in institutions, where they will remain for a long time to come.

Discussion

Who can ever understand the motivation of parents to do such harm to a child? Kim may never live anything close to a normal life, but the staff at the group home have high hopes. Use of behavior modification has reinforced positive changes in her behavior. By rewarding her use of language, first with candy and then with praise, Kim has developed a startling vocabulary, which is quite at odds with most theories that language develops very early in life, and that the longer the delay in learning language, the more unlikely it is to develop at all. The physical therapist has helped Kim develop physically by stretching and using limbs that had all but atrophied. She can now walk up to a mile and has begun to develop enough coordination to play kick ball. Her ability to get along with the other children is still fairly limited, and she exhibits extreme jealousy when she sees any of the staff spending time with the other children. During these times, she tries to pull the therapist away. When that doesn't work, she falls on the ground and has screaming temper tantrums that only subside when the staff member apologizes and provides her with the attention she craves. The staff thinks that her emotional development is at a 2-year-old level and that she's going through the "terrible twos." They have hopes that she'll progress, but they maintain a 24-hour watch on her to make certain that she doesn't hurt herself or others. Her emotions are still very primitive, and she still suffers from posttraumatic stress disorder (PTSD). Little things can release frightening memories of what her parents did to her. When this happens, she becomes so frightened and unmanageable that she has to be restrained. In one episode of PTSD, she severely bit a staff member. In another, she almost scratched the eye out of one of the orderlies. There is concern that perhaps she is far too disturbed to be handled in a minimum security setting and that her behavior is having a negative impact on the other children, all of whom have experienced serious abuse and are easily upset.

One year into treatment, Kim was found to have a very minor seizure disorder and was diagnosed with Epilepsy, Petit Mal (DSM-IV Code345.00, APA, 1994, p. 814). Although the neurologist didn't feel that Kim's management problems were a result of the epilepsy, within a month of the use of medication for the petit mal seizures, Kim's behavior improved markedly. Kim is now 13, hasn't had a menstrual cycle, and looks like she's age 9. Most new staff members think she's a boy because she has few external female features. The staff feels increasingly that Kim should be institutionalized with other children who have limited intellectual functioning and who sometimes are management problems. In a bizarre twist, Kim's parents requested a custody hearing to regain custody. Both had completed treatment and appeared to be functioning at a much healthier level. They said that they made her the way she is and owed it to her to provide care at a level she would never get in an institution. The court, against the advice of the treatment staff, allowed Kim to return home for a weekend visit under supervision. In the middle of the night, Kim smothered her parents to death and then bludgeoned them with an ax she found in the shed. The staff member assigned to supervise her was knocked unconscious. When Kim was found, she was covered with blood and was sucking her thumb and rocking herself back and forth. "Bad Kim," she kept saying, "Bad, Kim."

Treatment for Abuse and Neglect

Ducharme, Atkinson, and Poulton (2000) note that children from violently abusive homes display a number of "externalizing and internalizing" problems, including conduct problems, anxiety and withdrawal, and low self-esteem. Treatment, they believe, rather than helping the abusive family and the maltreated children, may "(1) exacerbate the child's oppositional difficulties; (2) increase the probability of parental violence in a violence-prone household; and (3) amplify the internalizing difficulties experienced by these children" (p. 995). However, in their work with abusive families, by teaching parents and children to avoid conflict in their interactions (in what the authors call an "errorless compliance strategy"), the authors were able to "prevent potentially abusive parental responses and remain sensitive to internalizing difficulties experienced in a family violence context" (p. 1002). Errorless compliance strategy is an approach to family conflict that teaches parents to handle noncompliance by children in a logical and noncoercive way. It builds on small, early gains to introduce compliance with more difficult and complex parent–child issues.

Moore, Armsden, and Gogerty (1998) report that a number of interventions have been developed to treat abusive parents and their children. Despite methodological problems, many studies show positive results for children and parents (DePanfilis, 1996; Kolko, 1996; Oates & Bross, 1995; Wekerle & Wolfe, 1993). However, Moore and colleagues note (1998, p. 4):

> The strongest evidence of efficacy comes from evaluations of treatment strategies aimed at increasing parenting abilities and improving the developmental status and interpersonal competencies of the children (Wekerle & Wolf, 1993). There is also empirical support for the value of interventions designed to improve parenting behavior of neglectful parents by reducing social isolation and improving social skills with individualized, one-on-one treatment programs (DePanfilis, 1996).

DePanfilis and Salus (1992), in their work for the National Center for Child Abuse and Neglect (a federal agency that is part of the U.S. Department of Health and Human Services), describe the treatment needs of children and their families. Treatment, they believe, is complex. Because the origins of abuse lie in a multiple number of reasons, many of them existing over a long period of time, the authors believe that "interventions need to address as many of the contributing factors [of abuse] as possible" (p. 61). They go on to say,

> Early research in child abuse and neglect treatment effectiveness suggests that successful treatment with maltreating families requires a comprehensive package that addresses both the intra-personal and concrete needs of all family members. . . . Recent research found that a broad range of therapeutic and other services for child sexual abuse exist including individual and group treatment, dyad treatment, family therapy, peer support groups, marital therapy, alcohol and drug counseling, client advocacy, parents aides, education and crisis intervention. (pp. 61–62)

DePanfilis and Salus (1992) suggest that issues to be addressed in the family include the history of abuse; family attitudes toward violence; problem-solving patterns; anger and impulse-control issues; definitions of acceptable sexuality; stress management; substance abuse; patterns of abuse in families that may be historical and cross several or more generations; impulse control and judgment problems within families; conflicts with authority at work and in the community; manipulative and self-indulgent behavior; acting-out behavior, with patterns of antisocial activities related to sexual and nonsexual behavior; demanding, controlling, and domineering behavior; a lack of the ability to trust; and reduced degrees of intimacy (pp. 63–64).

In evaluating long-term outcomes of treatment of abusing parents and their children, Moore, Armsden, and Gogerty (1998) noted, "The picture of long-term therapeutic outcomes is one of family strengthening and better parent–child interactions in which there is warmer, more responsive parenting as well as more positive parental perceptions, less difficult child behavior, or both" (p. 12). The authors also said that even in homes that continue to be abusive after treatment, that treatment has a positive impact in that it serves to lessen acting out that may lead to youthful violence.

Needed Societal Changes

There are no easy remedies for the problem of child abuse and neglect. Despite treatment efforts and more awareness of the impact of child abuse, much more must be done to correct this serious national problem. Prevention is one way to combat all forms of child abuse and neglect, and new programs must concentrate on prevention. The target populations for prevention efforts must include schools, families, professionals, and communities. Far more research needs to be done to develop effective approaches to child intervention when abuse and neglect have been committed. We still know too little about effective interventions, and we may be using incorrect approaches and services that ultimately cause harm. The following are actions that we can implement immediately:

1. *A no-tolerance law for child abuse and neglect.* Children are to be treated with concern for their emotional and physical health by all parents. Parents who abuse substances, are involved in family violence, punish children by using severe methods, and harm children emotionally, are intolerable. Whatever the cost, the protection and the safety of children should be our number one priority if we are ever to lessen the rate of violence in this country.

2. *A child protective services system that promptly investigates* all *child abuse complaints.* No one who makes a complaint to a child protective service agency should feel as if the complaint isn't taken seriously. Lag times of weeks or months before an investigation takes place are intolerable. Child protective service agencies should be held to the same standard as other governmental agencies. When they fail to perform, they should be liable for lawsuits and should never be allowed to hide behind confidentiality claims that often keep agency incompetence and neglect from becoming public.

3. *Trained workers with special training in the investigation and treatment of child abuse* are badly needed. This also includes workers willing to work with perpetrators. Although there are programs currently funded that provide financial incentives for MSW students to work in child protective services, few programs are funded to work with perpetrators of child abuse or the children who become violent offenders. Much more needs to be done to provide Americans with a core of professionally trained workers in the areas of child abuse and childhood violence.

4. *Training for mandated reporters* is a must. All teachers, nurses, doctors, helping professionals, and others who are designated as mandated reporters of child abuse and neglect need to have periodic training in child abuse detection and reporting. When a mandated reporter fails to report child abuse, he or she should be held legally liable.

5. There needs to be *mandated psychological evaluations of all children who have been abused or neglected,* with free treatment provided, if indicated. Children who have been abused or neglected are at high risk of violent behavior in schools and communities. They are also at high risk of living very unhappy lives. Children who have been abused and neglected need to be professionally evaluated to determine if they are at risk. If they are, the best, most efficacious treatment available should be provided for as long as it takes to help the child become well.

6. *An early-warning tracking system* is needed to make certain that victims of child abuse aren't becoming violent. This is such an obvious need that it's unclear why this isn't being done now. Perhaps a central clearing house might be used that would keep track of abused and neglected children who are at additional risk of offending.

7. *Mandatory parent training for the adult victims of child abuse who now want to have children* is badly needed, with early-warning indicators of violence, substance abuse, or other behaviors that place their children at risk. Having a child assumes responsibility. Children who have been abused are at high risk of abusing

their own children when they become adults. Help needs to be provided so that early signs of child abuse are dealt with quickly.

8. *Public education* is needed to let parents know the risk they may have of physical and sexual abuse of younger siblings by older siblings. Signs of difficulty in other areas of the older siblings' lives would be a key to determining that risk. Those signs include animal mutilation, bullying, sexual deviancy, poor impulse control, and an obsession with violence.

Summary

Child abuse and neglect are the primary reasons young children act out. Abuse of children, like domestic violence, is a problem that needs our full attention. The diagnostic signs of abuse and neglect must be taught to all mandated reporters, who must be sufficiently trained and willing to report abuse and neglect to child protective agencies, which must investigate every complaint. The few cases that are actually investigated each year suggest a system that is not protecting children at risk.

Integrative Questions _____

1. It seems very unlikely that child abuse and neglect, particularly when it is severe and long lasting, will not have a negative impact on children all along the stages of development. Do you think the concept of resilience is just another way of excusing the terrible conduct of parents toward children and that, eventually, even the most resilient people begin to experience emotional problems as a result of early childhood abuse?

2. In the case study of John, the child who had been severely abused and is now mutilating animals, do you think that animal mutilation is a precursor to violence against people, or might the two be separate and distinct behaviors?

3. How is it possible, as in the case of Kim, that parents who have so severely abused a child could ever be placed in the position of having custodial rights? Shouldn't parents who severely abuse children have their parental rights terminated forever?

4. Why does the child protective service system work so inadequately, or, in your view does it function well?

5. A number of physical and emotional symptoms of child abuse and neglect were listed in this chapter. Don't you think the length of the list serves to confuse child-care workers with normal children? What might researchers do to make this list more useful in assessing actual child abuse and neglect?

References _____

American Psychiatric Association. (1994). *Diagnostic and statistical manual of mental disorders* (4th ed.). Washington, DC: American Psychiatric Association.

Brokenburr, D. (1994). Personal interview.

Brown, J., and Brown, G. (1997). Characteristics and treatment of incest offenders. A review. *Journal of Aggression, Maltreatment and Trauma*, 1, 335–354.

Children's Bureau. (April 2002). *Summary of key findings from calendar year 2000, National Child Abuse and Neglect Data System.* Administration on Children, Youth, and Families. Washington, DC: Department of Health and Human Services. Available online at www.calib.com/nccanch/pubs/factsheets/canstats.cfm

DePanfilis, D., and Salus, M. (1992). *Child protective services: A guide for caseworkers.* National Center for Child Abuse and Neglect. McLean, VA: The Circle, Inc.

Dodge, K.A., Bates, J.E., and Petit, G.S. (1990). Mechanisms in the cycle of violence. *Science,* 28.

Dodge, K.A., and Richard, B.A. (1986). Peer perceptions, aggression and peer relations. In S. Pryor and G. Day (Eds.), *The development of social cognition* (pp. 35–58). New York: Springler-Verlag.

Ducharme, J.M., Atkinson, L., and Poulton, L. (August 2000). Success-based, noncoercive treatment of oppositional behavior in children from violent homes source. *Journal of the American Academy of Child and Adolescent Psychiatry,* 39, 995–1004.

Feller, J. (1992). *Working with the courts in child protection.* National Center on Child Abuse and Neglect. McLean, VA: The Circle.

Finkelhor, D., Hotaling, G.T., and Sedlack, A. (May 2000). *Missing, abducted, runaway and throwaway children in America. First report: Numbers and characteristics,* National Incident Report, 1988. Reported in 1999 National Report Series: *Juvenile Justice Crime Bulletin,* NCJ-180753.

Glicken, M. (1995). *Understanding and treating male abusive behavior.* Unpublished monograph.

Glicken, M.D., and Sechrest, D. (2003). *The role of the helping professions in treating and preventing violence.* Boston: Allyn & Bacon

Kessler, D.B., and Hyden, P. (1991). Physical, sexual and emotional abuse of children. *Clinical Symposia,* 43, 1.

Kolko, D.J. (1996). Individual cognitive behavioral treatment and family therapy for physically abused children and their offending parents: A comparison of clinical outcomes. *Child Maltreatment,* 1, 322–342.

Masten, A. (1989). Resilience in development: Implications of the study of successful adaptation for developmental psychopathology. In D. Cicchetti (Ed.), *The emergence of a discipline: Rochester symposium on developmental psychopathology* (pp. 261–294). Hillsdale, NJ: Lawrence Erlman Publishers.

Miller, L. (Summer 1999). Juvenile Crime Statistics 1998. *Victim Advocate,* U.S. Department of Juvenile Justice, U.S. Department of Justice. Washington, DC: U.S. Government Printing Press.

Moore, E., Armsden, G., and Gogerty, P.L. (1998). A twelve-year follow-up study of maltreated and at-risk children who received early therapeutic child care. *Child Maltreatment,* 3, 3–16.

Oates, R.K., and Bross, D.C. (1995). What have we learned about treating child physical abuse? A literature review of the last decade. *Child Abuse and Neglect,* 19, 463–473.

Paget, K.D., Philp, J.D., and Abramczyk, L.W. (1993). Recent developments in child neglect. In T. H. Ollendick and R.J. Prinz (Eds.), Advances in clinical child psychology (vol. 15, pp. 121–174). New York: Plenum.

Radke-Yarrow, M., and Brown, E. (1993). Resilience and vulnerability in children of multiple-risk families. *Development and Psychopathology,* 5, 581–592.

Sedlack, A. (1997). Risk factors for the occurrence of child abuse and neglect *Journal of Aggression, Maltreatment and Trauma,* 1(1), 149–181.

Straus, M.A., and Gelles, R.J. (1990). *Physical violence in American families: Risk factors and adaptations to violence in families.* New Brunswick, NJ: Transaction.

Tiet, Q.Q., Bird, H., and Davies, M.R. (November 1998). Adverse life events and resilience. *Journal of the American Academy of Child and Adolescent Psychiatry,* 37, 1191–1200.

Utah Public Television (July 1991). *Scared silent.*

Van Hasselt, V.B., Morrison, R.L., Bellack, A.S., and Hersen, M. (1988). *Handbook of family violence.* New York: Plenum.

Wekerle, C., and Wolfe, D.A. (1993). Prevention of child physical abuse and neglect promising new directions. *Clinical Psychology Review,* 13, 501–540.

Werner, E. (1993). Risk, resilience, and recovery. Perspectives from the Kauai longitudinal study. *Development and Psychopathology,* 5, 503–515.

Widom, C.S. (1989). Does violence beget violence? A critical evaluation of the literature. *Psychology Bulletin,* 106, 3–28.

6

Sexual Violence by Children

Few of us think of young children as predatory sexual offenders, but as noted in this chapter, a considerable amount of the adolescent and adult sexual offending, particularly child molestation, begins well before the onset on puberty. In studies discussed in this chapter, the average age of onset of sexual molestation may occur before the child is 10 years old. And because most of the children who begin their sexual offending at that early age molest their own younger siblings or the close friends of family, the sexual offending is very likely to continue at an ever more dangerous level as the child ages. The victims of molestation, in far too many cases, become the offenders as they age, and a cycle that should never have started, had teachers, parents, friends, and others in close contact with the child been more vigilant, continues until the molested child becomes the molester and is caught. How much suffering might have been prevented had parents and others been more aware of the early onset of sexual deviances and done something proactive to prevent it from happening? The intent of this chapter is to aid in that process.

Evidence of Sexual Violence by Children

Knopp (as cited in Araji, 1997), using the 1980 Uniform Crime Reports, found 208 children under the age of 12 who were arrested for rape. More recent surveys of sexually acting out children reveal much higher rates of sexually abusive behavior by preadolescent children. English and Ray (as cited in Araji, 1997) reported that the Washington Department of Social and Health Services had 641 active cases of children under the age of 12 who had raped, molested, or were involved in such noncontact sexual acts as exposing, masturbating in public, or peeping. Ryan et al. (1996) reported that in a sample of 616 adolescents seen for evaluation or treatment for committing a sexual offense, 25.9 percent had been sexually abusive prior to their twelfth birthday.

In self-reports by almost 500 juveniles being evaluated by the police for possible involvement in sexual offenses, Zolondek et al. (2001) found that over 60 percent reported involvement in child molestation, over 30 percent in pornography, and 10 percent to 30 percent in exhibitionism, fetishism, frottage, voyeurism, obscene phone calls, and phone sex. Juveniles reported involvement, on the average, in 9 to 46 incidents of sexual offenses. The average age of onset for the sexual offenses was between 10 and 12 years of age. Of the boys who reported never having been accused of molesting children, 41.5 percent reported that they had molested a younger child. The authors suggest that between 15 percent and 20 percent of all sexual offenses are committed by youth younger than age 18, and as many as 50 percent of all child molestations may be committed by youth younger than age 18 (Davis & Leitenberg, 1987; Furby, Weinrott, & Blackshaw, 1989).

Commenting on the very early age of onset of various sexual behaviors in their sample (9.7 to 12.4 years of age), Zolondek et al. (2001) noted that the average age of onset is considerably earlier than had been reported by other researchers, including Abel et al. (1985) and Weinrott (1996). Previous studies, they reported, relied on retrospective reports by adult offenders who may have been giving socially desirable responses or whose memories may have been poor. The authors believe that adolescents begin their sexual offending prior to puberty and that this finding is cause for concern, particularly because many of the offenders in their sample had been molesting younger siblings or close friends of the family. The authors call for early identification of youthful sexual offenders and point out that by the time young offenders are caught, they may have committed several offenses with several victims. Zolondek et al. urge clinicians and researchers to go back to the offender's preadolescent years, and caution that very early deviant sexual behavior is a strong predictor of later predatory sexual offending.

Caputo, Frick, and Brodsky (1999) report that juvenile sex offenses constitute a large number of all sex offenses. Groth, Longo, and McFadin (1982) note that juveniles have been identified as the perpetrators in more than 25 percent of all child sexual abuse cases. Davis and Leitenberg (1987) report that juveniles committed 20 percent of the forcible rapes reported to the FBI in 1981. Caputo, Frick, and Brodsky (1999) note that it is assumed that juvenile sexual offenses are merely exploratory and will not be repeated in adulthood, but Groth, Longo, and McFadin (1982) found that about a half of all adult sexual offenders report committing their first sexual offense as teenagers. Groth and colleagues (1982) further report that the patterns of the sexual offenses, in terms of the age and characteristics of the victim, the amount of force used, and other aspects of the assault appear to have first developed in adolescence and continue into adulthood.

Saunders et al. (1992) found that 44 percent of the respondents who were raped as children reported that the offender was younger than 21 years old. Berliner (1998) indicated that studies of adult sexual offenders have found that half of the offenders had begun having deviant sexual thoughts in adolescence or during preadolescence. Berliner also believed that juvenile and adult sex offenders have very similar characteristics. "They may engage in serious sexual crimes, have multiple victims, exhibit deviant sexual preferences, have comparable cognitive distortions, and lack victim empathy" (p. 645). Because the characteristics of juvenile sexual offenders are similar to those of adult offenders, Berliner noted that treatment programs for juveniles have also been similar to those of adults, without any strong evidence that an adult treatment model is necessarily the correct model for young offenders.

Snyder and Sigmund (1995) reported that the number of juvenile offenders arrested for sexual crimes increased steadily over the past decade. Barbaree, Hudson, and Seto (1993) indicated that studies estimate that juveniles are responsible for 15 percent to 20 percent of all rapes and 30 percent to 60 percent of all child sexual assault cases committed in the United States each year. Araji (1997) stated that reports of sexual aggression in children as young as ages 3 and 4 are not uncommon, with the most common age of the onset of sexual aggression appearing to be between ages 6 and 9. Girls are more likely to be early-onset sexual aggressors than older adolescents who have abused. The sexual acting out of early-onset female offenders is just as aggressive as that of young male sexual offenders. Victims of preadolescent sexual abusers have an average age of between 4 and 7, are most often female, and are usually siblings, friends, or acquaintances (Araji, 1997). Araji further noted that victimized children who have been sexually abused have been very frequently sexually abused, and, according to Pithers et al. (1998b), have higher rates of abuse and neglect victimization experiences than those found among their adolescent counterparts (English & Ray, as cited in Araji, 1997). The preadolescent victims of sexual abuse have also been found to have frequent academic and learning difficulties and impaired peer relationships (Friedrich & Luecke, as cited in Araji, 1997; Pithers and Gray, as cited in Araji, 1997). It almost goes without saying that many of the children who sexually abuse during childhood, adolescence, and adulthood have themselves been sexually abused. Pithers et al. (1998a) found that the families of children with sexual behavior problems tended to live with high levels of poverty and with the frequent existence of child sexual abuse and domestic violence.

English and Ray (as cited in Araji, 1997) compared preadolescent sexual offenders with adolescent offenders. Both groups had a high number of family risk factors related to repeat offending. The families of preadolescent sexual offenders had more family problems than the adolescent offenders. The younger children had much higher levels of social isolation and current life stresses than the adolescent offenders. Lane and Lobanov-Rostovsky (1997) found that girls represent 5 percent to 8 percent of the juvenile sex offenders and often sexually offend while involved in childcare. Mathews, Hunter, and Vuz (1997) compared 67 girls and 70 boys with sexual offense histories. While both male and female offenders were alike in many ways and both groups tended to molest young children of the opposite sex, girls had much more severe experiences as victims of childhood sexual abuse than did boys.

In discussing juvenile dating experiences, James, West, and Deters (2000) noted that half of all early adolescent children report some degree of violence in dating situations, including scratching, hitting, pushing, grabbing, or shoving their date. About 25 percent of the children did this an average of four to nine times a date. Thirty-three percent of the children in dating situations threw something that hit their dating partners, kicked them, and slapped them. Twenty percent of the children twisted their partners' arms, slammed or held their dating partner against a wall, bent their fingers, bit them, choked them, dumped them from a car, burned them, beat them up, and hit them with something harder than a fist (James, West, & Deters, 2000). Cascardi, Avery-Leaf, and O'Leary (1994) found that 32 percent of the males and 52 percent of the females in their study of high school students had used aggression against a dating partner, and O'Keefe (1997) found that 39 percent of the males and

43 percent of the females had been physically aggressive with a dating partner at least once. Foshee (1996) reported that females were more likely to be perpetrators of dating violence. Jezl, Molidor, and White (1996) found that 59 percent of their adolescent sample had experienced physical violence at least once in a dating relationship, 96 percent had experienced some form of psychological maltreatment, and 15 percent had been forced to engage in sexual activity. Significantly, more males than females reported being victims of physical abuse. Gray and Foshee (1997) found that about 66 percent of the adolescents who reported violence in dating relationships stated that it began with mutual consent and then escalated.

Veneziano, Veneziano, and Legrand (2000) studied the sexual behavior of adolescent sexual offenders. They believe that youthful offenders relive their own sexual molestations in their choice of victims, as well as circumstances in which they were molested. The authors were able to prove the following hypotheses guiding their study (p. 365):

> **Hypothesis 1:** Adolescent sexual offenders victimize children of an age close to the age that they had been when they were sexually abused. That is, if they had been victimized at age 6, they would be more likely to victimize a 6-year-old. **Hypothesis 2:** Adolescent male sexual offenders who had been sexually abused by a male would be more likely to victimize a male. **Hypothesis 3:** Adolescent sexual offenders victimize children related to them in the same way that they were related to their perpetrator. That is, if a relative had victimized them, they would victimize a family member. If a non-relative had victimized them, they would victimize a non-relative. **Hypothesis 4:** Adolescent sexual offenders engage in the same abusive behaviors with their victims as the abuse behaviors that had been forced on them. That is, if they had been fondled, they would fondle their victims.

Legal Definitions of Sexual Violence

The following definitions of sexually violent acts are a compilation of terms used by a number of reporting groups, including the National Crime Victimization Survey (NCVS), The Uniform Crime Reports (UCR), and The National Incident-Based Reporting System (NIBRS). The definitions are taken from the Bureau of Justice report entitled, "Sex Offenses and Offenders" (Greenfeld, 1997, pp. 31-33).

> **Forcible Rape:** The carnal knowledge of a person forcibly and/or against their will or where the victim is incapable of giving consent because of their age, mental status, or physical incapacity. Assaults and attempts to commit rape by force or threat of force are also included; however, statutory rape without force and other sex offenses are excluded.
>
> **Statutory Rape:** The carnal knowledge of a person without force or threat of force when the person is below the statutory age of consent.
>
> **Forcible Sodomy:** Oral or anal sexual intercourse with another person, forcibly and against their will or where the person is unable to consent because of age, mental or physical incapacity.

Sexual Assault with an Object: When the offender uses an instrument or object to unlawfully penetrate the genital or anal opening against a victim's will.

Forcible Fondling: Touching the private parts of another person against their will for the purpose of sexual gratification.

Incest: Non-forcible intercourse between persons who are related to one another as defined by not permitting marriage.

Lewd Acts with Children: Includes fondling, indecent liberties, immoral practices, molestation and other indecent behaviors with children.

Johnny, Sexual Violence and Child Molestation: A Case Study

Johnny is a 10-year-old boy living with his mother and three younger siblings. Johnny was sexually molested by his mother's boyfriend between ages 6 and 8. The boyfriend was sadistic in his molestation, and Johnny is an angry and deeply troubled boy. The molestation was never reported to the authorities, and the mother discontinued the relationship with the boyfriend when it became clear to her what was happening. The boyfriend threatened to kill Johnny if he told his mother, and Johnny all too readily believed him. A later investigation revealed that Johnny was reported to child protective services by his elementary school which, through an all too frequent glitch in the system, failed to investigate the case. Johnny was coming to school with many signs of neglect and physical abuse, including bruises on his hands, arms, and face and clothes that were dirty and threadbare.

The mother felt that the best way to help Johnny was to give him extra attention. She was fearful of seeking treatment, because she thought the worker would report the boyfriend to the authorities. Like Johnny, the mother was afraid that the boyfriend would harm her.

Johnny has begun to sexually molest younger children. He is sadistic in his molestation and often leaves bruises and cuts on his victims. He doesn't care if the victim is male or female and usually does damage to the child's genital areas by using pliers with young boys and bottles or broomsticks to penetrate young girls. Johnny feels a rage come over him before he molests a child. Sometimes he steals liquor from his mother to gain the courage to commit the molestation.

A teacher caught Johnny molesting a young boy in the restroom of his school. He is a withdrawn child, and when he was caught and the police were called in, he became silent and emotionless. The crisis worker who saw him initially diagnosed him as having Post Traumatic Stress Disorder (PTSD). There was no indication from the school that Johnny had violent sexual tendencies. He was considered a mild, introverted child by his teachers, on the low end of intelligence, and generally compliant. Like many overly compliant children, his quiet behavior hid a great deal of rage. Johnny was remanded to juvenile court and awaits disposition by the court following a presentence investigation.

Discussion

Johnny was seen initially by a forensic psychologist for psychological testing and then by a clinical social worker to gather a precise social history. During the history taking, it was determined that the mother's boyfriend had sexually and physically abused Johnny. Many of the sadistic things Johnny does to other children were first done to him by the boyfriend. The depth of Johnny's pathology was determined during the psychological examination when the psychologist wrote,

> Johnny is a 10-year-old Caucasian child who was sexually and physically molested by his mother's boyfriend from ages 6-8. He is a child with above-average intelligence who was developing normally before the molestation by the mother's boyfriend. He is deeply withdrawn and has repressed feelings of rage at the boyfriend and at his mother for not protecting him. He is now taking that rage out on other children. He knows that what he is doing is wrong but feels that he can't control the impulse to hurt others. He is unable to talk about his feelings at a level that would suggest potential success in treatment and isn't certain that what he is doing is personally wrong. He sees it as payback for not being protected. His prior molestation and his risk to others suggest that he should be placed in a closed facility with supervised treatment. The prognosis is very poor.

The social work report noted the following:

> Johnny's molestation by his mother's boyfriend was exacerbated by the mother's unwillingness to provide professional treatment for her child. Rather than seeking help, the mother compounded the boy's problems by overly sexualizing their relationship. Johnny slept with his mother after the boyfriend's departure and has memories of being touched and fondled by his mother, although the mother denies this. When Johnny molests other children, he has fantasies about being touched by his mother. Johnny needs supervised treatment in a protected facility where he can't do harm to himself or to others. He has an underlying depression that makes suicide or violence to others very likely. He is confused about who he should hurt and often thinks that it might be best to hurt himself. The prognosis for improvement is very poor. This is a highly traumatized child who needs a protected and safe environment for a very long time to come.

Johnny was found guilty of molesting children and was placed in a guarded and locked facility for violent children. He is withdrawn, unsociable, compliant, and a nonparticipant in group therapy. He has learned the system of the facility and seems relieved that he is finally getting some needed protection. He volunteers for extra work and seems almost happy. He refuses to see his mother or any members of his family and has become a believer in the Devil. He secretly worships with other believers in the facility and thinks he has found a philosophy of life that is satisfying. The staff of the facility has seen similar behavior in molested children and understands the harm that can be done by physical and sexual abuse. They also believe that 10 is too early an age to give up on a child and think that some children, particularly those like Johnny, who had some degree of normal development, have a chance to change their behavior as they mature. A good deal of the likelihood to change, they feel, has to do with continued help and the willingness of the staff to accept Johnny's current behavior as a sign of deep rage and resentment that may improve as he matures. The head therapist at the facility said the following about Johnny and children who have been molested:

> Lots of people talk about resilience and how wonderful the human spirit is. But when you see a child whose spirit is broken, you begin to understand the severe harm adults can do to children like Johnny. We're hopeful with Johnny, but the odds aren't good and traumas like the one Johnny suffered take a long time to heal, maybe forever.

Treating Youthful Sexual Offenders

Lab, Shields, and Schondel (1993) compared recidivism rates for juveniles in a specialized sex offender treatment program with recidivism rates for juveniles in nonspecialized programs for sex offenders. They found that recidivism rates for both groups were low and that specialized treatment programs were no more effective than nonspecialized programs for juvenile sex offenders. The authors concluded, "These results suggest that the growth of interventions has proceeded without adequate knowledge of how to identify at-risk youth, the causes of the behavior, and the most appropriate treatment for juvenile sex offending" (p. 543). However, Kimball and Guarino-Ghezzi (1996) found that juveniles receiving specialized sex offender treatment were more likely to accept responsibility for their behavior, to indicate remorse for what they had done, and to provide ideas that would suggest the ability to resist relapse. Follow-up to treatment suggested that involvement in a specialized program for adolescent sex offenders resulted in lower rates of reoffending.

Although anger is often cited as a primary reason for sexual acting out, particularly among child perpetrators, when Loza and Loza-Fanous (1999b) tested this assumption by reviewing the effectiveness of anger management programs in reducing violent behavior, including the violent behavior of rapists, they found

> no differences between violent offenders and nonviolent offenders and between rapists and non-rapists and nonviolent offenders on anger measures. These results supported the previous reports (reported earlier) that disputed the link between anger and violent behavior. The results also indicate that 73% of incarcerated violent offenders and 81% of incarcerated rapists were referred to an anger treatment program (in addition to the sex offender program) and that 74% of the nonviolent offenders and 76% of non-rapists and nonviolent offenders were not referred to anger programs. These results reflect the prevalence of the belief among correctional professionals that there is a link between anger and violence, rape, and recidivism. This situation exists despite the (a) supporting evidence against a link between anger and violent behavior among non-criminal populations and criminal offenders in particular, (b) lack of relationship between anger and criminal recidivism (Loza and Loza-Fanous, 1999), and (c) shortage of researches examining the role of anger in violent behavior and crime (Kroner and Reddon, 1992; Kroner et al., 1992). (p. 497)

Lea, Auburn, and Kibblewhite (1999) note that attitudes toward sex offenders and sex crimes vary among members of the different professional groups assigned to work with offenders. Akerstrom (1986) believes that prison staff may see sex offenders as outcasts in the prison system and may relate to them in ways that inhibit treatment. Hogue (1993) studied the attitudes of various staff working with sex offenders and found that probation officers and psychologists had more positive attitudes toward offenders than did prison officers and police officers. Not surprisingly, Hogue (1993) also found that sex offenders had more positive attitudes toward other sex offenders than did any of the professionals, suggesting that supervised peer groups might be an effective way to offer treatment. Hogue (1995) also found that police and prison officers who were selected for special training to work with sex offenders came away from the training with much more positive attitudes than they held before the training.

This finding may also apply to helping professionals who work with sex offenders but have no specialized training.

Hilton et al. (1998) reported on their experiences with high school students using half-day workshops to help reduce the amount of date rape and other forms of violence related to intimate and nonintimate relationships. Unfortunately, the authors found that self-report rates of sexual violence were as high for their sample attending a half-day workshop on sexual violence as they were for students who had no anti-date violence training. This was found to be so even though most students attending the workshop did not endorse sexual violence. The authors suggested that the workshops might have been more effective if only high-risk students had attended. Perhaps, the authors suggested, the material would have had more impact had it become part of the regular classroom curriculum and more opportunities for experiential work had been given. Lonsway et al. (1998) reported that college students gave better answers to hypothetical scenarios of sexual conflict and positive changes in attitudes after a semester-long date-rape education course. Hilton et al. (1998) believe that there is value in repeating emotional information such as the discussion of date rape. Resistance to discussing sexually violent behavior, which may describe the behavior of many of the participants, takes time to overcome. Hilton et al. (1998) warned that date-rape education courses should not be viewed as "innocuous," because they may actually make things worse. Programs to reduce sexual violence need to be carefully thought through, should use the available research as a guide, and must develop empirically sound forms of evaluation to determine whether they work.

A number of treatment approaches have been used with perpetrators of sexual violence, including those molesting children, and perpetrators of rape of intimates and of strangers. The literature suggests that the primary approaches used in various treatment settings include the following traditional and less traditional approaches: insight-oriented individual psychotherapy, group psychotherapy, family therapy, psychoeducational skills training, behavioral treatments, chemical castration, sexual addiction twelve-step recovery programs, relapse prevention, Parents United, and several model approaches that combine each of these. Several of the therapies used with sexual offenders are discussed here.

Chemical Castration

This controversial treatment is used primarily with very intransient adult offenders to decrease sexual obsessiveness by significantly lowering libido, erotic fantasies, erections, and ejaculations. Not a single study available in the literature suggests that this treatment should be used with children. One commonly used drug is Depo-Provera, a testosterone-suppressing agent. Side effects of this drug include weight gain, lethargy, cold sweats, nightmares, hot flashes, hypertension and elevated blood pressure, high blood sugar, and shortness of breath. Berlin (1982) reported an 85 percent effectiveness rate in eliminating deviant sexual behaviors, "as long as the medication was taken on a regular basis. It is not a cure and relapse often follows discontinuation of medication and is not recommended as an exclusive treatment" (reported in Brown & Brown, 1997, p. 347). Furthermore, the motivation to rape is often less sexual than it is hostility toward women. Consequently, perpetrators may continue to rape even though they lack any sexual or physical desire.

Psychoeducational Skills Training

Because sexual offenders as a group tend to be uninformed about human sexuality (Groth, 1978), and often have difficulty expressing their feelings, skills training groups focus on "multiple aspects of assertiveness skills, including making eye contact, duration of reply, latency of response, loudness of speech and quality of affect" (Becker & Hunter, 1997, p. 345). Rosen and Fracher (1983) also recommend teaching tension reduction and anger management to those offenders who may experience anxiety and anger before an assault. Groth et al. believes that the majority of offenders have very little awareness of the short- and long-range impact of sexual assault on their victims and suggests the use of empathy training to help offenders understand the impact of their behavior on the victim.

Behavioral Treatments

These interventions include covert sensitization, electrical aversion, odor aversion, chemical aversion, and suppression and satiation techniques. Covert sensitization is a procedure in which the therapist describes a deviant sexual scene followed by an aversive scene. The aversive scene may include going to jail, blood, odors, community responses, and other aversive stimuli the therapist determined to be effective in the screening interview. Scenes last about 10 minutes, and two scenes are presented at each session (Mayer, 1988). This same concept can be used with the addition of unpleasant odors or electric shock with the aversive scene. In satiation techniques, the offender is told to masturbate to nondeviant fantasies and then ejaculate. The client is then asked to continue masturbating to deviant fantasies for 45 minutes. Throughout, the client is asked to verbalize his fantasies, which are recorded and monitored for client compliance. Satiation procedures attempt to destroy the erotic nature of deviant urges by boring the client with his own fantasies (Johnson, 1992).

More traditional treatment approaches use insight, moral revulsion, concern for the victim, the consequences of continued sexual abuse, group treatment to reinforce the messages given during individual treatment, and empathy training to help youthful offenders recognize the harm done by their behavior through contact with victims who have been sexually assaulted. Most of these approaches have very limited effectiveness because they fail to replace deviant sexual attitudes and impulses with those that are more socially acceptable. Changing sexual orientations is difficult, particularly in youthful offenders whose sexual needs are considerable and whose fear of being caught may not as yet be very strong. When age and impulsivity are combined, the probability of behavioral change may not be high. Sexual assault may not be about sexual gratification as much as it may be about power, control, and humiliation. Nowhere is that more likely to exist than in prior victims of sexual abuse reliving their abuse as perpetrators rather than as victims.

Prendergast (1991) notes that children he has worked with in the sixth grade know virtually nothing about the fundamentals of sex. He suggests, therefore, that some sexual assaults may be a function of lack of knowledge in meeting and relating to others. He suggests that, in addition to the usual material presented in sex education courses, additional material should be included on the social aspects of dating and relationships, such as the following:

> How to meet someone and initiate a social conversation; how to successfully ask for a date; meaningful small-talk; how to say "no" in an acceptable and appropriate manner; how to be laughed at and not take it personally (this includes being the center of attention in a group, making an error or acting silly and laughing at yourself with the group); and all other aspects of a normal adult social life that may be suggested by the class. (p. 177)

The National Task Force on Juvenile Sexual Offending suggests the following approach to the treatment of youthful sex offenders (NAPN, 1993):

- Following a full assessment of the juvenile's risk factors and needs, individualized and developmentally sensitive interventions are required.
- Individualized treatment plans should be designed and periodically reassessed and revised. Plans should specify treatment needs, treatment objectives, and required interventions.
- Treatment should be provided in the least restrictive environment necessary for community protection. Treatment efforts also should involve the least intrusive methods that can be expected to accomplish treatment objectives.
- Written progress reports should be issued to the agency that has mandated treatment and should be discussed with the juvenile and parents. Progress "must be based on specific measurable objectives, observable changes, and demonstrated ability to apply changes in current situations."
- Although adequate outcome data are lacking, it suggests that satisfactory treatment will require a minimum of 12 to 24 months. (p. 53)

The primary goals in the treatment of youthful sex offenders, according to Cellini (1995), are community safety, control over abusive behaviors, increasing prosocial interactions, preventing further victimization, stopping the development of additional sexual problems, and helping youth develop appropriate relationships (Becker & Hunter, 1997). To accomplish these goals, highly structured individual and group interventions are recommended (Morenz & Becker, 1995). Treatment approaches include individual, group, and family interventions. Treatment content usually includes sex education, changes in thinking, victim awareness training, values clarification, impulse control, social skills training, reduction of deviant sexual arousal, and relapse prevention (Becker & Hunter, 1997).

As described previously, covert sensitization is a treatment approach that teaches juveniles to stop deviant sexual thoughts and to think about the negative consequences of their behavior (Freeman-Longo & Wall, 1986). Vicarious sensitization is a technique that shows juveniles audiotaped crime scenes designed to arouse the subject, followed by a video showing the negative consequences of their deviant sexual behavior. Research findings suggest that vicarious sensitization may be an effective approach for juveniles who are sexually aroused by prepubescent children (Weinrott, Riggan, & Frothingham, 1997).

Research by Izzo and Ross (1990) regarding the effectiveness of interventions with juveniles who commit various types of offenses, not just sex offenses, suggests that programs using cognitive therapy are twice as effective as those using other approaches. Lipsey and Wilson (1998) found that treatments focusing on interpersonal skills using behavioral approaches had the best results. Unfortunately, programs treating youthful sexual offenders experience high treatment attrition (Becker, 1990; Hunter & Figueredo, 1999). Hanson and Buissière (1998) found that failing to complete treatment correlated highly with a great deal of recidivism. According to Morenz and Becker (1995), there is little evidence that segregating sexual offenders from other offenders in treatment leads to better results.

Jean, Sibling Sexual Assault: A Case Study

Jean is a 9-year-old girl who has been sexually molesting her 5 year-old brother. Jean rubs her brothers penis with soap and warm water and is sometimes able to help her brother achieve a mild erection. Once her brother's penis is erect, she rubs his penis against her vagina. She finds this very exciting and has been able to achieve orgasms. Jean has many sexual thoughts and reads magazines with pictures of the naked bodies of very young boys. She can hardly wait until she is old enough to baby-sit, and has a little boy down the block chosen once this happens. Jean has not been sexually or physically assaulted but has begun having early signs of pubescence. She is aroused by little boys and often masturbates to orgasm thinking about them. Her brother has said nothing to his parents because Jean is older and tells him that the sexual contact they are having is a very special sign of the love brothers and sisters have for one another. She also tells him that it is their secret and brings her brother candy and other gifts she steals from local stores to reinforce that secret. In other respects, Jean's behavior is unremarkable. She is an average student, is not a behavioral problem at school or in at home, and has a number of friends at school and in the neighborhood. She was able to keep her secret hidden from her parents until they caught her one evening on top of her brother, naked, with his penis rubbing against her vagina.

The parents immediately took Jean to a child therapist specializing in sexual acting out. The therapist concluded that Jean felt no remorse for what she had done, would probably do it again if she had the chance, was not a good candidate for therapy because she didn't think she had a problem, was unmotivated to change, and thought the laws against sexual abuse of children were "silly." The therapist remarked that Jean thought that what she did for her brother was wonderful because it gave him so much pleasure. The therapist was required to report the molestation to child protective services, which placed Jean in an all-girl facility where she receives individual and group therapy and is closely supervised. She was also sent to juvenile court for additional psychological testing after she was found masterbating to pictures of little boys.

The testing psychologist for the juvenile court said the following in her report to the court:

Jean is a 9-year-old pedophile who has sex with male children below the age of 6. It is unknown how or when this behavior developed. She has been molesting her 5-year-old brother for almost a year. Jean has no known episodes of child abuse or neglect and comes from a strong, well-functioning, and intact family. Her parents had no evidence of Jean's sexual molestation of her brother or of her sexual inclinations. It is recommended that Jean be placed in a highly supervised setting where there are no young male children. While her pedophilia seems fixed on boys under 6, she is still developing, and it is impossible to know whether her fixation on boys will remain stable or whether it will shift to young girls, or even to older boys. Like most childhood sexual molesters, Jean's sexual behavior at 9 is a good predictor of her behavior in adolescence and adulthood. We know very little about girls who sexually molest children, but the behavior is a strong indication of continued molestation in the future. Given her lack of remorse and her belief that her victims enjoyed the experience, Jean isn't likely to respond positively to therapy. The prognosis for change in her sexual behavior is very poor. She certainly seems to have a fairly well developed Conduct Disorder with Sexual Aggression as a diagnosis at this point in time. In an adult pedophile, we would use a DSM-IV Diagnostic Code of 302.2. The specific indicators of this diagnosis are that the person has "intense sexual urges with pre-pubescent children, the urges cause impairment in functioning, and the person is at least 16 years old and 5 years older than the child they are molesting." (APA, 1994, p. 528)

Child Victims of Sexual Assault

Zolondek et al. (2001), in their sample of 500 juveniles undergoing evaluation for sexual offenses, found that when youth in the sample molested children, most of the children tended to be younger siblings or known nonfamily members. Juveniles in the sample used coercion and deception rather than force in the molestations and tended to select victims they knew and who were easily available. Ryan et al. (1996) found, in their sample of adolescent child molesters, that the victims were blood relatives in 38.8 percent of the cases, while Johnson (1988) found that 46 percent of the children molested by juveniles were family members. Many of the juveniles in this sample had engaged in child molestation that had gone undetected. A large number of youth in the sample had not been arrested for child molestation but for other sexual deviancies. The authors report that 42 percent of the sample arrested for sexual offenses, other than molestation, admitted that they had molested children before they were arrested. The authors therefore suggest that it is imperative that all juveniles arrested for sexual offenses should also be evaluated for possible molestation of children.

What makes victimization such a tragic situation is that prior childhood sexual molestation of sexual offenders is a frequent finding in both the adult and juvenile literature (Ford & Linney, 1995; Langevin, Wright, & Handy, 1989; Pierce & Pierce, 1987). We have knowledge from child abuse reports that almost 40 percent of all adolescent sexual offenders were sexually abused in childhood (Ryan et al., 1996). A study of very young perpetrators indicated that at least 49 percent were sexually abused (Johnson, 1988), while other studies found even higher rates (50 percent to 80 percent) of prior sexual abuse (Friedrich & Luecke, 1988; Ryan et al., 1987).

Victimization of children by sexual perpetrators not only results in a large range of symptoms to children along the developmental cycle, but also results in the high probability that the molested child might become a molester himself or herself. As Glicken and Sechrest note (2003), children who are molested often develop symptoms in childhood that worsen in adolescence and often become unmanageable in adulthood. Symptoms of childhood molestation include depression; suicidal thoughts; eating disorders; substance abuse; the inability to establish and maintain relationships; sleep disorders; anxiety problems with panic attacks; failure at school and at work; sexual deviancies; sexual acting out, including child molestation, rape, and prostitution; inability to form attachments with significant others; and a range of somatic concerns.

Physical and Emotional Repercussions to Victims of Sexual Violence

Sexual traumas, including rape, have serious emotional consequences for victims, such as depression, social isolation, fear of intimacy, a persistent feeling of disinterest in sexual activity, an inability to be physically touched, alcohol and drug abuse, eating disorders, panic attacks, continual feelings of apathy and lethargy, and posttraumatic stress disorder (PTSD) symptoms that sometimes result in physical problems that are often psychosomatic in origin but cause very real discomfort to the victim. There is a general sense that the more violent the sexual assault, the more serious and lasting the emotional symptoms will tend to be.

Many women report that rape results in the loss of relationships with the men in their lives, including their husbands. While outwardly sympathetic men often believe that in some subtle way, the woman either encouraged the rape or did too little to stop it. Some men even obsess that the woman actually enjoyed the rape and will ask numerous questions to try and find out if this is true. Intimacy is often a problem for victims following a rape, which can lead to problems in relationships. Often, the victim can't fully explain her feelings, and love relationships suffer from a nonspecific lack of communication, which ends in distancing and hurt feelings between both partners (Glicken & Sechrest, 2003).

Post-Traumatic Stress Disorder is the most common emotional result of sexual violence. It may occur whenever a person experiences a "traumatic event that is outside the range of usual human experience" (American Psychiatric Association, 1987). The DSM-IV (American Psychiatric Association, 1994) defines PTSD as, "the development of characteristic symptoms following exposure to an extreme stressor involving direct personal experience of an event that involves actual or threatened death or serious injury" (p. 424). In a sense, the traumatic event deeply upsets "the individual's psychological anchors, which are fixed in a secure sense of what has been in the past and what should be in the future" (Gilliland & James, 1993, p. 163). As a result, the victim is "thrust" into a state of crisis until the mind is able to reorganize, classify and make sense out of the experience. During the time of crisis, the sexual assault victim may experience a number of symptoms that are consistent with PTSD.

The symptoms of PTSD fall into four general categories: (1) reexperiencing the traumatic event, (2) avoidance of stimuli associated with the event, (3) numbing of general responsiveness, and (4) increased arousal (American Psychiatric Association, 1994). Reexperiencing the trauma can happen in many forms. One of the most common is frequent nightmares (Goodwin, 1987). Many victims of sexual trauma have difficulty falling asleep because they find that this is a time when their thoughts return to the traumatic event. However, once they do fall asleep, they often dream about the traumatic event and frequently wake up during the night. Many times, the victim may have recurring dreams that center around the physical and emotional trauma of the sexual assault. As a result of nightmares, many victims of sexually traumatic events suffer from sleep deprivation. To help achieve sleep, victims of sexual assaults may use alcohol or drugs to relax. The dependence on alcohol and drugs to help with sleep deprivation may lead to drug and alcohol abuse.

Another form of reexperiencing the event is through intrusive or obsessive thoughts. Intrusive thoughts may take the form of images that are introduced by sights, sounds, smells, or sensory experiences that bring the memory of the sexual assault into awareness (Gilliland & James, 1993). Some sexual trauma victims may repeatedly replay the sexual assault in their minds as they search for more positive outcomes to the experience (Goodwin, 1987). Victims of sexual assault also may avoid thoughts or feelings of the event that could potentially bring up memories of the event. For example, someone raped in an elevator may avoid taking elevators and may walk up many flights of stairs despite the inconvenience (Furey, 1993).

A third symptom of PTSD is a diminished responsiveness to the outside world, also referred to as "psychic numbing" or "emotional anesthesia" (American Psychiatric Association, 1987). The victim may feel isolated from other people, lose the ability to be interested in previously enjoyed activities, or experience difficulty with emotions associated with intimacy, tenderness, and sexuality (American Psychiatric Association, 1987).

The fourth category of PTSD symptoms is increased arousal. Many sexual abuse victims experience increased pulse rates, high blood pressure, or other forms of physical arousal when they are exposed to situations that remind them of the sexually traumatic event (Furey, 1993). They also may experience hypervigilance, difficulty concentrating or completing tasks, irritability, and fear of losing control (American Psychiatric Association, 1987).

Although there are a number of general symptoms related to PTSD, there are also a number of related symptoms. Rape victims often experience depression (American Psychiatric Association, 1987; Furey, 1993; Goodwin, 1987). In addition to depression, victims of sexual trauma may feel isolated from friends, peers, and family members, believing that others won't understand their emotional pain or that they will blame the victim for what has happened. It is not unusual for close friends and family members to be hypercritical of the rape victim for the way they are coping with the rape and, ultimately, to blame the victim for the rape itself (Furey, 1993).

Rape victims often experience anger over the changes the event has caused in their lives and over the unfairness of the event. The anger may be overt and result in outbursts over the slightest and most insignificant event, or it may result in psycho-somatic complaints such as headaches, stomachaches, generalized feelings of ill health, dizziness, and flulike symptoms, to give just a few examples. In general, victims of sexual assault may feel physically and emotionally fragile for weeks and even months afterward (Glicken & Sechrest, 2003).

Summary

The studies in this chapter suggest that sexual acting out may begin well before the onset of puberty and that much of it is directed at younger siblings or friends of family members. The victims of sexual abuse by older siblings, in turn, often begin molesting children, and a vicious cycle develops. There is a fairly imprecise and unreliable literature on the treatment of early childhood sexual acting out, much of it geared to older adults and, consequently, of questionable value for children. This chapter also considered the victims of sexual abuse and noted the subsequent frequent and long-term problems they experience throughout their lives.

Integrative Questions

1. Sexual abuse in families suggests that parents may be inattentive to their children. How could a child molest her sibling for a year, as the second case study indicates, without the family being aware of the behavior?

2. What might be some reasons that some children who have been abused are able to cope with the experience and do reasonably well in their lives?

3. Many people tend to think that pedophilia is untreatable and that the behavior is so fixed that pedophiles should be kept under very tight observation. What do you think after reading this chapter?

4. Sexual impulses are very difficult to change. Do you think any of the treatments discussed in this chapter are likely to change the robust sexual impulses of young sexual predators?

5. Why would a very young child act out sexually before they are biologically experiencing sexual feelings?

References

Abel, G.G., Mittelman, M.S., and Becker, J.V. (1985). Sex offenders: Results of assessment and recommendations for treatment in clinical criminology. In M.H. Ben-Aron, S.J. Hucker, and C.D. Webster (eds.), *The Assessment and Treatment of Criminal Behavior* (pp. 191–205). Toronto, Canada: M and M Graphic.

Akerstrom, M. (1986). Outcasts in prison: The cases of informers and sex offenders. *Deviant Behaviour*, 7, 1–12.

American Psychiatric Association. (1987). *Diagnostic and statistical manual of mental disorders* (3rd ed., Revised). Washington, DC: American Psychiatric Association.

American Psychiatric Association. (1994). *Diagnostic and statistical manual of mental disorders*, (4th ed., Revised). Washington, DC: American Psychiatric Association.

Araji, S. (1997). *Sexually aggressive children: Coming to understand them.* Thousand Oaks, CA: Sage.

Barbaree, H.E., Hudson, S.M., and Seto, M.C. (1993). Sexual assault in society: The role of the juvenile offender. In H.E. Barbaree, W.I. Marshall, and S.M. Hudson (Eds.), *The juvenile sex offender* (pp. 10–11). New York: Guilford.

Becker, J.V. (1990). Evaluating social skills and social aggression. *Criminal Justice and Behavior,* 514, 357–367.

Becker, J.V., and Hunter, J.A. (1997). Understanding and treating child and adolescent sexual offenders. *Advances in Clinical Child Psychology,* 19, 345.

Berlin, F.S. (1982). Sex offenders: A biomedical perspective. In J. Greer and I. Stuart (Eds.), *The sexual aggressor: Current perspectives on treatment* (pp. 83–126). New York: Van Nostrand Reinhold.

Berliner, L. (October 1998). Juvenile sex offenders: Should they be treated differently? *Journal of Interpersonal Violence,* 13, 645–646.

Brown, J.L., and Brown, G.S. (1997). Characteristics of incest offenders: A review. *Journal of Aggression, Maltreatment and Trauma,* 1, pp. 335–354.

Caputo, A.A., Frick, P., and Brodsky, S.L. (September 1999). Family violence and juvenile sex offending: The potential mediating role of psychopathic traits and negative attitudes toward women. *Criminal Justice & Behavior,* 26, 338–356.

Cascardi, M., Avery-Leaf, S., and O'Leary, K. (August 1994). Building a gender sensitive model to explain adolescent dating violence. Paper presented at the 102nd *Annual Meeting of the American Psychological Association,* Los Angeles, CA.

Cellini, H.R. (1995). Assessment and treatment of the adolescent sexual offender. In B.K. Schwartz and H.R. Cellini (eds.), *The Sex Offender: Vol. 1. Corrections, treatment and legal practice,* Kingston, NJ: Civic Research Institute. (pp. 6.1–6.12.)

Davis, G.E., and Leitenberg, H. (1987). Adolescent sex offenders. *Psychological Bulletin,* 101, 417–427.

Ford, M.E., and Linney, J.A. (1995). Comparative analysis of juvenile sexual offenders, violent non-sexual offenders, and status offenders. *Journal of Interpersonal Violence,* 10, 56–69.

Foshee, V. (1996). Gender differences in adolescent dating abuse prevalence, types, and injuries. *Health Education Research,* 11(3), 275–286.

Freeman-Longo, R., and Wall, R.V. (March 20, 1986). Changing a lifetime of sexual crimes. *Psychology Today,* 58–64.

Friedrich, W.N., and Luecke, W.J. (1988). Young school-age sexually aggressive children. *Professional Psychology: Research and Practice,* 2, 155–164.

Furby, L., Weinrott, M., and Blackshaw, L. (1989). Sex offender recidivism: A review. *Psychological Bulletin,* 105, 3–30.

Furey, J.A. (1993). Unknown soldiers: Women veterans and PTSD. *Professional Counselor,* 7, 33–34.

Gilliland, B.E., and James, R.K. (1993). *Crisis intervention strategies.* California: Brooks/Cole.

Glicken, M.D., and Sechrest, D.K. (2003). *The role of the helping professions in treating the victims and perpetrators of violence.* Boston: Allyn & Bacon.

Goodwin, J. (1987). *Readjustment problems among Vietnam veterans.* Cincinnati, OH: Disabled American Veterans.

Gray, H., and Foshee, V. (1997). Adolescent dating violence: Differences between one-sided and mutually violent profiles. *Journal of Interpersonal Violence,* 12 (1), 126–141.

Greenfeld, L.A. (February 1997). Sex offenses and offenders: An analysis of rape and sexual assault. Washington, DC: U.S. Department of Justice, Publication NCJ-163392.

Groth, N.A. (1978). Patterns of sexual assault against children and adolescents. In A. Burgess(ed.), *Sexual assault of children and adolescents* (pp. 3–24). Lexington, MA: D.C. Heath.

Groth, N.A., Longo, R.E., and McFadin, J.B. (1983). Undetected recidivism among rapists and child molesters. *Crime and Delinquency,* 128, 450–458.

Hanson, R.K., and Bussière, M.T. (1998). Predicting relapse: A meta-analysis of sexual offender recidivism studies. *Journal of Consulting and Clinical Psychology,* 66, 348–362.

Hilton, N., Zoe, H., Rice, G.T. et al. (December 1998). Antiviolence education in high schools. *Journal of Interpersonal Violence*, 13, 726–742.

Hogue, T.E. (1993). Attitudes towards prisoners and sexual offenders. In N.K. Clark & G.M. Stephenson (Eds.), *Sexual offenders: Context, assessment and treatment* (pp. 27–32). Leicester: BPS.

Hogue, T.E. (1995). Training multi-disciplinary teams to work with sex offenders: Effects of staff attitudes. *Psychology, Crime & Law*, 1, 227–235.

Hunter, J.A., Jr., and Figueredo, A.J. (1999). Factors associated with treatment compliance in a population of juvenile sexual offenders. *Sexual abuse: A Journal of Research and Treatment*, 11(1): 49–67.

Izzo, R.H., and Ross, R.R. (1990). Meta-analysis of rehabilitation programs for juvenile delinquents: A brief report. *Criminal Justice and Behavior*, 17(1):134–142.

James, W.H., West, C., and Deters K.E. (Fall 2000). Youth dating violence. *Adolescence*, 35, 455–465.

Jezl, D., Molidor, C., and White, T. (1996). Physical, sexual and psychological abuse in high school dating relationships: Prevalence rates and self-esteem issues. *Child and Adolescent Social Work Journal*, 13(1), 69–88.

Johnson, P. (1992). The effects of masturbatory reconditioning with non-familial child molesters. *Behavior Research and Therapy*, 30, 559–561.

Johnson, T.C. (1988). Child perpetrators—Children who molest other children: Preliminary findings. *Child Abuse and Neglect*, 72, 219–229.

Kimball, L.M., and Guarino-Ghezzi, S. (1996). Sex offender treatment: An assessment of sex offender treatment within the Massachusetts Department of Youth Services. *Juvenile Justice Series Report: No. 10*. Boston: Northeastern University, Privatized Research Management Initiative.

Kroner, D., and Reddon, J.R. (1992). The Anger Expression Scale and State-Trait Anger Scale: Stability, reliability, and factor structure in an inmate sample. *Criminal Justice and Behavior*, 19, 397–408.

Kroner, D., Reddon, J.R., and Serin, R.C. (1992). The Multidimensional Anger Inventory: Reliability and factor structure in an inmate sample. *Educational and Psychological Measurement*, 52, 687–693.

Lab, S., Shields, G., and Schondel, C. (1993). Research note: An evaluation of juvenile sexual offender treatment. *Crime and Delinquency*, 39(4), 543–553.

Lane, S., and Lobanov-Rostovsky, C. (1997). Special populations: Children, families, the developmentally disabled, and violent youth. In G.D. Ryan and S.L. Lane (eds.), *Juvenile sexual offending: Causes, consequences, and correction* (pp. 322–359). San Francisco, CA: Jossey-Bass Publishers.

Langevin, R., Wright, P., and Handy, L. (1989). Characteristics of sex offenders who were sexually victimized as children. *Annals of Sex Research*, 2, 227–253.

Lea, S., Auburn, T., and Kibblewhite, K. (March 1999). Working with sex offenders: The perceptions and experiences of professional and paraprofessionals. *International Journal of Offender Therapy & Comparative Criminology*, 43, 103–119.

Lipsey, M.W., and Wilson, D.B. (1998). Effective intervention for serious juvenile offenders: A synthesis of research. In R. Loeber and D.P. Farrington, *Serious and Violent Juvenile Offenders: Risk Factors and Successful Interventions* (pp. 313–345). Thousand Oaks, CA: Sage Publications.

Lonsway, K.A., Klaw, E.L., Berg, D.R., et al. (1998). Beyond "no means no": Outcomes of an intensive program to train peer facilitators for campus acquaintance rape education. *Journal of Interpersonal Violence*, 13, 73–92.

Loza, W., and Loza-Fanous, A. (1999a). Anger and predicting violent and nonviolent offender's recidivism. *International Journal of Interpersonal Violence*, 14, 1014–1029.

Loza, W., and Loza-Fanous, A. (1999b). The fallacy of reducing rape and violent recidivism by treating anger. *International Journal of Offender Therapy & Comparative Criminology*, 43(4), 492–502.

Mathews, R., Hunter, J.A. Jr. and Vuz, J. (1997). Juvenile female sexual offenders: Clinical characteristics and treatment issues. *Sexual Abuse: A Journal of Research and Treatment*, 9(3), 187–200.

Mayer, A. (1988). *Sex offenders: Approaches to understanding and management*. Holmes Beach, FL: Learning Perspectives.

Morenz, B., and Becker, J.V. (1995). The treatment of youthful sexual offenders. *Applied and Preventive Psychology*, 4(4), 247–256.

National Adolescent Perpetrator Network. (1993). *The Revised Report from the National Task Force on Juvenile Sexual Offending. Juvenile and Family Court Journal*, 44(4), 1–120.

O'Keefe, M. (1997). Predictors of dating violence among high school students. *Journal of Interpersonal Violence*, 12, 546–568.

Pierce, L.H., and Pierce, R.L. (1987). Incestuous victimization by juvenile sex offenders. *Journal of Family Violence*, 2, 351–364.

Pithers, W.D., Gray, A., Busconi, A., and Houchens, P. (1998a). Caregivers of children with sexual behavior problems: Psychological and familial functioning. *Child Abuse and Neglect*, 22(2), 129–141.

Pithers, W.D., Gray, A., Busconi, A., and Houchens, P. (1998b). Children with sexual behavior problems: Identification of five distinct child types and related treatment considerations. *Child Maltreatment*, 3(4), 384–406.

Prendergast, W.E. (1991). *Treating sexual offenders in correctional institutions and outpatient clinics: A guide to clinical practice*. New York: Haworth Press.

Rosen, R.C., and Fracher, J.C. (1983). Tension-reducing training in the treatment of compulsive sex offenders. In J.G. Greer and I. Stuart (Eds.), *The sexual aggressors* (pp. 144–159). New York: Van Nostrand Reinhold.

Ryan, G., Lane, S., Davis, J., and Isaac, C. (1987). Juvenile sex offenders: Development and correction. *Child Abuse and Neglect*, 11, 385–395.

Ryan, G., Miyoshi, T.J., Metzner, J.L., Krugman, R.D., and Fryer, G.E. (1996). Trends in a national sample of sexually abusive youths. *Journal of the American Academy of Child and Adolescent Psychiatry*, 33, 17–25.

Saunders, B., Kilpatrick, D., Resnick, H., Hanson, R., and Lipovsky, J. (January 1992). Epidemiological characteristics of child sexual abuse: Results from Wave II of the National Women's Study. Presented at the San Diego Conference on Responding to Child Maltreatment, San Diego, CA.

Snyder, H.N., and Sigmund, M. (1995). *Juvenile offenders and victims: A focus on violence*. Pittsburgh: National Center for Juvenile Justice.

Veneziano, C., Veneziano, L., and LeGrand, S. (April 2000). The relationship between adolescent sex offender behaviors and victim characteristics with prior victimization. *Journal of Interpersonal Violence*, 15, 363–374.

Weinrott, M.R. (1996). Juvenile sexual abuse: A critical review. Unpublished manuscript.

Weinrott, M., Riggan, M., and Frothingham, S. (1997). Reducing deviant arousal in juvenile sex offenders using vicarious sensitization. *Journal of Interpersonal Violence*, 12(5), 704–728.

Zolondek, S.C., Abel, G.F., Northey, W.F., and Jordan, A.D. (January 2001). The self-reported behaviors of juvenile sexual offenders. *Journal of Interpersonal Violence*, 16, 73–85.

7

Treating Violent Children
Clinical Approaches

This chapter considers clinical approaches to the treatment of child violence. Clinical approaches are defined as the interventions provided to individuals, families, and small groups by helping professionals. Chapter 8 addresses large-scale community, neighborhood, and school programs to treat childhood violence. As is noted in the following discussion, there is an underlying theme in the literature which suggests that clinical approaches may not be effective with children and adolescents who act out. This is a theme also noted in the literature on clinical work with adult perpetrators of violence (Glicken & Sechrest, 2003). The reality is that clinicians may often see violent children before they commit serious acts of violence. Many of the books and articles reviewed for this chapter suggested that violence and acting-out behavior are more effectively treated through large-scale prevention and treatment programs. Although many of these programs offer hope, it seems reasonable to believe that children who act out will be seen, at some point in the development of their behavior, by helping professionals whose interventions could reduce and even eliminate the possibility of violent behavior.

Clinical Approaches Used in Violence Intervention

Murray and Myers (1998) report that *conduct disorders* in childhood are frequently predictive of later delinquency and adult criminality. By age 6, family functioning is a strong indicator of delinquency. At age 9, the child's antisocial and aggressive behavior further predicts delinquent tendencies. Early assessment and intervention suggest the potential to inhibit the development of antisocial behavior among children with diagnoses of *Oppositional Defiant Behavior* and the more serious diagnosis of *conduct disorders*. This chapter provides research evidence on the effectiveness of clinical treatments.

Sprague and Walker (2000) believe that we have the diagnostic tools to identify children at risk of violence as early as age 5. As Fagan (1996) and Hawkins and Catalano (1992) reported, antisocial behavioral patterns coupled with high degrees of aggression early in a child's life are the best predictors of future violence. Many of these children will cause major acts of violence, and many more will have problems, throughout their lives, with domestic violence, substance abuse, employment, and mental health problems, as well as a host of social and emotional problems that, if identified and treated early, may be lessened, if not eliminated completely (Sprague & Walker, 2000).

There are many reasons why children develop behavioral problems at an early age. The two cases presented in this chapter explore several of those reasons. However, one reason remains significant: Violent children, or to use DiIulio's (1996a) term, *super predators*, grow up in an atmosphere of emotional poverty

> without loving, capable, responsible adults who teach you right from wrong. It is the poverty of being without parents, guardians, relatives, friends, teachers, coaches, clergy and others who habituate you to feel joy at others' joy, pain at others' pain, happiness when you do right, remorse when you do wrong. It is the poverty of growing up in the virtual absence of people who teach these lessons by their own everyday example, and who insist that you follow suit and behave accordingly. In the extreme, it is the poverty of growing up surrounded by deviant, delinquent, and criminal adults in chaotic, dysfunctional, fatherless, Godless, and jobless settings where drug abuse and child abuse are twins, and self-respecting young men literally aspire to get away with murder. (p. 3)

Studer (1996) suggests four catalysts of childhood violence that should be considered in treatment: biological reasons, family influences, messages from the media, and empowerment concerns.

Biological Variables

Testosterone and serotonin can trigger aggressive behavior. According to Lipsitt (1990), lower levels of serotonin seem to inhibit aggression and impulsivity. Violent behavior need not have a chemical base, however, because people without chemical imbalances may be violent (Myers, 1993). The need to understand biochemical reasons for violence suggests the positive benefits of a complete physical examination before treatment begins for children experiencing behavioral problems. One of the repeated biochemical issues noted in the literature on violence in children is the presence of hyperactivity. Medications for hyperactivity may prompt violence, or treatment using proper medications may decrease or eliminate violent behavior. Minimal organic brain damage, often associated with accidents and physical abuse, also may cause aggression and violence in otherwise emotionally healthy children.

Family Variables

The way in which the family provides structure, limit setting, and discipline can greatly influence the development of behavioral problems in children. When parents are harsh and use disproportionate violence to discipline their children, children come to believe that physical violence is a normal way of expressing love. It also teaches children that physical aggression is an acceptable way of resolving problems. When children suffer from physical or sexual abuse or neglect, the damage to them can be extreme. Even when the violence isn't directed at the child, as in spousal abuse, the child often suffers many of the same symptoms related to direct child abuse and neglect. As Herrenkohl and Russo (2001) indicate,

> the experience of harsh, physical discipline both terrorizes and humiliates the child, adding to the sense of worthlessness and providing a model for coping in social interactions. The child who is already angry in response to negative, inadequate nurturance and is seeking protection from a coercive family and a threatening world might be particularly susceptible to using aggressive behavior. (p. 10)

Many parents only have the example of their own dysfunctional parents to model child-rearing practices. Helping families understand beneficial child-rearing approaches may go a long way in helping children who begin to exhibit early signs of violence. Often, family life for children with behavioral problems is inconsistent and unpredictable. As Craig (1992) suggests, many of these young children are forced to gauge the moods of their parents and learn to respond to family life according to parental moods instead of consistent parental messages. Living with inconsistent parental behavior provides an early-life experience that forces children to take control of their environment. Craig suggests that, in the classroom, children from highly inconsistent homes may wait to react to any situation or event by first determining the mood of the teacher. Children who live in homes with inconsistent parenting may also become more aggressive when new and strange school routines force them to deal with situations that are out of their control. Craig believes that changes in the regular day, such as assemblies or class meetings, may elicit aggressive responses, because children experiencing inconsistent parenting are unprepared for the newness of the situation and may be unable to use their limited repertoire of behavioral responses to deal with unfamiliar situations and, consequently, may revert to aggression.

This need to control various environments cycles into the child's behavior at school and in the community, where the behavior may be seen as overly aggressive and controlling to an extreme. The adaptation to inconsistent family life not only affects the child, but also cycles on into later life. Griffin (1987) reports that children who demonstrate a large number of antisocial, developmental, and academic problems before age 9 are more likely to show aggressive tendencies as adults. Providing consistency in treatment should be a primary goal of all interventions with children who display behavioral problems.

Ducharme, Atkinson, and Poulton (2000) note that children from violent homes who might be at risk of committing violence show a variety of emotional difficulties that include conduct problems, anxiety and withdrawal, depression, and low self-esteem. One way of dealing with potential violence from children growing up in violent home situations is to provide help to parents in what the authors call "Compliance Training." This approach helps train parents (often mothers) in consistent parenting approaches that include equitable discipline, time outs when children are losing con-

trol, reduced attention for negative behaviors without scolding or blamin͜
dren, reduced family conflict, and focus on helping children to not use opposit.
fiant behavior to get their way. The authors noted improvement rates of o
percent in reducing child–parent conflict through the use of compliance training.

Television and Other Media

Huesmann et al. (1983) believe that overexposure to violence in the media has a de-
sensitizing effect on young children. Lipsitt (1990) thinks that the portrayal of life in
the media as wealthy, glamorous, and exciting creates a perception of the gap in
lifestyles between the child and the characters portrayed in the media that can lead to
anger, frustration, and deviant acts. Clinical work with children who act out and their
families should consider the influence violent material has on children with behavioral
problems. The mass culture may tend to reinforce an aggressive and hostile style of
personal interaction that the child is in the process of developing. A guiding principle
in treatment with families of violent children is to be aware of what children are
watching on television and in films and to note the impact it has on them. As Javier,
Herron, and Primavera (1998) state:

> As parents, we need to monitor what our children watch on television and watch with
> them. We need to engage them in conversation about what they see and help them un-
> derstand it and learn from it. Using television as a babysitter or a way of avoiding con-
> tact with our children may have greater detrimental results than we realize. It is our
> contention that the abdication of parental responsibilities and the erosion of the fam-
> ily are major contributors to the increasing number and the severity of the societal
> problems we face, including our subject, violent behavior. (p. 352)

Empowerment

Lipsitt (1990) believes that frustrated children act out aggressively to create a sense of
personal power and to provide an outlet, even if it is a socially harmful outlet, for their
need to achieve. According to Studer (1996), antisocial behaviors often occur when
children feel frustrated and lack other outlets for their frustration. Because children
with behavioral problems often feel inadequate and have poor self-concepts, one of
the guiding principles of working with children who act out is to enhance feelings of
adequacy and self-worth in treatment. One approach that is particularly effective in
accomplishing this is the strengths perspective (Glicken, 2004). In explaining the
strengths perspective, Glicken says the following:

> In our view, people do not improve when the locus of help is on what is wrong with
> them. They get better when the worker and the client actively identify the client's
> strengths: those behavioral processes, values, beliefs, cultural imperatives, religious in-
> volvements, spiritual convictions, support networks, friendships, and a host of more
> subtle life issues that move the client in a positive direction and whose focus permits a
> loving, tender, and caring relationship between helper and client. The positive behav-
> iors of the client form the basis of assessment and treatment. It is the strengths of the
> client that lead to improved functioning. (Preface)

Studer (1996) suggests that children with behavioral problems may benefit from learning anger management techniques, assertiveness training, problem-solving techniques, and conflict mediation.

1. **Anger Management:** Anger management is a cognitive therapy approach in which children learn to identify situations that lead to angry responses, recognize their physical reactions to anger (clenched fists, sweaty palms, heightened heart rate), and learn to rationally perceive their role in the situation so that the anger can dissipate or be dealt with appropriately.

2. **Assertiveness Training:** Assertiveness training is a way to help children learn to have their needs met without violating the rights or feelings of others. In distinguishing aggression from assertiveness, Baer (1976) notes that the purpose of aggression is to have needs met by violating the rights of others, while assertiveness helps children achieve those needs without disregarding the needs of others. Huey and Rank (1984) report that a class in assertiveness training was offered to disruptive eighth-grade urban male students. The class met one hour a week for four weeks for a total of eight hours. The students in the class showed decreased aggressive behavior and increased assertiveness. Mathias (1992) supports the use of assertiveness training for elementary students and notes that assertiveness training programs get overwhelmingly positive evaluations from children, teachers, and parents.

3. **Problem-Solving Training:** Problem-solving training helps children learn to think their way through difficult social situations and to increase empathy and sensitivity for others. Rundie (as cited in Goldstein & Glick, 1987) notes that when fifth-grade students were allowed to process actual life situations that affect most fifth graders (issues such as cheating, stealing, using drugs, and lying to parents), they did much better on group tasks than did children who were not involved in problem-solving discussions.

4. **Conflict Mediation:** Conflict mediation helps children learn to resolve conflicts with others by actually negotiating solutions. Schrumpt, Crawford, and Usadel (1991) outlined the following six basic steps in the mediation process: **Step 1:** Explain the ground rules and describe the conflict. **Step 2:** Gather information. Each person is permitted time to tell his or her story without interruption. **Step 3:** Focus on common interests: The purpose of this step is to help those in conflict identify common goals and to find out what each person views as a suitable resolution of the problem. **Step 4:** Create options. People in conflict are permitted to think the problem through, offer solutions, list possible options, and to provide a venue for joint problem resolution. **Step 5:** Evaluate options and choose a solution. Those in conflict are encouraged to agree on the list of options that come from step 4. **Step 6:** Write an agreement and close the mediation session. A written agreement is presented, which all parties sign, that spells out the conditions of the conflict resolution and each party's responsibility to abide by the agreement. As a further aspect of strengthening the agreement, the parties are asked to shake hands. Lane and McWhirter (1992) report that mediation improves potentially troubled behavior, helps children improve their listening skills, and enhances the climate of the school.

Mental health professionals have implemented a wide variety of treatment approaches in an attempt to address one or more of the many psychosocial risk factors associated with youth violence. The primary approaches include cognitive–behavioral skills interventions with seriously aggressive or violent youth, cognitive restructuring techniques, role-plays, therapist modeling, and behavioral assignments. All of these approaches attempt to reduce violent behavior in children by directly addressing risk factors within a child, such as ineffective problem-solving skills, deficits in moral development, incorrect or illogical perceptions of others, and feelings of insecurity and low self-esteem, to mention just a few. Unfortunately, according to Sechrest (2001), little significant impact on long-term recidivism has been demonstrated with these interventions.

Parent training models to help parents learn effective communication skills, conflict resolution, family problem solving, contracting, positive reinforcement, mild punishment, and modeling are effective in reducing child noncompliance and aggressive behavior among preschool- and elementary school–age children. These models attempt to reduce aggressive behavior by addressing the psychosocial risk factors that occur at the family level, including poor parental monitoring and discipline practices, as well as coercive family interactions. However, only slight improvements in family functioning occur in families of violent youth, and, again, no significant reduction in recidivism rates has been demonstrated (Sechrest, 2001).

Overall, mental health treatments have been most effective with younger, nonviolent, or mildly aggressive youth (Sechrest, 2001). However, they have been largely ineffective in reducing or preventing further violence with more serious or chronically violent offenders. As a result, many professionals and nonprofessionals are skeptical that the juvenile justice system and the mental health profession can rehabilitate violent children. It has been argued that the approaches previously reviewed have not been successful for two main reasons. First, they have included interventions that focus on only one or two psychosocial risk factors associated with youth violence (e.g., individual cognition, family relations) and have failed to simultaneously address the many other factors (e.g., peer, school, and neighborhood factors) that contribute to youth violence. Second, these interventions take place in only one location, such as a mental health clinic or a juvenile incarceration facility, and fail to address other influences on violent behavior, such as home life, school, or neighborhood.

Sechrest (2001) notes that one notable advance in the treatment of violent juvenile behavior is multisystemic therapy (MST). MST is a departure from such more traditional approaches as residential and inpatient treatment, detention and incarceration, and outpatient or clinic-based services. MST is offered in the juvenile's home, school, and neighborhood. The interventions are flexibly tailored to the psychosocial needs of each client and his or her family. MST targets the family system, by improving family emotional bonding and parental discipline strategies; the school, by increasing parent–teacher communication and child academic performance; peer relationships, by promoting involvement in extracurricular activities, structured sports, or volunteer organizations and; community organizations, by eliciting help from social service agencies.

Jenny, Treating a Conduct Disorder: A Case Study

Jenny is a 9-year-old girl who has been diagnosed with a severe childhood-onset conduct disorder. The diagnosis was made after five years of acting-out behavior in class, progressively more severe lying, stealing from classmates, cruelty to family and neighborhood animals, and a volatile temper that often results in physical aggression to members of her family, neighborhood children, and classmates at school. Jenny is presently suspended from school because of her violent outbursts and is being seen by a clinical social worker as part of her school's requirement that something be done about her behavior before she can return to class.

Jenny has many of the classic signs of a conduct disorder. In treatment, she is grandiose about her accomplishments, is highly manipulative, attacks the therapists verbally when she doesn't get her way, and sulks when the therapist suggests that she might be wrong about the way she views the world. Jenny externalizes blame for everything and can see only malicious intent in having to see a therapist. She frequently talks about getting back at the teacher and principal, who, she thinks, were responsible for her suspension from school.

The therapist has been using cognitive therapy (Beck, 1976) with Jenny. Cognitive therapy focuses on helping clients rationally think through solutions to social and emotional problems. It also helps clients analyze their thought processes as they critically evaluate irrational self-sentences about situations, which often result in dysfunctional behavior. Jenny has resisted therapy and tends to respond to the therapist in an exaggerated voice in which she mimics everything the therapist says in a squeaky and childlike voice. Nonetheless, the therapist has maintained his treatment plan, and at every session Jenny is encouraged to view her behavior as logically and as honestly as possible. This process of rationally reviewing her behavior is having a demoralizing impact on Jenny. After three months of treatment, she has begun to show signs of depression and regression. She often sits on the sofa curled up in the fetal position, clutching her doll, and sucks her finger and cries. Jenny's defenses are beginning to break down. Instead of the angry and aggressive child she presented initially in treatment, she has begun to show a frightened, troubled side that suggests the cognitive functioning of a much younger child.

The therapist believes that Jenny suffered a trauma when she was a very young child, but there is no evidence of child abuse or any of the other problems one associates with a developmental shutdown. The therapist thinks it's possible that the birth of a sibling when she was age 5 and the subsequent loss of her role as an only child may be partially responsible for the change in her behavior, but this is only a theory. After five months of treatment, Jenny is miserable and doesn't want to talk to the therapist. She complains to her parents that the therapist hurts her feelings and that he hates her, but changes are taking place in her behavior at school and at home. She has stopped acting out, is more thoughtful in her responses to others, and has begun to see the role she plays in the interactions with others that end in painful confrontations.

After eight months of treatment, the therapist has begun to see real changes in Jenny's behavior. She is more animated and engaged in treatment and is more willing to discuss her problems. Her anger has also begun to diminish. Jenny is acting in a more age-appropriate way. She can now discuss feelings and concerns. It is difficult to know why the change has taken place, because conduct disorders are often felt to be as difficult to treat as personality disorders in adults. The therapist now believes, after meeting her parents on a number of occasions, that Jenny lacks consistent parenting and that the birth of her sibling ushered in a degree of chaos in the family, which Jenny deeply resents. He also thinks that the therapeutic relationship has provided Jenny with a source of intimacy that has been missing in her life, and that the consistent, structured therapy she is receiving provides a caring substitute for her chaotic family life.

The changes in Jenny have been dramatic. She exhibits few of the symptoms she presented initially. After a year of therapy, she is progressing well in school and shows good social and emotional progress. But is she cured? The therapist hopes so but is inclined to wait and see. "Therapy doesn't produce miracles," he said,

> and when you treat acting-out children like Jenny, you hope for the best, but you temper it with reality. Jenny is still a troubled child who is about to enter the turbulent years of adolescence. Her underlying issues haven't changed, but her adaptation to the world has improved, probably as a result of the structure and consistency provided by the therapy. Jenny has shown amazing progress, and you always want to be optimistic with children. I suspect that the more treatment is able to help Jenny, the more she will progress as she enters adolescence. I would strongly recommend continued therapy for quite a long time to come, and a good deal of help to her family. She has a troubled, disorganized family. To be sure, they're loving and nonabusive, but they haven't much skill in setting limits or in providing consistent affection and support. All Jenny can see is in her family is chaos and disorganization, and it makes her angry and resentful. Like most children, Jenny craves consistency. You can't really expect Jenny to maintain her improvement in functioning without a similar improvement in the family. We have already begun to provide family therapy and parent education classes to the family, with excellent results. As with all clients, Jenny doesn't live in a vacuum. Her family environment affects her behavior. As the family improves, so will Jenny.

Pessimism Regarding the Effectiveness of Clinical Work with Violent Youth

It is interesting to note the general skepticism in the literature regarding the effectiveness of clinical approaches to treating children with early-onset violence. Rae-Grant, McConville, and Fleck (1999) write, "Because exclusive individual clinical interventions for violent conduct disorders do not work, the child and adolescent psychiatrist must seek opportunities to be a leader or team member in well-organized and well-funded community prevention efforts" (p. 338). Sprague and Walker (2000) complain about poorly matched treatment approaches that deny the severity of the problem. Elliott, Hamburg, and Williams (1998) report that counseling has no effect on the problems of antisocial and predelinquent youth. Steiner and Stone (1999) report widespread pessimism among clinicians regarding effective clinical work with violent youth, but believe that this pessimism is unwarranted. The authors indicate that treating childhood violence requires clinicians to practice with flexibility and to be cognizant of the need to develop treatment approaches that permit clinicians to offer interventions in many different settings, including schools, juvenile detention centers, prisons, and homes, as well as in the consulting room. Patterson and Narrett (1990) believe that there is strong evidence to support the effectiveness of family- and parent-based interventions in the elementary grades to reduce violence and related pathology. Myles and Simpson (1998) argue that because aggressive and violent children often experience a range of problems, we should provide services to meet children's academic and social needs. Those services should include counselors, psychologists, social workers, and treatment interventions that meet the social and emotional needs of aggressive and violent children.

In writing about therapeutic approaches to working with gang members, a unique subset of violent children, Morales (1982) provides the following reasons clinical interventions often do not work with gang members and, by extension, with violent youth in general:

> a) the belief by many clinicians that antisocial personality disorders and/or gang members are untreatable; b) the therapists' fear of violent people and the assumption that all gang members are violent; c) a belief in the lack of the psychological capacity for insight of poor and uneducated people, a cohort usually associated with gang activity; d) an over-appreciation of the value of treatment and a belief that every gang member can benefit; e) the opposite belief that gang members can't be treated and that all gang members are manipulative and dishonest; and f) the belief that the therapist has the power and hence will control the interview. (p. 142)

Morales (1982) explains that gang members entering treatment may have issues that must be understood by the therapist. They include (1) a distrust/dislike of authority figures, often the result of prior negative experiences with parents, teachers, and police; (2) a strong resentment to being forced into treatment involuntarily as the result of the justice system; (3) a feeling of discomfort with the therapist who might be of a different ethnic/racial group; (4) a sense of a generational, cultural, and perhaps language gap with the therapist; (5) the anticipation of looking forward to winning yet another struggle with a social control agent, or the notion of the therapist as a "Freudian cop" (p. 143).

Because many of the children who become violent come from abusive homes, it's interesting to note the lack of effectiveness in current approaches for work with abused children. Lukefahr (2001), in a book review of *Treatment of Child Abuse* (edited by Robert M. Reece, 2000), writes,

> Although there is a very strong effort throughout to base findings and recommendations on the available evidence, these chapters highlight the reality that this young, evolving specialty remains largely descriptive. A common theme of several authors is the prominent role of cognitive-behavioral therapy for child abuse victims, but therapists may be disappointed in the lack of specific protocols for implementing CBT. (p. 36)

Kaplan, Pelcovitz, and Labruna (1999) indicate that the effectiveness of treatment for children who have been physically and sexually abused "has generally not been empirically evaluated. In a review of treatment research for physically abused children, Oates and Bross (1995) cite only 13 empirical studies between 1983 and 1992 meeting even minimal research standards" (p. 1218).

Steiner and Stone (1999) suggest that whatever we may say about large-scale programs and the ineffectiveness of clinical work, violent clients, particularly children, almost always see a clinician at some point in their lives. To show the importance of early and effective intervention, the authors note that young men representing only 8 percent of the population commit almost half of all violent crimes. Many of these young men could be helped through clinical intervention if seen early enough, according to the authors, who go on to indicate that the cost of violence to victims and to taxpayers is "staggering." Mandel and Magnusson (1993) report that in the early 1990s, the lifetime cost for all Americans aged 12 and older, who were victims of violent crime, was estimated to be $178 billion a year, while the cost to taxpayers to incarcerate one juvenile was $32,000 a year in California, according to Butts (1994). Steiner and Stone (1999) believe that juvenile delinquency is a problem that presents a high probability of many pathologies, all requiring well-researched treatment approaches. The authors argue that without effective interventions, we will be unsuccessful in responding to continued episodes of violence throughout the life cycle.

Ellickson and McGuigan (2000) report that because early deviance and poor grades are useful predictors of later violence, violence intervention should begin as early as elementary school and should focus on issues of self-esteem, life choices, drug and alcohol abuse, and peer choices. These are issues with which clinicians routinely deal when treating children and adolescents. More significantly, Steiner and Stone (1999) write,

> Our understanding of how to help these children and adolescents is far from complete, and many more studies of interventions are necessary to advance science, clinical care, and public understanding. We need better tools to mitigate the human suffering of perpetrators and victims alike. Such a recommendation is not easily brought in line with the prevailing canons of the time, where we seek to prosecute children as adults and seek the death penalty for 10-year-olds. By involving our profession, which has a long and distinguished history of standing up for those who cannot do so for themselves. (p. 234)

Van Wormer (1999) suggests the importance of a strengths or positive approach to work with clients who act out and writes, "At the heart of the strengths perspective is a belief in the basic goodness of humankind, a faith that individuals, however unfortunate their plight, can discover strengths in themselves that they never knew existed" (p. 51). Van Wormer (1999) goes on to suggest the use of the following strengths techniques with clients who act out:

1. Seek the positive in terms of people's coping skills, and you will find it. Look beyond presenting symptoms and setbacks and encourage clients to identify their talents, dreams, insights, and fortitude.
2. Listen to the personal narrative. Through entering the world of the storyteller, the practitioner comes to grasp the client's reality, at the same time attending to signs of initiative, hope, and frustration with past counterproductive behavior that can help lead the client into a healthier outlook on life. The strengths ther-

apist, by means of continual reinforcement of positives, seeks to help the client move away from what van den Bergh (1995, p. xix) calls "paralyzing narratives."

3. In contradistinction to the usual practice in interviewing known liars, con-artists, and thieves, which is to protect yourself from being used or manipulated, this approach would have the practitioner temporarily suspend skepticism or disbelief and enter the client's world as the client presents it; showing a willingness to listen to the client's own explanations and perceptions ultimately encourages the emergence of the client's truth.

4. Validate the pain where pain exists. Reinforce persistent efforts to alleviate the pain and help people recover from the specific injuries of oppression, neglect, and domination.

5. Don't dictate: collaborate through an agreed upon, mutual discovery of solutions among helpers, families, and support networks. Validation and collaboration are integral steps in a consciousness-raising process that can lead to healing and empowerment (Bricker-Jenkins, 1991). (pp. 54–56)

Jason, Treating a Young Murderer: A Case Study

Jason is a 7-year-old child who killed a cousin while playing with his father's gun. Jason has no known emotional problems. Initially it was thought that the killing was an accident. With further investigation, however, it was discovered that when Jason was age 5, he killed a friend while playing with a gun. The family had been living in another state and moved after the shooting. When information about the prior killing was shared with the police, Jason was remanded to juvenile court and ordered to stand trial. He was found guilty of murder and placed in a facility for violent children.

Jason has none of the external characteristics of violent children. He is a sweet, intelligent, considerate child who seems thoughtful, empathic, and sensitive. He says that he is deeply sorry for the killing of two people and just guesses he shouldn't play with guns. He promises to never touch a gun again.

Jason has excellent peer relationships and is considered a leader among his peers, who like and respect him. No one has a bad word to say about Jason, and he is never in trouble. Many staff members have begun to doubt that he should be in the facility and have urged the administrator to seek his release to a group home where Jason can have access to his family and friends. One night, Jason smothered to death one of the boys in his dorm room. Jason said he was trying to help the boy breathe, because the boy was having an asthma attack on the night of the killing. "Boy, I have some kind of bad luck, don't I?" he said, and cried at the loss of his friend. The staff has asked that the petition to return the child to the community be voided, and Jason is in a confined and supervised setting away from other children.

In therapy, Jason is full of contrition and guilt. He reads the Bible and often shares biblical verses with his therapist to show his sense of moral regret. The therapist has gotten nowhere with Jason and thinks that his impulse to kill may be so unconscious that Jason is unaware of the reasons for his behavior. Jason seems disassociated from the murders. Talking to him, one gets the feeling that they were done by someone else. It might be possible that Jason has *Dissociative Identity Disorder* (DSM-IV Code #300.14, formerly known *as multiple personality disorder*), and the literature makes an argument that this may be the case (American Psychiatric Association, 1994, p. 487). It is also possible that Jason has no empathy at all and acts on impulses when he feels the urge to do harm. The therapist is uncertain, and Jason and his family aren't providing any assistance to help discover the reasons for the killings. Everyone the therapist has interviewed says that Jason is a "good boy" and that he could never hurt anyone. "He's a sweet boy," his grandmother told the therapist, "and he goes to church with me every Sunday. That child doesn't have a mean bone in his body."

One day in treatment, the therapist watched Jason undergo a personality change in reaction to question the therapist had asked. "His face went completely blank," the therapist noted in a report,

> and suddenly I could feel this malevolent force come over him. If he could, he would have killed me. He suddenly looked and even smelled differently. It was as if his body was sulfurous. And then, as quickly as the change took place, he was suddenly the gentle and sensitive child I had seen before. You read about these changes in the literature about some serial killers. I suspect that we have a long way to go before we fully understand the personality shifts made by children like Jason. Ninety-nine percent of the time, he's a considerate, loving, and sensitive child, and then, suddenly, he becomes a monster. How do you treat someone like that?

Discussion

The mental health field has no classification for "monsters." We believe that there are scientific reasons for Jason's behavior. A close look at Jason's family life reveals a very troubled and violent family. Jason's adolescent brother is in prison for a gang-related killing. His father spent 10 years in prison for beating a man to death in a barroom brawl. His mother has a history of alcoholism and addiction to crack cocaine. She is described by the authorities as violent, impulsive, and dangerous when she uses substances. It was discovered, as more information was gathered about the family, that Jason was diagnosed with a drug addiction at birth. His mother had been using crack cocaine and alcohol throughout the pregnancy. Jason suffered from a seizure disorder when he was a child and periodically "blacks out," according to his family. He has never been given medication, but a full neurological examination suggested that he suffers from petit mal seizures and frequently blacks out for time periods as long as several minutes. The neurologist thinks the seizure disorder might be associated with the violent episodes, and Jason has been placed on antiseizure medication. However, two more violent episodes in which he tried to kill a guard and attacked his therapist suggest that the problem is probably not related to his seizures.

Jason lives under close supervision. The staff keeps their distance and often thinks of the irony that his first name is the same as the character who wears a hockey mask in the *Halloween* horror movies. Jason continues to be a sweet, compassionate, and sensitive child and has continued on in therapy. He is cooperative in treatment but has no insight into his behavior and thinks that some demon must possess him when he kills. "I want somebody to get the Devil out of me," he tells his therapist. "Then I can go home and go to church with my grandma again. When I go to church, I know God will take care of me and I won't do anything to ever hurt anybody."

Summary

Although there is frustration and pessimism about the effectiveness of clinical intervention in the lives of violent children, a number of researchers agree that early intervention, when violence begins to show itself, might be beneficial. Several writers believe that the clinician's belief system sometimes presupposes such negative and stereotypic attributes of violent children that treatment is unlikely to help. Almost all of the data presented in this chapter suggest the need for more research in the area of effective treatment for early-onset violent behavior.

Integrative Questions

1. Do you think the pessimism toward clinical interventions described in this chapter is based more on a lack of proven clinical interventions or on the dislike clinicians appear to have for children who act out?

2. This chapter argues that the earlier the intervention, the more likely the child will not become overtly violent. Do you agree?

3. The case study about Jason seems to argue that he goes through a transformation in which a "malevolent" personality takes over and causes him to be violent. What might be some other reasons for his violence?

4. Children who act out with violence often come from abusive homes. Is it possible that most children show resilience and that violent homes are less important in understanding violence than the child's unique coping skills?

5. Referring to question 4, why do you think some children act out violently when abused, but other children show restraint and resilience and never act out violently?

References

American Psychiatric Association (1994). *The diagnostic and statistical manual of mental disorders* (4th Ed. Revised). Washington, DC: American Psychiatric Association.

Baer, J. (1976). *How to be an assertive (not aggressive) woman in life, in love, and on the job: A total guide to self-assertiveness.* New York: New American Library.

Beck, A.T. (1976). *Cognitive therapy and emotional disorders.* New York: International University Press.

Bricker-Jenkins, M. (1991). The propositions and assumptions of feminist social work practice. In M. Bricker-Jenkins, N.R. Hooyman, and N. Gottlieb (Eds.), *Feminist social work practice in clinical settings* (pp. 271–303). Newbury Park, CA: Sage.

Butts J.A. (1994). Offenders in juvenile court, 1992. *Juvenile Justice Bulletin*, OJJDP Update on Statistics.

Craig, S.E. (1992). The educational needs of children living with violence. *Phi Delta Kappan, 74,* 67–71.

DiIulio, J.J. Jr. (February 1996a). Fill churches, not jails: youth crime and super predators: Statement before the United States Senate Subcommittee on Youth Violence, February 28, 1996. Available online at: John DiIulio Testimony www./brook.edu/pa/hot/diiulio.htm

DiIulio, J.J., Jr. (July 1996b). Stop crime where it starts. *The New York Times*, July 13, 1996. Available online at John J. DiIulio, Oped. www.brook.edu/pa/hot/arttoppics/diiulio.htm

Ducharme, J.M., Atkinson, L., and Poulton, L. (August 2000). Success-based, noncoercive treatment of oppositional behavior in children from violent homes. *Journal of the American Academy of Child and Adolescent Psychiatry*, 39, 995–1004.

Ellickson, P.L., and McGuigan, K.A. (April 2000). Early predictors of adolescent violence. *American Journal of Public Health*, 90, 566–572

Elliott, D.S., Hamburg, B., and Williams, K.R. (1998). *Violence in American schools: A new perspective*. Boulder, CO: Center for the Study and Prevention of Violence.

Fagan, J. (March 1996). Recent perspectives on youth violence. Paper presented at the Northwest Conference on Youth Violence, Seattle, WA.

Glicken, M.D. (2004). *Using the strengths perspective in social work practice: A positive approach for the helping professions*. Boston: Allyn & Bacon.

Glicken, M.D., and Sechrest, D.H. (2003). *The role of the helping professions in treating and preventing violence*. Boston: Allyn & Bacon.

Goldstein, A.P., and Glick, B. (1987). Aggression replacement training: A comprehensive intervention for aggressive youth. Champaign, IL: Research Press.

Griffin, G. (1987). Childhood predictive characteristics of aggressive adolescents. *Exceptional Children*, 54, 246–252.

Hawkins, D., and Catalano, R. (1992). *Communities that care*. San Francisco: Jossey-Bass.

Herrenkohl, R.C., and Russo, M.J. (Feb. 2001). Abusive early child rearing and early childhood aggression. *Child Maltreatment*, 6, 3–16.

Huesmann, L.R., Eron, L.D., Klein, 1, Brice, P., and Fischer, P. (1983). Mitigating the imitation of aggressive behaviors by changing children's attitudes about media violence. *Journal of Personality and Social Psychology*, 44, 899–910.

Huey, W.C., and Rank, R.C. (1984). Effects of counselor and peer-led groups' assertive training on black adolescent aggression. *Journal of Counseling Psychology*, 31, 95–98.

Javier, R.A., Herron, W.G., and Primavera, L.H. (1998). Violence and the media: a psychological analysis. *International Journal of Instructional Media*, 25, 339–355.

Kaplan, S.J., Pelcovitz, D., and Labruna, V. (1999). Child and adolescent abuse and neglect research: A review of the past 10 years. Part I: physical and emotional abuse and neglect. *Journal of the American Academy of Child and Adolescent Psychiatry*, 38(10), 1214–1222.

Lane, P.S., and McWhirter, J.J. (1992). A peer mediation model: Conflict resolution for elementary and middle school children. *Elementary School Guidance & Counseling*, 27, 15–21.

Lipsitt, L.P. (Ed.). (January 1990). Violence and aggression in adolescence. *Brown University Child Behavior and Development Letter*, 1–6.

Lukefahr, J.L. (2001). Treatment of child abuse (Book Review). *Journal of the American Academy of Child and Adolescent Psychiatry*, 40(3), 383.

Mandel M.J., and Magnusson, P. (1993). The economics of crime. *Business Week*, December 13, 72–80.

Mathias, C.E. (1992). Touching the lives of children: Consultative interventions that work. *Elementary School Guidance & Counseling*, 26, 190–201.

Morales, A. (1982). The Mexican American gang member: Evaluation and treatment. In R. Becerra, M. Karno, and J. Escolar (Eds.), *Mental health and Hispanic Americans: Clinical perspective*. New York: Grune and Stratton.

Myers, J. (1993). *Social psychology*. (3rd Ed.). New York: McGraw-Hill.

Myles, B. S., and Simpson, R.L. (May 1998). Aggression cycle and prevention/intervention strategies. *Intervention in School and Clinic*, 33, 259–264.

Murray, B.A., and Myers, M.A. (April 1998). Conduct disorders and the special-education trap. *The Education Digest*, 63, 48–53.

Oates, R.K., and Bross, D.C. (1995). What have we learned about treating child physical abuse? A literature review of the last decade. *Journal of Child Abuse & Neglect*, 19, 463–473.

Patterson G., and Narrett, C. (1990). The development of a reliable and valid treatment program for aggressive young children. *International Journal of Mental Health*, 19, 19–26.

Rae-Grant, N., McConville, B.J., and Fleck, S. (March 1999). Violent behavior in children and youth: Preventive intervention from a psychiatric perspective. *Journal of the American Academy of Child and Adolescent Psychiatry*, 38, 235–241.

Reece, R.M. (Ed.). (2000). *Treatment of child abuse: Common ground for mental health, medical and legal practitioners.* Baltimore, MD: Johns Hopkins University Press.

Schrumpt, F., Crawford, D., and Usadel, H.C. (1991). *Peer mediation: Conflict resolution in schools.* Champaign, IL: Research Press.

Sechrest, D. (2001). Juvenile crime: A predictive study. Unpublished document.

Sprague, J.R., and Walker, H.M. (Spring 2000). Early identification and intervention for youth with antisocial and violent behavior. *Exceptional Children, 66,* 367–379.

Steiner, H., and Stone, L.A. (March 1999). Introduction: Violence and related psychopathology. *Journal of the American Academy of Child and Adolescent Psychiatry, 38,* 232–234.

Studer, J. (February 1996). Understanding and preventing aggressive responses in youth. Excerpted from *Elementary School Guidance & Counseling, 30,* Private Practice 194–203.

Van den Bergh, N. (Ed.). (1995). *Feminist practice in the 21st century.* Washington, DC: NASW Press.

Van Wormer, K. (1999). The strengths perspective: A paradigm for correctional counseling. Federal Probation, 63(1), 51–58.

8

Programs to Treat
Early-Onset Violence

In this chapter, we consider the programs that have been used to treat early-onset childhood violence. These programs approach early violence from an institutional and community perspective, and while they don't discount individual and group interventions, they are developed and applied to produce larger system changes. One might find programs such as those discussed in this chapter in school systems, communities, and troubled neighborhoods. As noted in Chapter 7, there is a sense among many clinicians that larger system change is the best intervention in the treatment of childhood violence.

Violence Prevention and Treatment Programs

Rae-Grant et al. (1999) reported that a number of programmatic interventions have been tried with youthful offenders with some success. Among these programs are school-based conflict-resolution training programs, gun-free zones around schools, evening curfews, weekend and evening recreational programs, summer camps, job and training programs for youths at risk, and community policing (Ash et al. 1996). Caplan et al. (1992) studied programs treating the early onset of drug use in teenagers. The outcomes of these programs resulted in better problem-solving skills, better control of impulsive behavior, and reduced alcohol use. Hansen and Graham (1991) found that fewer adolescents used alcohol and had better awareness of the risks of alcohol after drug and alcohol intervention. However, other programs were less effective. Mendel (1995) found that there was no relationship between the increase in guns obtained by the police and a decrease of violence in gun buy-back programs. Weil and Knox (1996), however, found programs limiting the flow of weapons across state lines to be effective. Kann et al. (1993) reported that a weakness of many of the programs developed to reduce youthful crime and violence is that they seem to work in the short term, but the gains made are not often significant in the long run.

Such popular but controversial programs as "Boot Camps" have not been shown to be effective (Henggeler & Schoenwald, 1994). However, Borduin (1999) reported that multifocused diversion programs providing services to repeat youth offenders before they enter the court system have shown positive results. Greenwood et al. (1996) indicated that programs focusing on prevention of crime in youthful offenders were more cost effective in lowering serious crime than were mandatory sentences for adult repeat offenders. For children with multiple risk markers to develop violent and/or antisocial behavior, many programs target specific aspects of the child's family life. Olds et al. (1988) provide an example of how an early infancy project for economically disadvantaged mothers with poor prenatal health, self-damaging behaviors, and poor family management skills can improve maternal diet, reduce smoking during pregnancy, result in fewer premature deliveries, increase the birth weight of babies, and result in significantly less child abuse. Johnson (1990) reports that providing social, economic, and health-related services to preschool children and their families with multiple risk markers improves academic success, reduces behavioral problems in at-risk children, improves parenting skills, decreases family management problems, and lowers the subsequent arrest rates for children in families provided services. However, Johnson cautions that some of these positive outcomes are only effective for several years after follow-up. Johnson suggests that the reasons for the lack of long-term effectiveness may be the result of diminished services to at-risk families, poor school experiences for children, and the multiproblemed lives of the families served. Weikart, Schweinhart, and Larner (1986), in a study of another preschool program, found similar results.

Rae-Grant, et al. (1999) noted that in elementary-grade school children, "interpersonal cognitive problem-solving programs gave rise to better problem-solving skills and fewer behavior problems in children with economic deprivation, poor impulse control, and early behavioral problems" (p. 338). Hawkins et al. (1992) reported that a social development program in Seattle for similarly at-risk grade-school children demonstrated positive results. Preschool and elementary school programs may be one proactive approach to preventing future delinquent and violent behavior.

Bilchik (1999) reports that a program in Rochester, New York, saw arrest rates for high-risk middle school students reduced by over 50 percent when youths had nine or more protective factors in their lives instead of six or fewer. Protective factors included family stability, a parent at home when the child returns from school, recreational facilities close to home, peer counseling programs, and a zero tolerance for violence program at school. Another program Bilchik (1999) reported on is a parent training and home visitation program by nurses in Elmira, New York, that resulted in early prevention of child abuse and delinquency through the use of nurses when pregnant women and new mothers were offered intensive training, guidance, and counseling regarding child care and parenting practices. Over a 15-year period in the Elmira study, there were 80 percent fewer instances of child abuse by the participating mothers, and the 15-year-old children of the participating mothers had half as many arrests as children whose mothers were not participants in the program. Henggeler (1997) reported similar results in a program in Charleston, South Carolina, that provided integrated, family-based treatment for adolescents demonstrating serious acting-out behavior. Only four years after completing the program, the rearrest rate was half that of comparable youths receiving traditional services (Henggeler, 1997).

Briscoe (1997) reports that the Texas State Legislature required the Texas Youth Commission to investigate the effectiveness of four specialized treatment programs for incarcerated youth, using the following criteria: one-year rearrest rates; one-year rearrest severity rates; one-year reincarceration rates; one-year rearrest rates for a violent offense, and three-year reincarceration rates. The findings of the study suggested that youth receiving specialized treatments applied to their specific needs were significantly less likely to marginally less likely to become recidivists than youth not receiving treatments matched to their needs. Programs treating chemical dependency showed the greatest effectiveness in three outcome measures: rearrest within one year, reincarceration within one year, and reincarceration within three years. A program for capital offenders reduced the likelihood of rearrest for violent crimes by 53 percent. It should be noted, however, that Texas has the highest rate of imprisonment in the United States (Gamboa, 2000). More persons are in jail in Texas than in California, a state with twice as many people. The encouraging statistics reported by Briscoe (1997) may not translate as well as youth move into adulthood.

Hagan and King (1992) considered recidivism rates with highly disturbed youths who had completed an intensive treatment program in a juvenile correctional facility. They found that following release and for a two-to five-year period, one-third of those treated did not reoffend after release, one-third offended but with less serious offenses, and one-third reoffended with crimes similar to those that led to their prior incarceration. Half of the youths treated were reincarcerated, either in jail or in prison, but, significantly, half were not.

Whitehead and Lab (1989), in an overall evaluation of the effectiveness of programs treating juveniles noted, "The results show that interventions have little positive impact on recidivism and many appear to exacerbate the problem" (p. 276). Izzo and Ross (1990), however, found that theoretically sound treatment programs, regardless of their orientation, were five times more effective than programs without a theoretical foundation. Programs using a cognitive theoretical base were twice as effective as those using other theoretical bases. Effective programs, according to Izzo and Ross (1990), have a positive impact on the way youthful offenders think about their behavior. According to Hagan et al. (1997), programs that used punishment, tried to treat underlying pathology, or considered violent youth crime as a problem stemming from poverty, social class differences, or cultural conflicts were not as effective as programs using cognitive/behavioral approaches. Similarly, Andrews et al. (1990) found that programs using cognitive/behavioral approaches providing anger management and conflict and substance abuse treatment were more effective than programs not using cognitive/behavioral approaches. Tate, Reppucci, and Mulvey (1995) found that the most effective treatment approaches were "child-focused, family-centered, and directed toward solving multiple problems across the numerous contexts" (p. 779).

Ellickson and McGuigan (2000) noted little in the research literature to suggest that programs developed for a specific ethnic or racial group have better results in lowering youthful crime and violence than do programs offered to the entire range of youthful offenders. However, they believe that programs must differentiate between the needs of males and females and suggest that gender differences require gender-specific intervention strategies. They also found that programs to reduce drug and alcohol use were effective with youthful offenders, particularly children in middle schools, who the authors characterize as being the most susceptible school-aged group to the influences of others in using and abusing substances.

The Roden Commission Report, a State of California report completed in 1982, begins by stating that most current approaches to youth violence address its symptoms and, consequently, accept the certainty of violence in society. The report concludes that the United States is the most violent Western, industrialized democracy; however, it states that the problem can be confronted. Certain negative aspects of our social and cultural condition encourage violence, "which, when identified, can be remedied. At the least we can begin to take scientifically-grounded action *to prevent* violence" (p. 1).

As Glicken and Sechrest (2003) note, the Roden Commission report (1982) saw the family as critical to personal development because it structures and "determines the nature and quality of subsequent social relations" (Roden, p. 6). Related to a poor family environment was their conclusion that "lack of self-esteem, negative or criminal self-image, and feelings of distrust and personal powerlessness are prevalent among violent offenders and highly recidivistic criminals" (Roden, p. 6). Other researchers, including Douglas and Olshaker (1995) and Ressler and Shachtman (1992), would agree that an attempt to regain or assert power is inherent in almost all crimes of violence.

The Roden report (1982) highlighted the way children become aggressive and violent, noting that the family is a critical training ground for values, rules, attitudes, and skills necessary for forming healthy social relations with others. A clear cause-and-effect relationship may not be proveable but a strong association was found between rejection, physical and sexual abuse, parental neglect, and lack of love and affection as key reasons for the development of violence in children.

The Roden report places considerable emphasis on training family members in child rearing. Early intervention for troubled families is also recommended and includes teaching nonviolent ways of resolving family conflicts in order to reduce "the risk that aggressive, combative attitudes and values espoused by parents may encourage aggressive behavior on the part of their children" (p. 27).

Constructing a Community Violence Treatment and Prevention Program: A Case Study

Lakewood, a moderately sized city in the Midwest, has been beset by extraordinarily high rates of childhood and juvenile violence in the community and in the school system. Lakewood is a middle-class community with few pockets of poverty, little unemployment, and citizens who are generally involved in community affairs. One cause of violence may be an escalating drug and alcohol epidemic among children and adolescents. Another is a complete breakdown in the school system, in which bomb threats and violence make it difficult for most children to get a respectable education. Rather than quickly adopting programs used by other communities with similar problems, the

Lakewood City Council brought in two tough-minded consultants. The Council asked the consultants to find and review programs that had long-term effectiveness and to return with recommendations. Council members had spoken to representatives from other communities who complained that programs they had developed on the advice of local consultants had very short life spans. Children seemed to improve as a result of treatment, but improvement rates were short lived and the overall crime rate was unaffected. The Lakewood City Council told the consultants that they wanted a report showing a connection between treatment and prevention strategies and lowered crime rates over the course of the life span—a tall order.

Two months later, the consultants came back with their report. It said, in effect, that there were few studies available showing lowered rates of violence over the life span. Furthermore, some programs actually increased rates of violence. (Some substance abuse programs actually found participants selling dangerous drugs to other participants, raising the violence level dramatically.) Not all programs were equal, the consultants said, and beyond that, one had to factor in the reality that programs had differential results based on the competency and length of employment of the staff. Most programs that worked were politically unpopular and often resulted in termination before long-term results were shown. A case in point was a program paying youth $150 for guns they turned in to the police. The consensus was that the guns were illegally obtained, so why should the community pay for illegal merchandise?

The cost of intervention and prevention would be very high, the consultants said, but compared with the cost of crime and violence, it was well worth the effort, even if the programs only helped a small cohort of children. Finally, it took time for programs to work. Changing long-term behaviors was difficult, and changing an environment that was currently experiencing high crime rates would also take time.

The consultants said that programs should be made available to everyone in the community, but the target population should be at-risk children because they had a greater probability of youth violence. *At-risk children* would include children who had been abused or neglected or were at risk of abuse and neglect; children whose parents abused substances; children with other siblings who had problems with violence; children from homes with poor health and nutritional practices; children whose parents undervalued or failed to support education; and children who were demonstrating early signs of aggression. The consultants went on to suggest the following programs, while making certain that the lack of definitive effectiveness data should be kept in mind:

1. Early assistance to at-risk families by providing financial, health, mental health, educational, and parenting skills services. At-risk families included families with an unusually high number of negative characteristics, including drug and alcohol problems, evidence of family violence, work-related problems, and unemployment.
2. Appropriate counseling services to individuals and families in the high-risk group. Treatment, the consultants said, was an important aspect of violence intervention and prevention.
3. A close working relationship between schools and community agencies. Instances of bullying, acting-out behavior, and evidence of child abuse or domestic violence were to be immediately referred to the appropriate agencies, with an oversite committee set up to monitor results.

(continued)

Continued

---

4. Providing recreational facilities close to neighborhoods, with professionally trained staff who could spot troubled behavior and provide immediate help through counseling or referrals to mental health professionals.
5. A no drug or alcohol tolerance policy for youth in schools and at community events.
6. Close supervision of high crime areas by the police and an immediate response at the first sign of violence.
7. A no-tolerance policy for weapons in the possession of youth, with mandatory sentencing.
8. A juvenile court that would enforce a no-violence community response to youth violence.
9. A no-violence policy in the school system, with a school board prepared to enforce the policy.

The consultants also told the Council a truism of all research: Because a program worked well in one location, it might not work well in another. Conditions varied in geographic locations and each community had its own set of dynamics that made it unique. Even so, the consultants said, it was wise to give the programs time to work, perhaps several years. Ongoing effectiveness evaluations were essential and should be used to make modifications to the programs as needed. If there was an immediate drop in violent behavior, the consultants noted, it would probably be the result of other forces and not the treatment programs. Perhaps, they suggested, the treatment programs would create concerns about violence, and those concerns would be enough to cause a sudden decrease in rates of violence. Sudden impressive changes would probably not last, and it would be a mistake to eliminate violence treatment and prevention programs before they had a chance to be evaluated empirically.

The consultants suggested, as a first step, that the City Council should try to find out why the violence rate in Lakewood had been increasing so dramatically. The reasons could be transient, or they could be related to problems in the community. Transient reasons for increases in violence might be contagion from nearby communities and could include mobile violence caused by nonresidents, rivalries with other communities, and copycat violence that was short-lived. Community-based violence was violence that had its origins in community difficulties and included high tolerance for child abuse and neglect, easy youth access to weapons, an overly tolerant police force, schools that didn't work cooperatively with the police or with child welfare agencies, easy youth access to drugs and alcohol, and increased gang and violent subculture activity.

Discussion

As the City Council was about to begin a search for a director of the programs to reduce violence in the community, youth crime and violence data from the police began to show a gradual but significant decline. The Council held off doing anything as they happily watched the violence statistics go from bad to acceptable levels of violence. No new programs were initiated, and the community settled back into a complacency about violence that was about to come to a dramatic and unhappy end. One of the children who would have been identified as an at-risk youth if the community had begun its violence program shot and killed two children and wounded 14 others at a local high school. The boy was arrested and brought to the city jail, where he spoke incoherently about voices in his head. An immediate search of his home found that he had also killed his parents. The boy had spoken for weeks about killing people, but in an unresponsive mood because violence figures had declined so steadily, no one took him seriously or did anything to stop his increasingly violent behavior.

In an attempt to find out whether the violence was specific to this youth or was the beginning of another cycle of violence in the community, the City Council asked the two consultants to return to the community and join the Council at a public meeting. The consultants told those present at the meeting:

> You have to think of violence as you would a health epidemic. You can't wish it away or think that it won't come back just because the problem seems to be better. The community has to be as proactive about violence as they would be if the water system was about to be polluted. There are social forces driving violence in this country. Whenever we think the problem is getting better, it comes back to remind us that it's not. Even though we've had declining violence in this community and elsewhere, violence rates are astronomical. The conditions that breed violence are still with us, and you can expect another round of increases in violence rates, perhaps not this year, but in the near future. Our advice to you is to initiate a violence plan, not because of this isolated instance of violence, but because of what will happen in the future if you don't."

The City Council voted to begin the violence program, although many community residents thought it was unnecessary and believed that one isolated instance of violence, bad as it was, did not justify the expense of a violence program in a community where violence rates had been declining. When this became a strong sentiment among many voters, the council issued some disturbing statistics. The community, they said, was at the national average for youth violence, an average many times higher than similar communities in Canada, England, and Australia. The drug addiction rate was much higher than in these three countries, as were the child abuse and neglect rates. The number of babies born alcohol or drug addicted was nearly as high in Lakewood as it was in major urban areas in America. And as a rating of community safety, Lakewood had recently seen its reputation sullied when a national publication wrote,

> Lakewood is a wonderful community. Housing is moderately priced, the climate is moderate, and the people are moderate. The only immoderate thing about Lakewood is that children have a tendency to assault and kill in Lakewood. If you don't mind a great deal of youth violence in a community that otherwise has many good things going for it, Lakewood is the place for you.

As a result of the publication, a major company changed its mind about relocating its headquarters to Lakewood. As one company executive said, "We want our kids to live in a safe community. Lakewood has been remiss by doing nothing to deal with youth violence."

Youth Violence Programs

Guetzloe (1999) suggests that youth violence should be treated as a public health concern and that prevention of youth violence may be seen as primary, secondary, or tertiary, depending on the progression of the problem. Primary prevention tries to reduce the rate of certain problems and to keep those problems from occurring. Secondary prevention involves the early location of youth violence with appropriate interventions. Tertiary prevention concerns itself with youth who are chronically violent.

Primary prevention attacks youth violence at its point of origin and suggests that violence may be caused by any number of problems, including brain injury, mental illness, chemical abnormalities, availability of weapons, exposure to media violence, and the acceptance of violence in a particular society or culture (Guetzloe, 1999).

Guetzloe (1999) notes that secondary prevention may be achieved by intervening in home, school, and community issues that may contribute to youth violence. She gives the following examples of secondary prevention: (1) providing resources and services to ensure the physical and psychological safety of all youth, (2) making certain that all students develop the skills necessary for academic and social achievement, (3) working cooperatively with parents and community agencies, (4) providing effective training for everyone involved in preventing and treating violence, and (5) making appropriate referrals to provide youth with the best possible intervention based on the problems they are experiencing.

Tertiary prevention provides protection of the population from violent behavior and may include prison sentences or other "containment" approaches to maintain a healthy community. Guetzloe (1999) notes,

> Regardless of the specific origins of their behavior, the prognosis for chronically violent individuals is generally poor, and provisions must be made for interventions such as imprisonment and incarceration as well as rehabilitation. The primary goal of incarceration is to isolate violent individuals to protect the rest of the population. Young people who feel pleasure—or nothing at all—in the slaughter of other human beings need a complete emotional overhaul. The only hope for many violent offenders lies in changing their thinking, a process that requires a lengthy period of time and total supervision. (p. 22)

However, in an interesting reversal of the way most research on violence is done, Sells (1995) asked students their ideas of what caused aggression and violence perceptions. Thirty-nine percent of the students surveyed indicated that group or gang membership was a significant contributor to violence. The Center for the Study of Prevention and Violence (1994) noted that several primary factors influencing aggressive and violent behavior were race, gangs, drugs and alcohol, weapons, and family issues. The Office of Juvenile Justice and Delinquency Prevention (1994), in a similar report, found that factors that contribute to delinquent behavior include delinquent peer groups, weak family attachments, neighborhoods with high rates of crime, poor school performance, and inconsistent discipline.

Violence Programs That Appear to Work

Fagan (1990) reported the results of the Violent Juvenile Offender (VJO) Program, which verified that programs that were well implemented produced lower recidivism rates. The VJO Program was offered to youth identified as violent as a result of their crimes (completed or attempted homicide, aggravated assault, armed robbery, and forcible rape). The major purpose of the effort was to provide treatment services to youth in the critical months after their return to the community, when most failures occur. Experimental and control groups were used. When program implementation was strong, lower rearrest rates were found. Conclusions from the VJO study were that

> the social integration factors that initiate or maintain delinquency may be unrelated to its cessation. . . . Intervention had little discernable effects on the social indicators of school, work, or family, nor did it strengthen the social bonds thought to be part of the etiology of delinquency. Yet there were indications of reduced recidivism for experimental youths. Accordingly, there is reason to believe that some aspects of program participation may have contributed to these effects, though without significantly altering the social status or social integration of the participants. (p. 100)

In his research on the best candidates for treatment programs, Alexander (2000, p. 216) found that youths whose offenses resulted from conflict with friends, family, classmates, and others in the community were most likely to benefit from treatment. Aggression Replacement Training (ART), is a promising new treatment for highly aggressive children developed by Goldstein and Glick (1996). ART has three components that are integrated into course content on a weekly basis for ten weeks: (1) skill streaming, (2) anger management, and (3) moral education. Skill streaming teaches 50 skills that form the basis of prosocial behaviors taught through "modeling, role-playing, performance feedback, and transfer training" (Alexander, 2000, p. 217). Anger management helps teach youth ways of responding positively to situations that may provoke anger in aggressive children and adolescents. Moral education focuses on concerns for the rights of others and fairness. When using approaches like ART, Alexander (2000) found that programs relying on systematic reinforcement helped speed up the process of developing prosocial behaviors. Approaches such as ART are sometimes called *strength-based approaches* and *cultural competence* programs and are modeled after programs used with adults such as drug courts (Alexander, p. 77).

Greenwood et al (1996) cite Lipsey's (1992) metaanalysis of more than 400 juvenile program evaluations, which:

> found that behavioral, skill-oriented, and multi-modal methods produced the largest effects, while some methods actually produced negative effects, such as deterrence programs [like] "shock incarceration" and "scared-straight" techniques. . . . Positive effects were larger in community rather than institutional settings. (p. 13)

Lipsey's metaanalysis determined that of the 400 programs reviewed, the average reduction in recidivism was only 5 percent. In a more current analysis, Lipsey, Wilson, and Cothern (2000) examined 200 experimental and quasiexperimental intervention studies using juvenile justice system personnel, mental health personnel in public or private agencies, and other counselors, laypersons, or researchers. Lipsey et al. (2000) found the most effective treatments to be interpersonal skills training, individual counseling, and behavioral programs.

Mihalic et al. (2001) reviewed more than 500 programs meant to reduce violence, drug use, and overly aggressive behavior. Programs with the most positive results were: functional family therapy, multisystemic therapy, and, multidimensional treatment foster care (Mihalic et al., 2001). Programs for younger juveniles not as yet in the criminal justice system seemed to work less well raising some concerns about early intervention before violent behavior becomes destructive.

In summary, the treatment programs that seemed to most effectively reduce youth are:

1. Programs to reduce gang membership and activity.
2. Programs to improve family functioning and parenting skills.
3. Programs to assess and treat children using drugs and alcohol.
4. Programs to improve school performance and school-related conduct.
5. Anger management programs to help aggressive children deal with conflict.
6. Individual and group therapy and counseling to provide a more individualized approach to problems of aggression and violence when needed.

The following case study demonstrates the use of these six points to reduce violence in a community experiencing an outbreak of youth violence with racial and gang-related overtones.

A Youth Violence Prevention Program with Teeth: A Case Study

Jamestown, a city in the southeastern part of the United States, had a serious outbreak of youth violence in the early 1990s when violence nationally was coming to a peak. Much of the violence centered around two issues: gangs and racial conflicts. The violence was becoming so significant that police officers were sent to local elementary and secondary schools to conduct weapons checks and to search lockers for guns, something more common today but very controversial at the time in Jamestown, a community that prided itself on good racial relations and civility. To complicate matters, the two high schools and half of the elementary schools were closed during the middle of the semester because of gang and racial violence. In one episode of violence, a lunchroom turned into a gang fight with hundreds of students involved. Damage to the school was over a million dollars.

Community leaders, including those from the opposing racial groups involved in the disturbance, were brought together to discuss a way of resolving the problem. A local university professor with group leadership skills was asked to help organize and run the meetings. At first, tensions were so high it didn't appear likely that anything would be resolved. Members of the two minority racial groups came to meetings with armed guards, and there were frequent "walkouts" when problems became too difficult to resolve. With patience and much talk and work, the group began to devise a plan to calm tensions in

Jamestown and to resolve youth violence. The plan was comprehensive and included considerable time and money spent to right the social inequities between the two major racial groups involved in the violence. There were promises made and kept of new jobs for minority adults and youth, and complete access to quality education for all children in Jamestown. There were promises made and kept that a tight lid would be placed on potential sources of violence. A violence mediation team was organized, the purpose of which was to immediately deal with violence when it seemed likely to become a problem. The school system promised to quickly begin correcting inequities in the quality of education received by the two minority groups. Individual families with problems of family violence and drug abuse were identified, and the local child welfare agency sent social workers out to begin the long and difficult task of correcting these problems. The city agreed to a mandatory arrest policy for domestic violence and child abuse, and began enforcing the policy immediately. Everyone felt a sense of urgency to reopen the schools because youth crime was escalating, as many children who were out of school began committing crimes while their parents were at work.

The police force and the community relations department began a concerted effort to modify gang behavior. Meetings were held with gang members, agreements were reached, and trust began to develop. There was agreement that gangs could exist but that illegal or violent behavior was intolerable. Facilities were provided for gang meetings. Suggestions were made for more socially responsible gang behaviors. Gang recruitment of new members at school was curtailed, and gang members agreed not to wear gang colors or write gang signs in and around schools. Schools agreed that bullying and intimidation were preludes to violence and began cooperating with the police to modify this behavior through treatment or, if that didn't work, through more formal involvement with the juvenile court. Use of illegal substances, particularly in and around schools, was considered intolerable. Stiff penalties were provided for anyone supplying minors with alcohol, and drug laws were strictly enforced, particularly those pertaining to drug selling near school grounds. Counselors trained in the treatment of violence were hired by the school system, with help from community funding, to offer treatment to children and adolescents showing signs of potential violence. The counselors had the right to include parents in treatment sessions as a mandatory expectation of the child continuing in school. The school board issued a "no tolerance for violence policy" that included sanctions for bullying, intimidation of other students and school faculty and staff, and fighting. Conflict resolution experts were brought in to teach children and adolescence the essence of conflict and anger management. Guidelines were sent to parents, suggesting limits on watching violence on TV, in video games, and in films, and suitable alternatives to violent programs were suggested.

The program began working and within a year, Jamestown had returned to a peaceful, cooperative, and much more cautious community. Once having experienced violence on the order that Jamestown had, the community was unwilling to become complacent and continues to have one of the most successful and comprehensive violence control programs in the country. Like too many American communities, violence rates are still much too high for any community to feel completely safe, but the upswing in youth violence has been reduced and today's violence is often the result of economic factors that leave young adult males out of work with little hope for the future. On that score, Jamestown has not fared well, and like many communities with high youth and young adult unemployment, Jamestown has more than its share of preventable drug- and alcohol-related domestic violence, automobile accidents, and random violence.

Summary

The mixed evidence of success in many of the programs developed to treat and prevent childhood violence suggests the need for continued development and evaluation of new programs. Unfortunately, a close look at some of the programs discussed in this chapter suggests that they are old ideas clothed in new language. Clearly, there is a role for individual, group, and family treatment at a fairly early point in the development of childhood violence. Programs to decrease family violence are absolutely essential, as are early and aggressive reporting and intervention into child abuse and neglect. Programs to decrease school violence very early in a child's life are also essential and should begin in preschool and continue on. Programs that treat adolescent crime as if the child were immune from violence before adolescence make little sense. Violence begins early in the lives of children, and the best way to treat it is to develop creative, well-funded, and well-researched programs that prevent violence through early education, training, and intervention. It might also be wise to consider how other countries contain childhood violence and to develop programs that use the wisdom of countries with low rates of childhood violence.

Integrative Questions

1. A good deal of childhood violence seems to originate in poorly functioning and violent homes. Why should normal children suffer the abuse and disruption of a few troubled children? Shouldn't children from violent homes be isolated and taught in special classes?

2. Programs to treat violent children seem as unsuccessful as the clinical interventions described in Chapter 7. Is it possible that violence is an untreatable problem?

3. Shouldn't children from violent homes be taken out of those homes as soon as violence is detected and be raised in healthy, violence-free environments? Wouldn't that reduce childhood violence considerably?

4. Programs to treat violence may appear logical and effective, but what chance do they have of succeeding when staff members frequently move and children have to constantly relate to new staff members with whom they may not have as productive a relationship?

5. The most recent reports of childhood and adolescent violence suggest that we have less violence among these groups than we had 10 years ago. Do you feel that your school, neighborhood, and community environments are safe from youth violence?

References

Alexander, R. Jr. (2000). *Counseling, treatment, and intervention methods with juvenile and adult offenders*. Pacific Grove, CA: Brooks/Cole.

Andrews, D., Zinger, I., Hoge, R. et al. (1990). Does correctional treatment work? A clinically-relevant and psychologically-informed meta-analysis. *Criminology, 28,* 369–404.

Ash, P., Kellermann, A., Fuqua-Whitley, D., and Johnson, D. (1996). Gun acquisition and use by juvenile offenders. *JAMA, 275,* 1754–1758.

Bilchik, S. (January 1999). Breaking the cycle of juvenile crime. *Trial*, 35, 36–41.

Borduin, C.M. (1999). Multisystemic treatment of criminality and violence in adolescents. *Journal of the American Academy of Child and Adolescent Psychiatry*, 38, 242–249.

Briscoe, J. (September 1997). Breaking the cycle of violence: A rational approach to at-risk youth. *Federal Probation*, 61, 3–13.

Caplan, M., Weissberg, R.P., Grober, J.S. et al. (1992). Social competence promotion with inner-city and suburban young adolescents: Effects on social adjustment and alcohol use. *Journal of Consulting Clinical Psychology*, 60, 56–63.

Center for the Study and Prevention of Violence. (Spring 1994). *Overview and report progress*. Boulder, CO: Institute for Behavioral Sciences.

Douglas, J., and Olshaker, M. (1995). *Mind hunter: Inside the FBI's elite serial crime unit*. New York: Scribner.

Ellickson, P.L., and McGuigan, K.A. (April 2000). Early predictors of adolescent violence. *American Journal of Public Health*, 90, p. 566–572

Fagan, J. (1990). Social and legal policy dimensions of violent juvenile crime. *Criminal Justice and Behavior*, 17(1), 93–134.

Gamboa, S. (August 28, 2000). Texas incarcerates most, fastest in U.S. *San Antonio Express News*, 1A.

Glicken, M.D., and Sechrest, D.K. (2003). *The role of the helping professions in treating the victims and perpetrators of violence*. Boston: Allyn & Bacon.

Goldstein, A.P., and Glick, B. (1996). Aggression replacement training: Methods and outcomes. In C.R. Hollin and K. Howells (Eds.), *Clinical approaches to working with young offenders* (pp. 151–179). Chichester, England: John Wiley & Sons.

Greenwood, P.W., Model, K.E., Rydell, C. P., and Chiesa, J. (1996). *Diverting children from a life of crime: Measuring costs and benefits*. Santa Monica, CA: Rand Corporation.

Guetzloe, E. (Fall 1999). Violence in children and adolescents—A threat to public health and safety: A paradigm of prevention. *Preventing School Failure*, 44, 21–24.

Hagan, M., and King, R. (1992). Recidivism rates of youth completing an intensive treatment program in a juvenile correctional facility. *International Journal of Offender Therapy and Comparative Criminology*, 36, 349–358.

Hagan, M.P, Cho, M.E., King, J.A. et al. (December, 1997). An assessment of the effectiveness of an intensive treatment program for severely mentally disturbed juvenile offenders. *International Journal of Offender Therapy & Comparative Criminology*, 41, 340–349.

Hamparian, D.M. (1985). Control and treatment of juveniles committing violent offenses. In Loren Roth, (ed.), *Clinical treatment of the violent person*. Washington, DC: U.S. Department of Health and Human Services, Public Health Service, Alcohol, Drug Abuse, and Mental Health Administration.

Hansen, W.B., and Graham, J.W. (1991). Preventing alcohol, marijuana, and cigarette use among adolescents: Peer pressure resistance training versus establishing conservative norms. *Preventative Medicine*, 20, 414–430.

Hawkins J.D., Catalano, R.F., Morrison, D.M., et al. (1992). The Seattle Social Development Project: Effects of the first four years on protective factors and problem behaviors. In J. McCord, and R. Tremblay (Eds.), *The prevention of antisocial behavior in children*. New York: Guilford.

Henggeler, S. (May 1997). Treating serious antisocial behavior in youth: The MST approach. *Juvenile Justice Bulletin*, 1, 12.

Henggeler, S., and Schoenwald, S. (1994). Boot camps for juvenile offenders: Just say no. *Journal of Child and Family Studies*, 3, 243–248.

Izzo, R., and Ross, R. (1990). Meta-analysis of rehabilitation programs for juvenile delinquents, a brief report. *Criminal Justice and Behavior*, 17, 134–142.

Johnson, D.L. (1990). The Houston parent–child development center project: Disseminating a viable program for enhancing at-risk families. *Prevention in the Human Services*, 7, 89–108.

Kann L., Warren, W., Collins, J.L. et al. (1993). Results from the national school-based 1991 Youth Risk Behavior Survey and progress toward achieving related health objectives for the nation. *Public Health Rep*, 108(Suppl 1), 47–67.

Lipsey, M.W. (1992). Juvenile delinquency treatment: A meta-analysis inquiry into the variability of effects. In T.D. Cook, Cooper, D.S. Cordray, (Eds.), *Meta-analysis for explanation: A casebook* (pp. 83–127). New York: Russell Sage.

Lipsey, M.W., Wilson, D.B., and Cothern, L. (April 2000). Effective intervention for serious juvenile offenders. *Juvenile Justice Bulletin.* Washington, DC: Office of Juvenile Justice and Delinquency Prevention. Available online at www.ncjrs.org/html/ojjdp/jjbul2000_04_6/contents.html

Mann, D. (July 1976). *Intervening with convicted serious juvenile offenders.* Santa Monica, CA: Rand Corporation.

Mendel, R.A. (1995). *Prevention or pork? A hard-headed look at youth-oriented anti-crime programs.* Washington, DC: American Youth Policy Forum.

Mihalic, S., Irwin, K., Elliott, D., Fagan, A., and Hansen, D. (July 2001). *Blueprints for violence prevention.* Juvenile Justice Bulletin. U.S. Department of Justice, Office of Juvenile Justice and Delinquency Prevention. Available online at http://ncjrs.org/html/ojjdp/jjbul2001_7_3/contents.html

Office of Juvenile Justice and Delinquency Prevention. (1994). *Comprehensive strategy for serious, violent, and chronic juvenile offenders.* Washington, DC: Office of Juvenile Justice and Delinquency Prevention.

Olds, D.L., Henderson, C.R., Tatelbaum, R., and Chamberlin, R. (1988). Improving the life-course development of socially disadvantaged mothers: A randomized trial of nurse home visitation. *American Journal of Public Health*, 78, 1436–1444.

Rae-Grant, N., McConville, B.J., and Fleck, S. (March 1999). Violent behavior in children and youth: Preventive intervention from a psychiatric perspective. *Journal of the American Academy of Child and Adolescent Psychiatry*, 38, 235–241

Ressler, R.K., and Shachtman, T. (1992). *Whoever fights monsters.* New York: St. Martin's Press.

Roden, S. (1982). *Ounces of prevention, toward an understanding of the causes of violence.* Final Report to the People of California 1982. Sacramento: State of California Commission on Crime Control and Violence Prevention.

Sells, R.D. (Ed.). (1995). *Dealing with violence: What schools and communities need to know.* Bloomington, IN: National Educational Service.

Tate, D., Reppucci, N., and Mulvey, E. (1995). Violent juvenile delinquents, treatment effectiveness and implications for future action. *American Psychologist*, 50, 777–781.

Weikart, D.P., Schweinhart, L.J., and Larner, M.B. (1986). A report on the High/Scope preschool curriculum comparison study: Consequences of three preschool curriculum models through age 15. *Early Child Research*, 1, 15–45.

Weil, D.S., and Knox, R.C. (1996). Effects of limiting handgun purchases on interstate transfer of firearms. *JAMA*, 22, 1759–1761.

Whitehead, J., and Lab, S. (1989). A meta-analysis of juvenile correctional treatment. *Journal of Research in Crime and Delinquency*, 26, 276–295.

9

The Relationship between Early-Childhood-Onset Violence and Adolescent and Adult Violence

In order to appreciate fully the magnitude of childhood criminality as a social destructor, it is best to begin at the endpoint—the terrible people that violent antisocial kids are likely to become. Young psychopaths comprise a substantial portion of the children who devolve into serious, habitual criminals. And what criminals they become! The cruelest, most calculating felons. Blithe killers, strong arm virtuosos, industrious career miscreants viewing crime as their profession, unfettered by conscience or conviction or the threat of distant punishment as they wreak misery and pain on the rest of us. They're not spurred by poverty—They do it because they love it. They do it because they can.

—Jonathan Kellerman, *Savage Spawn*, 1999, p. 19

This chapter covers the compelling evidence that early-childhood violence cycles on to serious adolescent and adult violence in fully half the children designated as violent before age 12. In a large number of the remaining children, many will have substance abuse problems, be perpetrators of family violence, abuse children, have poor work records, and generally perform badly throughout the life cycle. If not treated early in life, childhood violence is a serious and long-lasting problem that tends to increase in severity and frequency. At the same time, many children who appear to have early signs of violent behavior do well in adolescence and adulthood. The last part of this chapter suggests the need for caution when working with very young children, and reminds us that children need room to grow and change as they mature.

The Evidence

As noted throughout this book, there is considerable evidence that early-childhood violence cycles on to serious adolescent and adult violence. Johnson et al. (2000) conducted a community-based, longitudinal study to determine whether personality disorders during adolescence were associated with higher risk for violent behavior during both adolescence and early adulthood. Their findings confirmed that adolescents with personality disorders were far more likely to act out in violent ways than are adolescents who had not been diagnosed with personality disorders. Because personality disorders are usually not used as a diagnosis until a youth is age 18, this cohort of adolescents were more serious in their acting-out behavior and had earlier onset of violent behavior than did adolescents with late-onset conduct disorders.

Herrenkohl et al. (2001) report that individuals involved in early-onset violence in childhood are at a very high risk of committing violent crimes in adolescence and adulthood. The risk for later violent behavior increases the younger the violence begins. Elliott (1994) found that 45 percent of the children who commit violent offenses by age 11 go on to commit violent offenses in their early 20s. The older the age of onset of violence, the less likely children are to commit violent offenses in adulthood. According to Thornberry, Huizinga, and Loeber (1995), almost twice as many children committing violent acts before age 9 end up committing violent acts in adulthood, as compared with children between the ages of 10 and 12.

Sprague and Walker (2000) note that antisocial behavior and high levels of aggression characterized by high frequency and extreme severity in a number of social situations (family, school, neighborhoods) occurring early in a child's life are strong predictors of violent behavior in adolescents and adults. The authors suggest that early-onset violence often leads to victimizing others (offenses to persons), drug and alcohol abuse, generalized violence, school failure and dropouts, and delinquent acts. Sprague and Walker write, "Over the developmental age span, these behavior patterns become more destructive, more aversive, and have much greater social impact as they become elaborated" (p. 368).

Hagan and Foster (2001) report that even though homicide rates have been declining in America, adolescent murder rates are six times higher in the United States than they are in neighboring Canada. Furstenberg (2000) believes that "advanced industrial societies create adolescence and early adulthood as life stages in ways that inevitably render them problematic" (p. 897). Tanner and Yabiku (1999) suggest that for American adolescents, "the economic climate and changing social norms have . . . complicated a once well-worn path from adolescence to adulthood" (p. 254).

For many youth, Hagan and Foster (2001) believe that, "the transition to adulthood is Hobbesian: nasty, brutish, and short" (p. 874).

Moffitt (1993) suggests that violent young children who continue their violent behavior into adolescence and adulthood often have neurological problems that affect healthy development, including poor reading and problem-solving skills, memory problems, extreme inattentiveness, and impulsivity. These characteristics are often not present in later onset violent adolescents whose acting out begins in adolescence and often ends in early adulthood. Moffit believes that predispositions to violence in young children are exacerbated by harmful peer contacts and other environmental influences. Moffitt distinguishes early starters of violence who are predisposed to violence from later starters of violence and thinks that children who become violent in adolescence have a positive social orientation but give in to peer influences that sometimes include violence. This may be true of gang members who are initiated into violence in their early teens but leave gang life as they mature. For many late starters, violence acts to negate adolescent feelings of inadequacy. In essence, Moffitt believes that early-childhood starters of violence are much more likely to continue violent behavior into adolescence and adulthood and that late starters usually diminish and end violent behavior as they mature. To reinforce Moffit's theory of late-onset violence, Csikszentmihalyi and Schmidt (1998) wrote, "It is common for adolescents to feel that they are 'second-class' citizens, estranged from decision making and societal power. For teenagers, one result of being marginalized is that the seeking for respect, especially among young males, can reach pathological levels" (p. 13).

In a study of the differences between early and late starters of violence, Vitelli (1997) reported that early violence starters have preadolescent diagnoses of conduct disorders with antisocial behavior. Early-starter delinquency appears linked to poor parental and family functioning. Late-starter delinquency seems more influenced by deviant peer group associations. Early starters of violence have a greater likelihood of adult offending than do late starters. Early starters often show a pattern of family dysfunction coupled with explosive behavioral and school problems. This combination is very predictive of later offending (Patterson, Capaldi, & Bank, 1991; Patterson, Crosby, & Vuchinich, 1992). Stattin and Magnusson (1989) found that teacher ratings of aggressiveness in children as early as age 10 were strong predictors of later juvenile and adult offending, with the majority of repeat offenders coming from the early-starter group.

Family difficulties in early childhood that predict future delinquency include poor child-rearing practices, past records of family involvement in crime, impulsive behavior by parents and other family members, and low parental achievement in school and at work (Farrington, 1994). Towberman (1994) identified lack of parent–child attachment, foster home and institutional placements early in life, abuse in foster and institutional placements, drug use when committing crimes, and poor school records as contributors to chronic youth violence. Dembo et al. (1992) reported similar family problems but also found that being a victim of childhood physical and sexual abuse contributes to early substance abuse and delinquency.

Jane, Early-Onset Child Violence Leading to Adolescent Violence: A Case Study

Jane is a 15-year-old Caucasion adolescent with a long history of violent behavior that first began when she was age 5. Jane pushed a cousin off a tree, fracturing the cousin's leg. A year later, she pushed her 3-year-old brother into the path of an oncoming car. The boy was badly injured and has severe brain damage. Two years later, on a home visit from a residential facility Jane had been sent to by the juvenile court, she put insecticide in her mother's soft drink.

Jane has been in and out of treatment facilities since she was age 6 and appears unchanged. She has flat affect, has no remorse for her behavior, and is unable to describe the emotions she feels when she harms people. Others experience her as cold, aloof, and emotionless. Her classmates call her "The Robot" and stay away from her. Periodically, Jane commits an act of violence and then, for periods of months or longer, appears nonviolent and reasonable. Because of her age, the diagnostic categories available to adults to describe her behavior seem unrealistic. One diagnostician, however, went out on a limb and diagnosed her as having *Intermittent Explosive Disorder* (DSM-IV Code # 312.34, APA, p. 612). This disorder is characterized by "several episodes of failure to resist aggressive impulses that result in serious acts of destruction and are grossly out of proportion to any precipitating stressors. The aggressive episodes are not better accounted for by another mental disorder" (APA, 1994, p. 612). This seems like an overly nonspecific diagnosis for someone who has many episodes of violent behavior with no real precipitating cause. In explaining the choice of diagnosis, the therapist who did the initial diagnosis wrote,

> Sometimes children like Jane are unusual in that their violent behavior seems to occur for no particular reason. You could argue that it is a manifestation of some unknown biochemical reaction, or that it stems from some unknown process or illness we have yet to uncover or understand. When Steinbeck wrote *East of Eden*, he described a character with many of Jane's symptoms, and while I object to Steinbeck's use of the word "monsters," surely there are people who enter the world capable of doing great harm for reasons that are unrelated to abuse, poor family functioning, traumas that cause neurological damage, or any of the other usual reasons for such violent and unprovoked behavior. What Steinbeck wrote seems to describe Jane and I'm quoting from his description of a character in *East of Eden*:
>
> > I believe that there are monsters born in the world to human parents. Some you can see, misshapen and horrible. . . . And just as there are physical monsters, can there not be mental or psychic monsters born? As a child may be born without an arm, so one may be born without kindness or the potential of conscience. To a man born without a conscience, a soul-stricken man must seem ridiculous. To a criminal, honesty is foolish. You must not forget that a monster is only a variation, and that to a monster the norm is monstrous. (John Steinbeck, *East of Eden*, 1992, p. 72)

The therapist goes on to note,

> Jane has a confusing set of symptoms for a young adolescent. There is no precise diagnosis for her behavior. Surely, she has a severe personality disorder with psychotic and/or bio-chemical features. She tests negative for both but, in children, this may just mean that the problem hasn't become robust enough to make an accurate diagnosis. For the time

being, Jane needs to be kept under close supervision to protect others. Residential treatment is suggested but Jane may not be able to utilize treatment because she sees no connection between her acts of violence and any specific feelings of anger toward her victims. Certainly, she needs to be held in a secure facility with tight supervision, and she needs ongoing observation and assessment to find out if there are other reasons for her violent behavior that haven't been found thus far.

Discussion

Jane was seen by the author in a closely supervised interview. Jane is of average height and weight. Her dress was age appropriate. She seemed neither engaged nor disengaged in the meeting, just physically present. She seldom changed expressions and almost appeared to be wearing a mask. Her voice seemed flat and expressionless. She sat slouched in her chair and asked if I had a "smoke." When I said that I didn't, she shrugged. "No biggie," she said. I wondered if she could explain the violent acts she's committed over the years. "I just felt like doing it," she said. I wondered if perhaps she had regrets about any of the harm she had done. She shrugged, looked right at me and asked, "Why?" I wondered if it didn't bother her that she had hurt people in her family. She shook her head. "They were there. It could have been someone else. Their tough luck." Could she explain why she felt no remorse? "What's remorse?" she asked. I explained that it meant guilt or regret. "I don't know what that feels like," she said. I said that it felt like you wished it hadn't happened and that maybe you were to blame. "I don't feel that way. I don't mind that it happened, and I don't feel guilty. Why should I? People know I get weird. They should stay away from me. It's their fault, not mine." Didn't that seem like an unusual way to feel about family members? "All the kids in this place feel the same way. Why is it unusual?" Was it true they all felt that way? "Most of them, sure. They hurt people on purpose. I don't do it on purpose, it just happens. It's like a volcano. You can't say it hurts people on purpose but sometimes it, like, explodes, just like me." She looked at me and seemed as unemotional and disengaged as ever. I asked if she was angry when she had these violent episodes. "Nope. Sometimes it feels good to hurt people. It's fun sometimes to see them in pain. I enjoy the looks on their faces like, I didn't think this kid could hurt me, but they're wrong, I can." I wondered if she felt the same way about other people hurting her. "It doesn't bother me. I like it when people hurt me. Sometimes it makes me get wet, you know." It gives you pleasure? "Yeah, like that."

Did she feel she was different from other people? "No," she said, "I'm honest and they're not. People like to hurt people. I see it all the time. They like to feel stronger than other people. They like to feel they're like the big shits and you're not." Everybody? "Yeah, everybody." Do people hurt you? "Sure. The guards rape me all the time and some of the boys come in and make it with me, sometimes three or four at a time. I like it though." You're kidding me, now, aren't you? "Why should I tell you anything? What do you care?" I'm writing a book. I hope to make people more aware. "Just tell them to throw kids like me away. We're just evil. I think I was supposed to be another person, maybe somebody who hurts people. I read this story about guys in South America who put electricity in guy's dicks. I'd like that job." Really? "Yeah, really."

Jane slouched back in her chair and stared at me. "You sure you ain't got a smoke?" she asked. "I'd tell you a lot more if you gave me a smoke." The truth? "Hey, you never know, do you?"

The Continuation of Early-Childhood Violence into Adult Violence

Reiss and Roth (1993) believe that children often learn that violent behavior "works" by observing their parents or their peers, or from media portrayals of the effectiveness of violent solutions. Many Americans seem to find portrayals of these aggressive and violent solutions to their problems as models for their own behavior. Popular culture has responded to a growing fascination with violence by producing television shows and films in which violence and life-threatening situations are standard fare. Nonetheless, Reiss and Roth (1993) cite evidence from longitudinal studies indicating that "children who show aggressive behavior at around age 8 are more likely than others to exhibit delinquent, criminal, or violent behavior in adolescence and adulthood" (p. 103). Longitudinal studies by Widom (1999) and McCord (1999) support the concern about aggressive behavior at an early age, especially its connection to child abuse and neglect. McCord (1999), whose study of families and child rearing spanned 30 years, found that parental responses to aggressive behavior in their sons was critical to later aggressive behavior (p. 169). The more lenient and encouraging parents were regarding their child's aggressive behavior, the more that behavior became apparent in the child's school conduct, in his or her behavior in athletics, and in the way the child reacted to others when there were disagreements.

Johnson et al. (2000) note that adolescents with a greater number of DSM-IV cluster A or cluster B personality disorder symptoms had a higher probability of committing violent acts during adolescence and early adulthood. Cluster A symptoms include "Paranoid, Schizoid, and Schizotypal Personality Disorders. Cluster B symptoms include Antisocial, Borderline, Histrionic and Narcissistic Personality Disorders" (APA, 1994, pp. 629–630). The authors report that their definition of violence included arson, assault, breaking and entering, initiating physical fights, robbery, and threats to injure others. The authors also found that paranoid, narcissistic, and passive-aggressive personality disorder symptoms during adolescence were associated with violent acts and criminal behavior during adolescence and during early adulthood. The authors suggested that children and adolescents with diagnoses of conduct disorders and personality disorders (clusters A and B) might be prime candidates for treatment. When early treatment is provided, it could help us determine whether treatment might reduce the potential for violence during adolescence, in young adulthood, and in later life.

Interestingly, Johnson et al. (2000) believe that the tendency not to use the term *personality disorder* as a diagnostic category in youth under the age of 18 seriously reduced the size of their sample. There were clearly children with behavior consistent with a diagnosis of personality disorder who were acting out and who had a great deal of potential for adolescent and adult violence, but who were given less serious diagnostic labels because they were not yet age 18.

The unwillingness to use adult diagnostic labels with children is admirable, in our view, because it suggests the ability of children to change and the reluctance to saddle children with an adult diagnosis that may unfairly affect them later in life. However, this practice also lends itself to incorrect diagnoses, because behavior at a lesser age that has all of the diagnostic characteristics of an adult disorder should at least be used as a secondary diagnoses to describe the behavior as serious enough to provide needed help to the child and protection to the community.

Moffitt (1993) suggests that early initiators of violence often experience neuropsychological problems that affect their development. As mentioned previously, neuropsychological problems, according to Moffitt, show themselves in the form of poor reading and problem-solving skills, memory difficulties, inattentiveness, and impulsive behavior. All of these behaviors increase the risk for violence throughout the life cycle, according to Moffitt, who believes that exposure to dysfunctional social and environmental influences may reinforce negative conduct.

The entire issue of diagnostic labeling with violent children is something we need to spend much more time researching and discussing. In reading the articles and books that helped develop the ideas for this book on violent children, it soon became clear that the only two diagnostic categories used with children who act out were *Conduct Disorder* and *Oppositional Defiant Behavior*. Neither are satisfactory terms because both imply behavioral problems, even serious behavioral problems, but with the sometimes unrealistic caveat that serious behavioral problems in children don't exactly mean the same thing as they do for adults. That's a very positive way of viewing the issue, but it doesn't help the clinicians, school administrators, and juvenile court personnel who must make predictions about a child's future behavior and react accordingly. Frankly, after comparing the long list of characteristics of school shooters prepared by the FBI with the very different list of characteristics of *actual* school shooters, it became evident that there are compelling reasons why we need to develop highly descriptive and predictive diagnostic categories for children who are beginning to show early-onset violent behavioral problems. While we don't want to stigmatize children by using labels that may have implicitly negative connotations, for the sake of effective treatment and prevention, we certainly want to be accurate and realistic about the child's potential for future violence.

John, Early-Onset Child Violence and an Adult Personality Disorder: A Case Study

John is a 26-year-old man who has just been arrested for the fourth time for domestic violence. John has been severely battering his 22-year-old girlfriend and now faces the possibility of a mandatory sentence of five years in state prison. John is not contrite and argues that his girlfriend asked to be battered because of her disrespectful and demeaning behavior. He told the police that she'd called him an "asshole" and that had prompted John to beat her to the point of unconsciousness.

John has a long history of violent behavior, beginning at age 6. He had been expelled from school for bomb threats, bullying, hitting a teacher, drug use, drug sales on school grounds, stealing, cheating on tests, and other problems that have followed him throughout adolescence and into adulthood. John has a volcanic temper and has been in so many fights that he has scar tissue all over his face. He is proud of the way he looks and has taken to calling it, "the look of a warrior." John's family is a violent one. Three of the sons and one of the daughters have abused their boy friends, since early

(continued)

Continued

adolescence. John and his siblings watched their father beat their mother and then beat and sexually assault each of them. John now believes that women like to be beaten and that they respect a man who knows when things have gone far enough and a beating is in order. He is happy to oblige all women who feel that way, he says.

John was diagnosed with a severe Childhood-Onset Conduct Disorder at age 8, but as a 15-year-old teenager, after he had beaten a classmate to unconsciousness with a baseball bat because the classmate wouldn't give John his lunch money, John was diagnosed with the adult diagnosis of an Antisocial Personality Disorder (DSM-IV Code #301, APA, 1994, p. 649). DSM-IV defines an antisocial personality disorder as

a pervasive pattern of disregard for and violation of the rights of others occurring since 15 years of age, as indicated by 3 or more of the following (APA, 1994, pp. 649–650):

1. Failure to respect lawful behaviors with repeated acts that are grounds for arrest.
2. Lying and conning others.
3. Impulsivity.
4. Repeated physical fights.
5. Reckless disregard for others.
6. Repeated failure to sustain consistent work behavior or honor obligation.
7. Indifference to the suffering of others.
8. The individual is at least 18 years of age.
9. There is evidence of a Conduct Disorder before age 15.

John has been in therapy since he was a child. He is persistently argumentative, condescending, and unmotivated in treatment. He attends therapy to amuse himself and lets everyone know how useless he thinks the entire process is. John hates therapists and believes that had any of them been any good, they would have stopped the beatings and sexual abuse he and his family endured when he was a child. He thinks they're all bureaucrats who work for agencies who "don't give a flying screw about people. They just care about their jobs and doing as little as they can. It's like them guys on the railroad. They call it featherbedding. That's what them therapists do, they featherbed. They look at you like they care, but inside, they think we're scumbags. Hell, I think we're scumbags, too."

When you have a diagnosis that implies a defect in character, the prognosis for improvement is often poor. The therapist who is working with John finds him unmotivated to change but certainly suffering from signs of depression.

It's a mistake to think that people who have been diagnosed with antisocial personality disorders are unfeeling. The opposite is the case. Often, when their goals are thwarted and they find that life is going in a downward spiral, old feelings of insecurity, low self-esteem, and estrangement from others begin to show themselves. Remember that John was battered and sexually abused as a child. No one comes out of that experience with highly positive feelings about themselves. In fact, not a few felons with antisocial personality disorders attempt suicide in prison. It is when people like John are in deep despair that they are most likely to hurt themselves, or others. A gigantic upheaval is one way to stabilize emotions and for many people like John, this is when serious and harmful acting out is most likely to take place. The notion that you have to knock people down before you can build them up again when you're working with violent people is completely invalid. What you need to do is to begin showing them a positive side of their "Self" that has merit and worth. To quote Saleebey (2000), "Every maladaptive response or pattern of behavior may also contain the seeds of a struggle for health." (p. 129)

Discussion

John was sentenced to a mandatory five-year sentence in state prison. The state in which he lives has very tough domestic violence laws, and John's case created a great deal of publicity. John feels the publicity caused the tough sentence. In talking about his life, John told the author,

> What did you think I would turn out to be, a minister or something like that? I had a childhood from hell. There wasn't a day I wasn't beaten up or raped, or it didn't happen to my brothers or sister. Hell, my ma was just a bag of broken bones by the time she was thirty. She couldn't do nothin' to help us out. But the school and the welfare and the cops, they didn't do nothin' to help us, neither. We was comin' to school with bruises all over. What did they think was going on? So I ain't got no feelings for people who say I should be in jail for beating up my girlfriend. I treated her good and she paid me back by sleeping with my best friend and putting a drug rap on me. Five years in jail? If anybody should be in jail five years it's them caseworkers at the welfare department who didn't even come to the house to investigate. Too busy, too many cases. Well, you got an example of what happens when a kid is livin' in hell. My life hasn't been so great, and I done a lot of harm to people to get back at them for what was done to me. But being in prison is like being buried alive and if I make it out of here, it'll be a miracle. I got this new therapist. He ain't so bad. He listens and he reminds me that I ain't always been bad and I got some good qualities. He's the first one who ever said that to me. I'll hang in there with him. Maybe it'll help, but I'm holding back on my judgment until I'm sure he's OK. I feel real down right now. They got me on some drugs to make me feel better. It's OK, I'll make it, but you know, I wish when I was a kid someone had come to my house, said this was a kid worth saving, and took me away and put me with some good people to raise me. Maybe that would have helped. I think so.

Does Early-Onset Violence Necessarily Lead to a Continuation of Violence throughout the Life Cycle?

A key factor in this book has been the belief that the earlier childhood violence begins, the more likely it is to continue into adolescence and adulthood. A large number of writers agree, but is it necessarily true? The answer is that early indicators of violence are not absolutely predictive that violence will occur throughout the life span but serve to alert us to potential problems in the future. A good indication that early markers of violence do not necessarily lead to violent behavior may be found in the work of Werner and Smith (1982). The authors discovered that one of every three children who were evaluated by several measures of early-life functioning to be at significant risk for adolescent problems, including violent behavior, actually developed into competent and confident young adults by age 18. In their follow-up study,

Werner and Smith (1992) reported that two of three of the remaining two-thirds of the children at risk had turned into caring and healthy adults by age 32. One of the primary outcomes of their research was the belief that people have "self-righting" capabilities that lead to self-correction in life and that these capabilities can be identified early in life. The most important self-righting capability develops through meaningful personal relationships that offer the child a sense of protection and serve as a catalyst for change. Werner and Smith (1992) believe that it is never too late to move from defeat and hopelessness to a sense of achievement.

A number of studies have been presented in this book, arguing that early life experiences, particularly child abuse, have a long-term deleterious effect on behavior and frequently lead to violence and other serious problems. However, Rind and Tromovitch (1997) conducted a metaanalysis of the impact of child sexual abuse on the emotional functioning of adult victims and concluded that the impact was limited:

> Our goal in the current study was to examine whether, in the population of persons with a history of CSA [child sexual abuse], this experience causes pervasive, intense psychological harm for both genders. Most previous literature reviews have favored this viewpoint. However, their conclusions have generally been based on clinical and legal samples, which are not representative of the general population. To address this viewpoint, we examined studies that used national probability samples, because these samples provide the best available estimate of population characteristics. Our review does not support the prevailing viewpoint. The self-reported effects data imply that only a small proportion of persons with CSA experiences are permanently harmed and that a substantially greater proportion of females than males perceive harm from these experiences. Results from psychological adjustment measures imply that, although CSA is related to poorer adjustment in the general population, the magnitude of this relation is small. Further, data on confounding variables imply that this small relation cannot safely be assumed to reflect causal effects of the CSA. (p. 253)

Granted, this is a controversial finding, but it should give us pause to consider that many children from violent homes do not become violent and are amazingly resilient. In a review of the factors associated with resilience to stressful life events, Tiet, Bird, and Davies (1998) noted that higher IQ, quality of parenting, connection to other competent adults, an internal locus of control, and social skills have been identified as protective factors that allow children to cope with stressful events. According to the authors, protective factors act as primary buffers between the traumatic event and the child's response. However, Tiet, Bird, and Davies (1998) believe that even resilient children respond inconsistently to stressful events and that another way to look at resilience is to show the relationship between the specific traumatic event and the response. Many of the maltreated children studied for resilience were evaluated solely on school-based outcomes that included grades, deportment, and the degree of involvement in school activities. However, Luthar and Zigler (1991) reported that while resilient children do well on many school-based outcomes, many suffer from depression. Interestingly, however, although many of the maltreated children studied showed signs of depression, they still did well on behaviorally oriented outcomes measures such as grades and school conduct.

In summarizing their findings on resilient children, Tiet, Bird, and Davies (1998) wrote,

> In conclusion, resilient youth tend to live in higher-functioning families and receive more guidance and supervision by their parents and other adults in the family. Other adults in the family may complement the parents in providing guidance and support to the youth and in enhancing youth adjustment. Higher educational aspiration may also provide high-risk youth with a sense of direction and hope. Although IQ had no impact in youth at low risk, youth at high risk who have a higher IQ may cope better and therefore avert the harmful effects of adverse life events. (p. 1198)

Violence and Male Behavior

One of the concerns in writing this book was the fear that encouraging early recognition of violence could lead to labeling that would stigmatize children and result in self-reinforcing behavior. Children need emotional room to grow and develop. If behavior that may eventually self-right itself is incorrectly assumed to be violent, children may not have the emotional room to develop in unique and positive ways. D'Antonio (1994) suggests that young males, the primary population of children showing signs of early violence, are often denied the very characteristics for which they were formally praised. "Once celebrated for their natural aggression and high spirits," D'Antonio wrote (p.20), "now they are branded as hyperactive, incorrigible thugs. Is society making boyishness pathological?" In taking this argument even further, D'Antonio (1994) stated,

> [M]any mothers and teachers don't understand the natural assertiveness of boys. Too often, boys are made to feel inferior or even disturbed. This notion that boys are bad is reinforced by a stream of feminist thought that argues that women are natural peacemakers while male aggression—in the form of patriarchy—is the main source of war, pollution, poverty, virtually every kind of suffering in the world. (p. 20)

Tiller (1967) believes that when boys are unable to understand or successfully define masculinity and male behavior, they learn to compensate for their confusion through exaggerated male behavior. Tiller calls exaggerated behavior in young males "compensatory masculinity." The boy striving to become a man and who feels fearful and insecure about the process may copy male verbal patterns or the way men they admire walk. Young boys may see this as a way of proving to others that they are men. They may drink or smoke at an early age to exaggerate their need to be seen as real men. When the need to prove masculinity is overpowering because of peer or family pressures, compensatory masculinity may lead boys to violence. It is no small coincidence, according to Tiller (1967), that violence among very young boys occurs in those whose home life is highly chaotic or where there is an absence of healthy male figures to help socialize young boys. Writing about compensatory masculinity, Harrison, Chien, and Ficarratto (1989) noted,

One way children cope with anxiety derived from sex-role expectations is the development of compensatory masculinity (Tiller, 1967). Compensatory masculinity behaviors range from the innocent to the insidious. Boys naturally imitate the male models available to them and can be observed overemphasizing male gait and male verbal patterns. But if the motive is the need to prove the right to male status, more destructive behavioral patterns may result, and persist into adulthood. Boys are often compelled to take risks that result in accidents; older youth often begin smoking and drinking as a symbol of adult male status; automobiles are often utilized as an extension of male power; and some men find confirmation of themselves in violence toward those whom they do not consider confirming their male roles. (p. 306)

Harrison, Chien, and Ficarratto (1989) went on to note that as much as three-fourths of the seven-year difference in life expectancy between men and women is attributable to socialization:

Parents assume that male children are tougher than female children, when in fact, they may be more vulnerable than female children. Male children are more likely to develop a variety of behavioral difficulties such as hyperactivity, stuttering, dyslexia, and learning disorders. Male socialization into aggressive behavioral patterns seems clearly related to the higher death rate from external causes. Male anxiety about the achievement of masculine status seems to result in a variety of behaviors that can be understood as compensatory. (p. 306)

An additional alternative reason for male violence was noted by Marin (1991), who reported that 80 percent of the homeless in America are males. Of the many interesting reasons for the number of male homeless, Marin suggested, "Poor families practice a form of informal triage. Men, at very early stages of life, are released into the streets" (p. 85), where life is often fraught with danger and violence. Marin went on to say,

When men work (or when they go to war—work's most brutal form) we grant them a right to exist. But when work is scarce, or when men are of little economic use, then they become in our eyes not only superfluous but dangerous. We feel compelled to exile them from our midst and banish them from our view. We are so used to thinking of ours as a male-dominated society that we tend to lose track of the ways in which some men are even more oppressed than women. [Men of color who constitute 50% of the homeless], suffer endlessly from forms of isolation and contempt that often exceed what many women experience. (p. 87)

In considering the helping approaches one might use with violent children, Scher (1990) believes that most forms of treatment are based on notions of introspection and insight that are more appropriate for female clients than for boys or men. Treatment, Scher believes, is not an alternative to male guidance and that "what it means to be a male in our culture and what impact that has on males as clients in psychotherapy has frequently not been addressed" (p. 322). O'Neil (1981) suggested similar concerns when he wrote:

Many men [as children] are taught that masculine power, dominance, competition and control are essential to proving one's masculinity; that vulnerabilities, feelings, and emotions in men are signs of femininity and are to be avoided; that masculine control of others, self and the environment are essential for men to feel safe, secure and comfortable; and that men seeking help and support from others show signs of weakness, vulnerability and potential incompetence. (p. 240)

Franklin (1992) acknowledges that black men, like most men, have very low participation rates in therapy. He believes that the reason for low participation rates are explained by a belief that therapy indicates weakness, something many young children are also taught to believe. Franklin suggests that therapy is not a traditionally male way of resolving problems and that while black males may seem to be intimately involved in treatment, particularly group treatment where concern and interaction with others is so important, "doubts and inadequacies of the inner self are tightly guarded secrets. Men are not likely to share personal vulnerabilities [because] seeing a therapist is perceived as an abdication of a man's fundamental right and ability to solve his own problems" (p. 352).

Robertson and Fitzgerald (1990) reported that males with traditional masculine attitudes are less willing to accept professional help and are resistant to descriptions of therapy that use insight techniques or focus on reliving early-life experiences. The authors found that when treatment is described as a class, seminar, or course, males are much more likely to attend. The authors hypothesize that male socialization makes it very difficult for even very young men to admit problems, seek help, and then follow through on the help if it is framed in ways that force self-awareness or insight. Males, according to Robertson and Fitzgerald (1990), are more likely to stay in treatment when the service offered is supportive, reinforcing, instructional (advice giving), and nonconfrontational.

Brannon (1976) believed that one of the reasons men resist therapy and the helping process can be explained by the gender role messages boys are taught as very young children. Many gender role messages are given to boys in sports and are internalized before the first grade, making boys resistant to therapy very early in life. Brannon (1976) believed that there are four primary messages given to boys at such an early age that they know the messages well enough to have mastered them, to some extent, by puberty:

1. *No sissy stuff:* the need to be different from women
2. *The big weed:* the need to be superior to others
3. *The sturdy oak:* the need to be self-reliant and independent
4. *Give 'em Hell:* the need to be more powerful than others, through violence, if necessary

While gender role messages that therapy is feminizing may make treatment more complex with boys, it should also suggest that we need to develop uniquely male approaches to treatment. Perhaps we are at the same stage in developing treatment approaches for young male children as we were when women began to suggest that therapy was driven by male beliefs that were inconsistent with the needs of women and the realities of their lives.

Summary

There is compelling evidence that early-onset violence often leads to violence throughout the life span and to such nonviolent problems as substance abuse, work failure, and depression. As adults, many violent children become the primary perpetrators of child abuse and family violence. Caution is urged in labeling children as violent before their behavior is well developed. Children evolve, and many children who appear violent become well functioning and healthy adolescents and adults. Young boys, who make up the largest portion of the violent child population, often need time to develop their sense of masculinity, suggesting the need for male mentoring and treatment approaches that are uniquely male in their orientation. Much more work needs to be done on how male children are socialized, their reluctance to use treatment, and how help can be offered and used that results in positive change.

Integrative Questions _____

1. Do you favor a watch-and-see attitude toward children demonstrating early signs of violence, or would you immediately provide diagnostic and treatment services as a way of being proactive?

2. What are some possible reasons why children might be violent at age 6 but be absolutely nonviolent and normal by age 18?

3. Early diagnosis of violence could lead to labeling that stays with children throughout their lives. Do you believe that labeling is stigmatizing? If so, what might be some alternatives to labeling violent behavior in young children?

4. An argument was made that gender role messages given to boys early in life make it difficult for them to utilize therapy. Do you agree with this? If so, what might an alternative therapy for young boys consist of in terms of the approach used?

5. In one of the case studies, John blamed the courts and the child welfare system for allowing child abuse to continue in a home where all the children developed serious problems. Do you believe that early intervention by the courts might have prevented this client from becoming so abusive in his relationships with women?

References _____

American Psychiatric Association. (1994). *Diagnostic and statistical manual of mental disorders.* (4th ed). Washington, DC: American Psychiatric Association.

Brannon, R.C. (1976). No "sissy stuff": The stigma of anything vaguely feminine. In S. Sailid and R. Brannon (Eds.), *The forty-nine percent majority.* Reading, MA: Addison-Wesley.

Csikszentmihalyi, M., and Schmidt, J.A. (1998). Stress and resilience in adolescence: An evolutionary perspective. In K. Borman and B. Schneider (Eds.), *The adolescent years: Social influences and educational challenges* (pp. 1–17). Chicago: National Society for the Study of Education.

D'Antonio, M. (December 16, 1994). The fragile sex. *Los Angeles Times*, p. 20.

Dembo, R., Brown, C.H., Schmeidler, J., Williams, L., and Wothe, W. (1992). The role of family factors, physical abuse, and sexual victimization in high-risk youths' alcohol and other drug use and delinquency: A longitudinal model. *Violence and Victims*, 7(3), 245–266.

Elliott, D.S. (1994). Serious violent offenders: Onset, developmental course, and termination: The American Society of Criminology 1993 Presidential Address. *Criminology*, 32:1–21.

Farrington, D.P. (1994). Early developmental prevention of juvenile delinquency. *Criminal Behaviour and Mental Health*, 4(3), 209–227.

Franklin, A.J. (1992). Therapy with African American men. *Families in society: The journal of contemporary human services*, pp. 350–355.

Furstenberg, F. (2000). The sociology of adolescence and youth in the 1990s: A critical commentary." *Journal of Marriage and the Family*, 62, 896–910.

Hagan, J., and Foster, H. (December 2001). Youth violence and the end of adolescence. *American Sociological Review*, 66, p. 874–899.

Harrison, J., Chien, J., and Ficarratto, T. (1989). Warning: Masculinity may be dangerous to your health. In M. Kimmel and M. Messner (Eds.), *Men's lives*. New York: MacMillan.

Herrenkohl, T., Huang, I., Kosterman, B. et al. (February 2001). A comparison of social development processes leading to violent behavior in late adolescence for childhood initiators and adolescent initiators of violence. *Journal of Research in Crime & Delinquency*, 38, 45–63.

Johnson, J.G., Cohen, P.S., Kasen, E.S. et al. (September 2000). Adolescent personality disorders associated with violence and criminal behavior during adolescence and early adulthood. *American Journal of Psychiatry*, 157, 1406–1412.

Kellerman, J. (1999). Savage spawn: Reflections on violent children. New York: Ballentine.

Luthar, S., and Zigler, E. (1991). Vulnerability and competence: A review of research on resilience in childhood. *American Journal of Orthopsychiatry*, 6, 6–22.

Marin, P. (July 8, 1991). The prejudice against men. *The Nation*, p. 85–91.

McCord, J. (1999). Family relationships, juvenile delinquency, and adult criminality. In F.R. Scarpitti and A.L. Nielson (Eds.), *Crime and criminals: Contemporary and classic readings* (pp. 167–176). Los Angeles: Roxbury.

Moffitt, T.E. (1993). Adolescence-limited and life-course persistent antisocial behavior: A developmental taxonomy. *Psychological Review*, 100, 674–701.

O'Neil, J.M. (1981). Patterns of gender role conflict. *Personnel and Guidance Journal*, 60.

Patterson, G.R., Capaldi, D.M., and Bank, L. (1991). An early starter model for predicting delinquency. In D. Pepler and K.H. Rubin (Eds.), *The development and treatment of childhood aggression* (pp. 139–168). Hillsdale, NJ: Lawrence Erlbaum.

Patterson, G.R., Crosby, L., and Vuchinich, S. (1992). Predicting risk for early police arrest. *Journal of Quantitative Criminology*, 8(4), 335–355.

Reiss, A.J. Jr., and Roth, J.A. (Eds.). (1993). *Understanding and preventing violence*. Washington, DC: National Academy Press.

Rind, B. and Tromovitch, P. (1997). A meta-analytic review of findings from national samples on psychological correlates of child sexual abuse. *Journal of Sex Research*, 34(3), 237–255.

Robertson, J., and Fitzgerald, I. (1990). The mistreatment of men: Effects of client gender role and life style on diagnosis and attrition on pathology. *Journal of Counseling Psychology*, 37, 3–9.

Saleebey, D. (2000). Power in the people; strength and hope. *Advances in Social Work*, 1, 127–136.

Scher, M. (Fall 1990). Effect of gender role incongruencies on men's experiences as clients in psychotherapy. *Psychotherapy*, 27, 322–326.

Sprague, J.R., and Walker, H.M. (Spring 2000). Early identification and intervention for youth with antisocial and violent behavior. *Exceptional Children*, 66, 367–379.

Stattin, H., and Magnusson, D. (1989). The role of early aggressive behavior in the frequency, seriousness, and types of later crime. *Journal of Consulting & Clinical Psychology*, 57(6), 710–718.

Steinbeck, J. (1992). *East of Eden*. New York: Penguin Books.

Tanner, J., and Yabiku S. (1999). Conclusion: The economies of young adulthood—One future or two?" In A. Booth, A. Crouter, and M. Shanahan (Eds.) *Transitions to adulthood in a changing economy* (pp. 254–269). Westport, CT: Praeger.

Thornberry, T.P., Huizinga, D., and Loeber, R. (1995). The prevention of serious delinquency and violence: Implications from the program of research on the causes and correlates of delinquency. In J. C. Howell, B. Krisberg, J.D. Hawkins, and J.J. Wilson (Eds.), *A sourcebook: serious, violent, and chronic juvenile offenders* (pp. 213–237). Thousand Oaks, CA: Sage.

Tiet, Q.Q., Bird, H., and Davies, M.R. (November 1998). Adverse life events and resilience. *Journal of the American Academy of Child and Adolescent Psychiatry*, 37, 1191–1200.

Tiller, P. (1967). Parental role division and the child's personality. In E. Dahlstrom (Ed.), Changing roles of men and women. New York: Beacon.

Towberman, D.B. (1994). Psychosocial antecedents of chronic delinquency. *Journal of Offender Rehabilitation*, 21(l), 151–164.

Vitelli, R. (December 1997). Comparison of early and late start models of delinquency in adult offenders. *International Journal of Offender Therapy & Comparative Criminology*, 41, 351–357.

Werner, E., and Smith, R.S. (1982). *Vulnerable but invincible*. New York: McGraw-Hill.

Werner, E., and Smith, R.S. (1992). *Overcoming the odds: High-risk children from birth to adulthood*. Ithaca, NY: Cornell University Press.

Widom, C.S. (1999). The cycle of violence. In F.R. Scarpitti and A.L. Nielson (Eds.), *Crime and criminals: Contemporary and classic readings* (pp. 332–334). Los Angeles: Roxbury.

10

Case Studies of the Continuation of Early-Childhood Violence through the Life Span

The following short case studies were shared with the author by clinicians who have worked in forensic, health, and mental health agencies with older clients who have committed early-childhood violence. While accurate diagnosis for young children is imprecise, at best, the author has attempted to provide an early-childhood diagnosis when the original offense was committed and a current diagnosis. Although many of the clients in this chapter have *personality disorders*, they may not be of the antisocial subtype. Some of the clients in this chapter have an adult diagnosis of *Borderline Personality Disorder* (DSM-IV Code #301.83; APA, 1994, p. 654) or *Narcissistic Personality Disorder* (DSM-IV Code #301.81, APA, 1994, p. 661). Many older adults who have committed childhood violence are thought to have a form of personality disorder; however, in some instances this may not be true. Some clients have shifting diagnoses throughout the life span, while others may have more serious disorders that now appear to suggest mental illness or behavior associated with brain trauma. For the moment, however, let's consider the cases of older adults with a current diagnosis, in some form, of a personality disorder. The DSM-IV defines a personality disorder as follows:

> An enduring pattern of inner experience and behavior that deviates markedly from the expectations of the individual's culture. This pattern is manifested in two (or more) of the following areas: 1) In ways of perceiving self, others and events; 2) in the range, intensity, lability and appropriateness of the response; 3) in interpersonal functioning; and 4) in impulse control. The enduring pattern is inflexibly and impairment in many important areas of functioning that can usually be traced back to early childhood and is of a long duration, and is not caused by a mental or physical disorder or brain trauma. (APA, 1994, p. 633)

143

Jack: A Child Arsonist

Jack is a 64-year-old man who was seen by a hospital social worker while he was undergoing treatment for end-stage cancer of the liver. When he was age 11, Jack killed a family when he set fire to their house. Prior to this event, he had a long history of animal cruelty, arson, and theft. Jack was sent to a treatment facility but was unmotivated for treatment. While in the facility, he raped a younger boy. On release, Jack molested children and used drugs and alcohol continually. He married when he was age 18 and physically and sexually abused his wife, who left him with a 2-year-old daughter whom he physically and sexually abused until she was taken from him at age 15.

Jack has served time in prisons throughout his life for various crimes, most of them under the influence of drugs and alcohol, and many of them violent. He has no remorse and can never remember feeling guilty about anything he's ever done in his life. When his cancer was diagnosed, Jack went to live with his daughter. The daughter and her husband abused Jack and sometimes withheld his pain medication. The daughter and her husband are full of rage that Jack is living with them and only continue to allow him to be at their home because of the disability checks he receives. Jack tried to rape his 8-year-old granddaughter but was too weak to complete the act. His daughter poured scalding water on Jack's legs as punishment and let the burns go without being cleaned so that Jack developed a secondary infection, for which he is being treated in the hospital along with his liver cancer. Jack is an unlikable patient, and the nurses stay their distance. He likes to touch their bodies when they get too close. He's also stolen money from the rooms of some of the patients. As Jack describes his life, he says,

> Hell, I've been bad all my life. My ma and pa kicked me outta the house when I was 6. Said I was a bad seed and could never amount to nothing. I sure proved them right. I ain't afraid of dying. I been dying from the day I was born. People like me, God must have meant for some purpose, I guess. I don't know what that is since all I ever thought about was havin fun and getting my way. I guess that's what everybody wants, but they're too scared to do. So screw 'em. I'm dying but I sure had a good time.

Discussion

Jack has a severe antisocial personality disorder (DSM-IV Code# 301.7; APA, 1994, 645). He has no empathy for the feelings of others, is entirely self-centered, has an amoral value base, and takes what he needs from others without feelings of guilt. Jack is one of those people who even the most optimistic helping professional might give up on. He shows none of the requisite signs of the ability to use treatment, is unmotivated to change, and is unlikely to consider introspection a desirable quality. He lives for the fullfillment of his impulses and, as such, isn't likely to change his behavior. This is not to say that antisocial behavior doesn't change. There is some evidence that antisocial behavior begins to moderate itself after age 30, but not always. In Jack's case, his violent impulses are as robust as ever. They are impulses that often end up with others getting harmed. Incarceration is an expensive and unreliable way to treat people with Jack's problems, but until we have more effective approaches, it could be argued that incarceration is the only real way of protecting the public from Jack's predatory conduct. While we may protect the public by incarcerating Jack, one wonders about the pain he would inflict on a prison population.

Al: A Child Killer

Al is a 61-year-old Caucasian man currently being treated in a community mental health clinic for severe depression and alcoholism. Al killed his brother during a fight when Al was age 10 and the brother was age 12. Al hit his brother over the head with a brick he found in the backyard of his parent's home. Al was a troubled child from birth. He had many childhood physical problems, including asthma. He began stealing, lying, and exhibiting animal cruelty at an early age. As an adolescent, Al can recall being in small trouble most of the time. "Nothing big, just the same old stuff. The teachers thought I was a trouble maker and I guess that's true," he told his counselor. He continued,

> I guess what nobody cared to know is that killing my brother made me very depressed and I was using alcohol and drugs to deal with the depression. I wasn't a bad kid most of the time but I had a bad temper and I was taking it out on everybody around me. I never was very successful. My wife divorced me because of my drinking and sometimes I was pretty mean to her and the kids. The kids haven't spoken to me in years. I always worked and never was in much trouble after high school, but I always had this depression and this drinking problem. Both problems have made my life hell. I don't know how many times you have to pay for a mistake, but I've been paying since I was 10. My parents disowned me, my friends stopped being friends, I spent three or four years in state institutions, and if I wasn't bad before, I sure was after. They taught me to be a crook and to think of myself like I was one. I never stopped thinking that way about myself. When things would go good for me, this voice in my head would tell me what a bad person I'd been. When I drink, I feel numb. I don't think I've had much fun in my life. I tried religion and that helped some, but maybe God doesn't care much for me, either. I don't know. You should be cut some slack in life when you make a mistake instead of paying for it all your life. I think about killing myself. If I had the guts, I would. Therapy helps some and I'm learning about myself, but maybe when you're my age, you don't expect to change and I guess I'll carry this feeling about myself inside of me until the day I die.

Discussion

Al has changed. His behavior no longer seems consistent with a diagnosis of an antisocial personality disorder, although there are some features of the disorder in the abuse of his wife and children. But at this point in time, a more useful diagnosis might be *Alcohol Dependence* (DSM-IV Code #303.90; APA, 1994, p. 195) with *Severe Depression* (DSM-IV Code #296.3; APA, 1994, p. 345). Because *Antisocial Personality*

Disorder often leads, in time, to depression and substance abuse, some clinicians would not change the diagnosis but would just point out the evolving nature of the disorder over time. In Al's case, he isn't talking like someone with a personality disorder. He sounds contrite, viscerally upset about his life, and trying to use admirable methods of seeking some closure on his past. It isn't unusual for personality-disordered people to do this in the later stages of their lives. Some clinicians believe that this attempt to change later in life is half-hearted and that the major characteristics of the disorder are still present in the self-centered and uncaring behaviors of the person. Other clinicians would take a chance on Al by focusing on his desire for change and for closure on the painful events in the past. It's possible to be too pessimistic in treatment, something that helps no one.

Ruth: *Abuser of Children She Was Babysitting*

Ruth is a 59-year-old woman who was physically abusing the children she was caring for when she was 10 to 12 years of age. She is currently being seen in treatment for severe anxiety and panic attacks. A family friend sexually molested Ruth when she was age 8 and though she told her parents, they did nothing about it. That started Ruth off on a number of years of serious acting out, drug abuse, and depression. Ruth has been married five times and feels nothing for any of the men she's been with. She doesn't find sex satisfying and thinks of intimacy as more trouble than it's worth. Ruth has been involved in a number of criminal activities, including shoplifting, theft, and prostitution. She was thought to have sexually molested one of her sons when he was age 2, but there was insufficient evidence to prosecute her. Ruth has two children, both of whom live with her ex-husbands. She has no desire to see either child and has been out of touch with them for years. Her anxiety attacks coincided with the end of her last marriage.

It has become increasingly clear to Ruth that she is miserably unhappy, but she doesn't know what to do about it. The panic attacks have resulted in frequent visits to the emergency room, where she is repeatedly told to seek treatment for her anxiety-related problems. Ruth believes that she is going to die and that God will send someone into her life to kill her. She told her therapist, "I'm going to get paid back for all the misery I brought to other people. It's just a matter of time before someone evil comes into my house and kills me." Ruth is afraid to leave her house and only comes for therapy if she can travel by cab. She has started wearing scarves over her face so the evil person who she thinks is being sent to kill her won't know who she is.

> I was an OK kid before that bastard molested me and then everything went wrong. I should have gotten some help but my parents were old-fashioned people who believed that family secrets were nobody's business. They thought anyone who needed help for an emotional problem was a disgrace to the family and would reflect badly on all of them. They treated me like I had a disease. Here someone does an unspeakable thing to me and it's somehow my fault. I know I'm going to die and I know that no one in my family will care. To die without anyone, that's the worst part of this whole thing.

Discussion

No diagnosis is likely to be accurate throughout the life cycle. It's possible that Ruth had another form of disorder during childhood, but the history Ruth provides suggests one of the common diagnoses related to sexual child molestation: *Borderline Personality Disorder* (DSM-IV Code #301.83; APA, 1994, p. 654). A Borderline Personality has all of the elements of a personality disorder, but it includes five or more of the following symptoms: (1) a pattern of unstable relationships; (2) unstable self-image or identity; (3) self-destructive impulsivity; (4) suicidal behavior; (5) irritability, anxiety, and severe swings in mood; (6) chronic feelings of emptiness; (7) difficulty controlling anger and (8) transient paranoid ideations or dissociative symptoms (APA, 1994, p. 654). Clients with Borderline Personality Disorder may also experience numerous unfulfilling relationships, sexual acting out, behavior that sometimes appears to demonstrate signs of mental illness, and severe ongoing depression and/or anxiety. People with Borderline Personality Disorders are difficult to treat because their symptoms are transient, their trust level is low, and their desire to manipulate is high. None of these symptoms bode well for treatment. In Ruth's case, as in the case of many clients with Borderline Personality Disorder, there was a severe disruption in her social and emotional development as a result of sexual abuse—followed by family rejection and acting-out behavior. While many clinicians believe that the antecedents to Borderline behavior may be noted in childhood with symptoms that parallel adult symptoms, this may not necessarily be the case. Some people with Borderline Personality Disorder appear to have successful childhoods and adolescence but begin experiencing emotional difficulty in early adulthood.

Ruth has not responded well to past psychotherapy. Although she has an experienced clinician working with her, Ruth is emotionally labile. She constantly shifts the emphasis of her problem so that a focus on any one symptom is difficult. She is often unable to attend interviews and seems so confused at times that her speech becomes garbled. For these reasons, many clinicians often misdiagnose Borderline behavior with a form of mental illness. Perhaps in some Borderline clients this is true. Borderline behavior runs the gamut emotionally, and those on the highly disturbed end of the continuum may appear to be mentally ill. The literature isn't overly optimistic about the use of talking therapies. Much more research needs to be done on this disorder before interventions are found that appear to work.

Lucille: An Accomplice to Robberies

Lucille is a 65-year-old Caucasian woman currently receiving treatment for clinical depression. Lucille was involved in a series of childhood and adolescent robberies in which she accompanied a male partner, although, she never directly took part in the robberies. Lucille was not diagnosed with a *conduct disorder* as a child or as an adolescent, nor has she demonstrated antisocial behavior as an adult. Like many other clients with *Narcissistic Personality Disorder* (DSM-IV Code #301.81; APA, 1994, p. 658), Lucille often forms relationships with men who accept and respond to her need for excessive admiration. Many of these men have antisocial personalities, and the gifts and attention she receives, even in the absence of a caring or loving relationship, appeal to her need to think of herself as someone very special. She is often grandiose in her thinking, has fantasies of success and power, is unempathic to the feelings and the needs of others, exploits other people, and is arrogant to such an extreme that most people dislike her immediately. Many people like Lucille suffer rejection and avoidance by others and are often unable to form satisfying or emotionally intimate relationships. As her pattern of failed relationships has become all too clear to Lucille, she has developed a deep clinical depression that seems unresponsive to therapy or medication. Her inability to take responsibility for her behavior and her tendency to blame others for her situation make treatment very difficult. In commenting on her early involvement in violent crime and her failures in life, Lucille said,

> Nobody really understands my special gifts. I wasn't a bad girl but I was in love with adventure and with the people who did exciting things. You must take risks in life to develop your special talents, and the boys I was with were kind and gentle to me and gave me gifts and love that nurtured my spirit. I knew they were limited boys, but while they were good to me, I had everything a girl could ever want. People don't understand that I have special abilities, and think that I'm arrogant. Maybe I am. Maybe God has been kinder to me than most. I know something wonderful will happen to me to take away this heavy burden of sadness I bear. It's awful that God would burden me with depression when I could offer so much to the world. I have greatness in me, and all the adventures I've had would make a wonderful book. I told a dear friend once that I would write a book about my adventures with the criminal element, and he said, "Lucille, that would make a marvelous book." He was a wonderful man, but like all the men I know, they just never knew how to treat a lady with my gifts. I can't permit myself to be with anyone who isn't as talented as I am or who doesn't recognize my specialness. One of the boys who used to rob stores, he told me that I was his muse. He couldn't get inspired to rob unless I would go along with him. I think that's one of the most adorable things anyone has ever said to me.

Discussion

Needless to say, not everyone with a narcissistic personality disorder becomes involved in childhood violence. And not all people who display narcissistic characteristic can be classified as having a Narcissistic Personality Disorder. The DSM-IV notes that one should only use this diagnostic category when "these traits are inflexible, maladaptive, and persisting and cause significant functional impairment or subjective distress" (APA, 1994, p. 661). Lucille displays most of the characteristics associated with Narcissistic Personality Disorder, but how does one explain her involvement in early-childhood violence? Probably, by taking her explanation at face value. The boys who robbed stores intrigued her. She liked the attention, but she disassociated the harm it might have done to others and saw it as romantic. Such views of life hardly make for good treatment results, and while Lucille has not been involved in violence as an adult, her narcissism has hurt others, particularly the men who have fallen in love with her and have found her endless need for praise and adulation offensive to the point of feeling suffocated. One of her six ex-husbands, who sometimes cares for her when she is too depressed to move from her bed, told her therapist:

> Dealing with Lucille is like trying to satisfy the hunger of a shark. She is the most needy person I've ever known. She isn't able to show appreciation for your help and can only see her own problems. She was an impossible wife, and, in all the time I've known her, I can't remember a single time she ever showed concern for anyone but herself. She treats her problems when she was a kid like a romance story and every one of her ex-husbands, including me, like scum. She thinks she's doing me a favor for taking care of her. I think people like Lucille are killers. They kill your spirit, and they take everything that's good out of you.

Oscar: A Violent Gang-Banger

Oscar is a 58-year-old resident of a group home who has been in and out of emergency rooms since he was in late adolescence. Oscar suffers from *Severe Bi-Polar Disorder* with psychotic features (DSM-IV Code# 296.89; APA, 1994, p. 359). As a child and adolescent, Oscar was involved in several gangland murders and was a member of a notoriously violent gang until he was age 18. At that point, his behavior began to deteriorate and his level of violence increased to such an extent that his fellow gang members were afraid he would kill *them*. It was at this point that Oscar sought psychiatric help, and the diagnosis *of Severe Bi-Polar Disorder* was made. Oscar has been in and out of jail for violent behavior throughout his adult life. Once on medication, he can be a sweet and considerate man who gets along well with others, but when he cycles off his medication, as is often the case when he moves into manic phases, his behavior becomes violent and the disorder begins to have psychotic features. His social worker said that Oscar needs constant assistance with medications. He doesn't like the way he feels when he's medicated. As he begins to experience manic episodes, he tells his social worker, "It's like having sex. I feel like a million bucks." When asked about his violent behavior, Oscar said,

> I got this problem. I get off my meds and it makes me do stuff. When I'm on the meds, I don't do bad stuff but I feel like my head is messed up. I can't think straight. When I go off my meds, I start to feel real good and then, I don't know, I go psycho. Everybody pisses me off. Noise makes me go nuts. Sounds, like sounds from the street, they make me mad. Sometimes I chase cars that beep their horns cause I'm so pissed off at the noise they make. I get so mad sometimes, I just hit people. I don't mean to and I feel bad afterward, but it's this mental thing I got. I done things when I was a kid nobody should do. I don't know why I done them but maybe I had this mental thing then— this bi-polar thing—and I didn't know it. I want to apologize to them people I hurt. You tell them people I'm sorry. It's rotten to live on meds that make you feel like you're wacko just to be sure you don't do bad stuff. I grew up in a nice family. They loved me, but what could they do? I was pretty whacko right from when I was a little kid.

Discussion

Many people confuse Bi-Polar Disorder with Psychosis. People with Bi-Polar Disorder often have severe mood swings that sometimes have psychotic features (DSM-IV Code # 296.89, APA, 1994, p. 359). But Bi-Polar Disorder often responds well to medication. This isn't to say that people with severe bi-polar disorder are necessarily moderate in their behavior once on medication, but it does suggest that most extreme behavior can be controlled. Oscar clearly has a severe Bi-Polar Disorder. His violence and his inability to deal with external stimulation such as noise and street sounds suggest that once off his medication, Oscar can be extremely dangerous. His treatment regimen includes constant supervision to make certain that he takes his medication, anger management sessions, learning helpful techniques to navigate daily life issues, and day treatment that includes planned social activities. Oscar loves to cook and often helps out in the day program kitchen. A day program patient antagonized Oscar by taunting him. In retaliation, Oscar stabbed him with a kitchen knife. He is apologetic and realizes he did the wrong thing but can't control his anger once it reaches a certain point. His social worker told us,

> Oscar is a gentle and sweet man most of the time when he's on his medications, but he has a very low tolerance for frustration and often loses control. He can't be in the kitchen anymore, and after his jail sentence has been served, he'll come back into the program. This is a constant cycle with many of our violent clients. We've learned to be patient and always hope that they will get better. Sometimes they do, even folks like Oscar with violent tempers. It's what makes the job so worthwhile.

Robert: Murderer of a Friend

Robert is a 61-year-old patient in a state hospital for the emotionally impaired. He has been institutionalized for over 15 years for killing his parents. When Robert was age 11, he shot and killed his best friend, whom he claimed was "driving him crazy" by tape recording voices and playing them in Robert's room while Robert tried to sleep. The voices were in a foreign language, and Robert thought they were alien voices. An early diagnosis of *Childhood-Onset Schizophrenia* is unusual, but not unknown. The DSM-IV reports, "The onset of Schizophrenia typically occurs between late teens and the mid-30's with onset prior to adolescence rare although cases with age of onset of 5 and 6 have been reported" (APA, 1994, p. 281). Robert has been in and out of institutions since he was age 11 because of mental illness. The problem grew progressively worse through adolescence, with Robert experiencing paranoid delusions and hallucinations. Robert believed that people were following him and trying to kidnap him. The delusions make him extremely violent. On three occasions, he has beaten people he thought were going to harm him. The killing of his parents occurred during a time in Robert's life when he thought his parents were secretly communicating with aliens so that they could experiment with his body.

When Robert was 18 years old, he was hospitalized for attacking a schoolmate. He was psychiatrically evaluated and diagnosed with Paranoid Schizophrenia (DSM-

IV Code #295.3; APA, 1994, p. 287). The symptoms of schizophrenia include "delusions, hallucinations, disorganized speech, social or occupational dysfunction serious enough to affect work, school, or social interactions, with a continuation of symptoms for 6 months or more" (APA, 1994, p. 287). The additional symptoms of Paranoid Schizophrenia include one or more delusions or frequent hallucinations. In Paranoid Schizophrenia, "delusions are typically persecutory or grandiose, or both, but delusions with other themes (jealousy, religiosity) may also occur" (APA, 1994, p. 287). Unlike other forms of schizophrenia, people with Paranoid Schizophrenia may show none of the usual behaviors associated with other forms of schizophrenia such as flat affect, garbled speech, or disorganized or incoherent thinking. People with Paranoid Schizophrenia may be able to work or have intimate relationships with others, but when the symptoms become severe, as in Robert's case, the psychotic features of the disorder become very evident. When threatened, people with Paranoid Schizophrenia may strike out at others. The DSM-IV (APA, 1994) notes that this form of schizophrenia is more treatable than other forms (p. 287). This has not been the case with Robert, however.

Discussion

Robert believes there is a vast conspiracy working against him. He trusts no one and thinks that his caseworker at the institution is an alien in disguise. Robert wears sunglasses to protect himself from the "gamma rays" he suspects are aimed at him from alien vessels high in the atmosphere. He told his caseworker that he would kill the first person who tried to enter his body with a probe. "You try and touch me with one of those probes," he said, "and I'll kill you with my bare hands." Although medication may help Robert, he typically "tongues" his medication and spits it out when the nurse isn't looking. There is a lucrative trade in psychotropic medications at the institution, and Robert often sells his medication to an orderly who provides extra money or other benefits that Robert uses to make his life more comfortable. Even though Robert is a deeply disturbed man, he is also very intelligent and, in some areas of his life, very successful. Mental illness has taken Robert's freedom away, but in his small world, he lives comfortably, is seldom disruptive, and has a sense of order that keeps his fears and more violent tendencies from becoming uncontrollable. As his caseworker said, "Robert is a lifer. He will probably never be able to leave the institution because of his violent behavior. Some people think of mental institutions as warehouses, but for someone like Robert, they can be safe havens where the community is protected and patients can live with some degree of comfort and order."

Jackie: A Child Molester

Jackie is a 56-year-old woman who sadistically sexually abuses children. She was caught abusing her 3-year-old sister when she was age 9. Jackie enjoys inflicting pain on the children she molests and is sexually aroused when she hurts children. When Jackie first began sexually abusing children, it was not thought that women were sexually abusive to children. Jackie received little in the way of counseling for abusing her sister other than a lecture from her minister. When she was a teenager, Jackie was caught bruising the vaginal area of a child she was babysitting with a beer bottle. She was sent to juvenile court and served a three-year sentence in a juvenile facility. She received no treatment for her problem and while in the facility, frequently sexually molested younger girls. There is nothing in her history to suggest that she was molested or that she suffered any other traumas to explain her behavior.

At age 25, Jackie was caught molesting a young girl in the restroom of a restaurant. The court ordered a presentence psychiatric evaluation, which indicated that Jackie was a robust *Pedophile* (DSM-IV Code #302.2; APA, 1994, p. 527) with the additional diagnoses of *sexual sadism* and *antisocial personality disorder*. Pedophilia is defined as an intense sexual arousal for children who are 13 years old and younger by people over the age of 16 when sexual arousal causes impairment in functioning (APA, 1994, p. 528). A Sexual Sadist (DSM-IV Code #302.84), according to the DSM-IV, is someone with ongoing fantasies about hurting others: "When sexual sadism is severe, and especially when it is associated with antisocial personality disorder, individuals with Sexual Sadism may seriously injure or even kill their victims" (APA, 1994, P. 530). Jackie has sadistically sexually abused hundreds of girls under the age of 6.

When Jackie was 50 years of age, she was caught molesting a child she was babysitting and sentenced to 10 years in jail. Jackie is happy in jail. Many of the women in her dormitory have fantasies involving hurting people. For a few cigarettes, she is always able to find a good storyteller who will provide sexual fantasies about hurting and molesting children. She also has access to a computer and to the Internet and watches child pornography and masturbates when sadism involved. Like many sexual molesters, Jackie believes that the children she molests and hurts love her. She only seeks out needy children who have been abandoned or neglected by their parents, and provides them, she believes, with love and tenderness. "Children enjoy what I do. They think it feels good," she says. "I've always known that. It's the kind of uptight world we live in that doesn't allow me to take those poor unloved kids out there and provide for them. I could love them fine and take care of them instead of them being out in the streets where anyone could hurt them. It's just a pure shame, if you ask me."

Discussion

We are in our infancy in the treatment of perpetrators of child molestation. There are few approaches that seem to work at all, other than incarceration to protect children and public identification of child molesters. We usually think that pedophilia happens as a result of child molestation, but that isn't necessarily the case with all molesters. Still, it is far too common for children who have been molested to molest other children during and after childhood and adolescence. Jackie is the exception, and in work with violent people, it is always necessary to consider the exceptions that don't neatly fit into our notions of why violence occurs. Sometimes, there are reasons that are deeply rooted in past events that no one knows about, and sometimes people act in ways that have no rational explanation. In such instances, it is best to treat the symptoms. Jackie is receiving "empathy training," also known as "victim awareness training," which attempts to confront her with the harm she has done. Jackie is a hard sell and doesn't believe a word she hears from the victims who come to the prison and talk about the havoc brought on by the pain inflicted on them by people like Jackie. Jackie is actually sexually aroused when she hears about the pain her behavior causes and can hardly wait to get back to her room to masturbate. She also receives cognitive therapy, but her motivation to look at her behavior is minimal. From Jackie's point of view, she's lived a happy life. Her stints in prison have all been "fun," and she says that most of her best friends are "girls I met in the joint. You get to know some very solid ladies in jail."

David: A Career Criminal

David is a 61-year-old Caucasian man who is in jail for driving his truck into a group of people a year earlier. Luckily, no one was seriously injured. David felt like hitting the people because they were walking across the street when he had a green light. He feels nothing about what he did other than to wish he'd been faster on the getaway to escape arrest. David stole his father's car when he was 10 years old and drove it into an oncoming car, killing three people and badly injuring three others.

He had a long history of antisocial behavior leading up to the auto accident and was sent to a juvenile facility, where he stayed for two years. He was never a model prisoner and got into repeated fights in the facility. After his release, David was frequently in trouble, with increased violence. By the time he was 18, he was serving time for armed robbery, assault with a deadly weapon, simple assault, and assault with intent do bodily harm. Since then, David has been in and out of jail for a variety of offenses, most of them involving violence. He has been diagnosed with *Severe Antisocial Personality Disorder* with episodes of violence (DSM-IV Code #301.7; APA, 1994, p. 649). The DSM-IV also provides for a diagnosis of *Adult Antisocial Behavior* (DSM-IV Code #V71.01; APA, 1994, p. 683), but that diagnosis is limited to adult criminal behavior that is not due to a mental disorder, including antisocial personality disorder. Given David's long history of antisocial behavior, the better diagnosis would be *Adult Antisocial Personality Disorder* described in the DSM-IV as a pervasive disregard for others since age 15 with repeated unlawful behavior, evidence of a prior Conduct Disorder, lack of remorse, disregard for the safety of others, and impulsivity (DSM-IV Code #301.7; APA, 1994, p. 650).

David sees himself as a "professional crook." He enjoys giving others pain and likes the power he has in frightening weak people. He showed his therapist an article one day about the September 11, 2001, bombings of the World Trade Center. In it, a former soldier remarks about a colleague who died while helping many others leave the burning building. "I don't buy this bullshit about dieing for other people, but listen to what this soldier says, because it's what I believe:

> People like Rick, they don't die old men. They aren't destined for that and it's not right, by God, for them to become feeble, old and helpless sons of bitches. There are

certain men born in this world, and they're supposed to be setting an example for the rest of the weak bastards we're surrounded with. (Stewart, 2002, p. 65)

"I set an example for other crooks who are getting old and have lost their steam. I'm the old fart who still scares the shit out of people," David said, and continued,

> I think that's a good example. It means when you get old you can still be strong. You don't have to walk around bent over like some old creep ready to die. I feel like I'm doing the world some good and that I set an example for other crooks. You can grow old and not get yourself beat down by the system. And you can do what you feel like doing and nothing happens to you except a little time in the slam. Any of us who have been in jail before, we do our time, have as much fun as we can, and get on with it. If you're afraid of jail, you shouldn't be a crook. Not being afraid of jail lets me be as mean, as nasty, as tough, as shitty, as wild as I want to be. Sometimes, me and my buddies, we howl at the moon like wolves. Nobody can stop us, we're invincible.

Discussion

David is one of the people with antisocial personality disorder whose behavior doesn't change with time. It's difficult to give up on people, but David needs a confined setting where he won't hurt others. His behavior is fixed and unlikely to moderate itself through experience or treatment. Does that mean we should give up? Not at all. David should continue receiving treatment in jail and should be challenged about his behavior. When a level of discomfort sets in, David may look more carefully at his behavior and moderate it. One has to keep trying on the assumption that time, the situation, and internal pain may all come together and result in change.

Janice: A Gang Leader

Janice is a 66-year-old former gang leader of one of the most vicious female gangs in Los Angeles history. The gang Janice led was tied to 13 murders, drug sales to children, school violence, random shootings, armed robberies, and many other violent crimes. Janice spent much of her young adult life in prison for killing a rival gang member. In prison, however, she underwent a metamorphosis. She discovered that she had strong religious beliefs and became a devout Christian. She finished high school and began working on a college degree. She read voraciously and became a leader in her dormitory, where she successfully encouraged many other young women to end their criminal lives. Many of these women have done well in their lives and are still close friends of Janice. Janice completed a doctorate in Sociology when she left prison. She became involved in community politics and is a competent and highly respected member of the local school board. She just retired from her college position as Associate Professor of Sociology and has published many well-received articles on gang behavior.

Janice isn't alone in changing her behavior. This is not to say that early-childhood violence goes away in all cases, but in many cases, it does. For reasons about which we aren't entirely certain, people often change their violent behavior and become productive citizens, parents, spouses, and family members. Hughes (1997) believes that violent gang-bangers often change because they fear for the lives of their children and families. Other writers suggest that antisocial behavior changes as people mature. Janice has a somewhat different perspective. She told the author,

> I can't tell you the day I decided to change. It wasn't as if I had an epiphany or anything. I was too tough and angry then to have epiphanies. I was attending religious services to get out of doing some work in the slam, and one day, maybe after six months of going to services, I started listening to what was being said. It moved me to tears and you have to understand how tough I was and how I would never cry in public, but I did. I was just overcome with emotion. I think that day I saw how useless my life was, and I had a glimpse of how much better it could be if I followed a different path. Maybe it *was* an epiphany of sorts. I just felt so humble and overcome with love, I never wanted to hurt anyone again.
>
> I went back to my dormitory and I wrote letters to everyone I knew, apologizing to my victims. I sent them to my lawyer and asked her to mail them, and she did. Cleansing the soul is an important part of contrition, and you can't move away from what you've been until you apologize for the harm you've caused others. Not just with words, but with deeds. I decided I was going to do good in the world, and when I made that decision, the rest of prison flew right by. I was too busy getting an education and becoming a decent person to think about jail. I thank God for letting me see the light, and I apologize everyday when I wake up and every night when I go to sleep for the pain I've caused. I taught Sociology for 30 years. They're the best years anybody could ever have, and I'm thankful that God helped me so I didn't hurt another person. Why did I change when others don't? I can't say for certain. Maybe my wonderful mother helped through her early training. Finding God definitely helped. Maybe I had a certain resilience and could see things from a different perspective. You should never lose hope. Just because someone is a bad kid doesn't mean they'll be bad adults. It's a long way from childhood to real adulthood, and too many people make the transition well for me to be pessimistic.

Summary

The case studies in this chapter were provided to show the violent behaviors in early childhood and the resulting behaviors during adolescence and adulthood. There were also diagnoses provided and a discussion of the changes in diagnosis sometimes required by changes in behavior during the person's life cycle. Although many of the cases presented here had negative outcomes, this isn't always the case. A special reminder was made that people change and that unless we're optimistic and supportive, we won't be able to work with the violent people we see in the early stages of the life cycle, when change is very often possible.

Integrative Questions _____

1. What life events could change violent behavior in childhood to positive behavior in adulthood?

2. Many of the people described in this chapter's case studies appear to have no remorse about their conduct. Do you think that lack of remorse is one of the primary reasons people are violent across the life cycle?

3. Children who act out sexually need early attention. What interventions would you suggest for children like Jackie and Ruth?

4. Several of the cases presented in this chapter provide a glimpse of the way people with severe antisocial personality disorder think. Can you suggest ways of helping young children with developing antisocial tendencies to think more about the feelings of others and the impact their behavior may have on friends, families, and victims?

5. Oscar, the client with bi-polar disorder, is a dangerous person, even when he's taking his medication. Is it safe to keep people like Oscar in fairly open community group homes where they aren't supervised to the extent they would be if they were in a locked facility?

References _____

American Psychiatric Association (1994). *Diagnostic and statistical manual* (4th Ed.). Washington, DC: American Psychiatric Association.

Hughes, M.J. (June 1997). An exploratory study of young adult black and latino males and the factors facilitating their decisions to make positive behavioral changes. *Smith College Studies in Social Work, 67*, 401–414.

Stewart, J.B. (2002). The real heroes are dead. *The New Yorker,* February 11, pp. 52–65.

11

Mr. R: An Autobiographical Account of Early Violent Behavior through the Life Cycle

The following case history was written by a student who was taking my domestic violence course, an irony that will become clear as the case unfolds. He was an exceptionally good student, and his contribution to class discussion had the ring of someone who knew what he was talking about. He was a remarkably handsome man in his late 50s and he had returned to school late in his life. For his final paper, he asked if he could write an autobiographical account of his own experiences with violence, domestic and other forms. I readily agreed, and this case study is the result. Unfortunately, four months after submitting the paper, he had a heart attack and passed away just as he was finding the love of career and family that had so eluded him throughout his life. Although it is a long account, I think it will be difficult to put down. Following the case itself, there are a few reflective comments that might help the reader consider some alternative ways of understanding the case material. The only changes made in Mr. R's account of his life relate to names and places; otherwise, these are Mr. R's words as he wrote them.

Personal History: The Early Years

I was born on the East Coast in January of 1941. My father, a Presbyterian minister, was the pastor at two small churches in that largely rural area. I have a sister born two years previous to me. My mother had rheumatoid arthritis and was bedridden much of the time. My memories of that period are few. I do recall hating any kind of change. When winter ended, I didn't want to change my clothing to spring apparel, nor in the fall did I want to change to winter clothing. I fought any and all changes.

The most notable incidents during the first five years of my life were related to me, in much later years, by my sister. She told me once that when I was about a year old, I had an accident in which I broke my leg. I was told I cried for days but, for whatever reason, my parents would not take me to a doctor. When a visitor stated they heard my bones grating together, I was then taken to the hospital. I never really knew the nature of the accident. I do know that my father, one of 10 children, was raised in some poverty and was always reluctant to spend money for any circumstance, doctors included. I recall an incident when I was about 5 or 6 years. I had, for reasons unknown, set fire to a field of tall grass behind our home. Because I reported it to my mother, my consequences were minimal; however, I do recall much discussion at the time about the incident.

When I was 6, our family moved west. I recall my father's angry silences at having to leave his home and all of his family members because of my mother's need for a dry climate. My mother was always at odds with my father's family and enjoyed a miraculously fast recovery from her arthritis. My father, who had been affectionate with me prior to our move, changed after arriving in Idaho. I was, of course, too young to understand that which I learned later. He essentially gave me over to my mother, and he took my sister for his confidante. My mother and I became very close, as did my father with my sister. At that time of life, I was okay with that arrangement, but in later years, when I looked to my father for some male guidance, he was not available and I was definitely not okay any longer with the arrangement. It was far too late for any change in that area of our lives.

My memories of our family's three years in Idaho are also few. I began school and, for reasons I cannot recall, seemed to spend much time in punishment under the teachers desk. I remember myself as being shy, fearful, and a little small for my age. It rather surprised me when I began to experience some incidents of violence that seemed to transcend the typical schoolyard scrap. When I was 7, I had two fights with the neighborhood bully. In the first, he cut my head with a can lid he had picked up. I bled so much I thought I might die, and I have that scar to this day. In our second fight, I got a broken board with a sharp end and stuck it in his neck. I remember chasing him home with that board flapping as he ran. I can't recall any consequences of that incident. I had others fights with kids, and I recall always being so afraid that I would use any weapon to defend myself. To this day, I don't really understand why or how I became involved in those kinds of incidents other than the fact that I sometimes had to defend being the preacher's kid, which I always hated.

When I was 8, an incident occurred that greatly upset my mother. A cat had born a litter of kittens under our house, and I heard my father talk of getting rid of them. Consequently, I dug a small hole in the back yard, filled it with water, and drowned the kittens. It had my father's blessing, but it unhinged my mother. She never forgot that incident.

During my family's stay in Idaho, my father enjoyed some moderate success in his profession. He built a small church, literally, where there was none prior to his arrival. It seems the only thing that marred that success was my ongoing propensity to get into trouble. No one could understand why a quiet, shy, and, at most times, gentle child kept having these kinds of problems. I understood least of all.

When I was age 9, my father was moved again, this time to a little ranch and university town in New Mexico. I entered the fourth grade at a school that seemed mostly Hispanic. Although I felt lost, (I always felt lost), there was something about those Mexican kids I liked and envied. I learned my first Spanish from them so that I could play with them. Their homes were rough and poor, but I loved going to them. I felt more comfortable in their homes than I did in my own.

My father continued to experience success at his new church. The congregation grew, and I remember people telling me what a fine man my father was. I didn't have a clue as to what they could mean. My behavior continued to be a source of trouble and embarrassment for my family. While my sister was outgoing and loved being the center of attention at church activities, I dreaded every time I had to appear at church, which was often. I was told frequently that I must support my father's ministry. My heart was not in that activity. I once discovered that the not too distant university provided an inexhaustible supply of empty soda bottles that could be redeemed for a penny apiece at the little Mexican market in the neighborhood I liked best. Folks at the school even put them in these neat wooden cases that were easy to carry. I had a lucrative little enterprise going for several weeks until the campus police intervened by delivering me home to my father. My poor folks. I don't recall ever trying to embarrass them, but it just seemed to continue to happen. My father, a man who always preached nonviolence, was driven to violate that policy on a regular basis, but only on me. He would use a coat hanger, his belt, or a stick he kept for just that purpose. While he would whip me rather severely (the marks lasted a week or better), I never felt physically abused, then or now. It was just the way things were done in those days. He never whipped me without a reason, usually a good one. But while I never felt physically abused, I had a great, smoldering anger over the fact that he never had the time of day for me except to punish me.

One summer day, the district superintendent of the church came to visit for the afternoon. Much preparation had been done to prepare for this occasion. I was told they had a son my own age and I was to entertain him outside. That son arrived dressed in a full cowboy outfit complete with two cap pistols. I really wanted one, just one, but he refused my request. For some reason I felt it necessary to beat him up, bad. The superintendent left early that day, and I paid the price. I always felt my father never forgave me that one. People just couldn't understand my behavior, and neither could I. I never recall feeling mean or aggressive, but these things just continued to happen.

After two years in the small New Mexico town, my father was again moved, this time to Albuquerque. He was to build a new church, and it was quite an opportunity for him. My parents and sister were excited. For me, it was one more change, and I hated all change. In Albuquerque, I started the sixth grade. I was never more then an average student and that didn't change for me. My parents continued to be called to school for my behavior. That also didn't change. I don't know why I remember these events as landmarks, it's just that way. I was allowed to roam throughout the church at any time. This included the office where the Sunday service collections were put after church service. For every parishioner who told me how wonderful my father was, for every blue-haired lady who patted my head, for every Sunday school teacher who threatened to tell my father on me, I charged the church a dime, which I collected from those plates. Eventually, I gave myself a raise to a quarter. I had more money than most kids, and nobody ever knew. One might wonder why my father didn't notice my prosperity, but then he only noticed me when some authority brought me to his attention. My mother loved me and I knew it; however, so much of her time was given to the church and promoting my father's success that she didn't notice my early journeys into thievery.

The Adolescent Years

And succeeding he was. Within eight years of moving to Albuquerque, he built one of the largest churches in the city and received an honorary doctorate from a university. But as his star rose, mine continued to descend. In my freshman year in high school, I was suspended for a week. I had fought a kid in the bleachers at our first home basketball game, which temporarily halted the contest. My father had to petition the school principal to get me back in. By this time, I was feeling angry and frustrated nearly all the time. I sensed my father was desperate to find a solution and afraid for the future. And so was I. Many years later, in Alcoholics Anonymous, I heard someone say that they "felt like they were on the wrong planet without an instruction manual." That statement summed up my feelings during those years and for many years to follow.

In my early teens, I developed a raging interest in cars, hot rods to be exact. I found I had some mechanical ability and proceeded to build, as my finances allowed, a procession of hot rods. What parts my friends and I couldn't purchase, we stole. My father, seeing a yard full of parts one day, accused me of being "a fence," as he put it. Then he let it go. The sheriffs were at our door several times. I would wave goodbye to my mother from the back seat of their car but always returned home shortly. I found I had a knack for talking my way out of most situations.

When I turned 17, I was a junior in high school. Age 17 also provided an opportunity for my father to implement a solution for me, his problem child. He took me out to lunch one day with a man he introduced as Major Jones, a member of the church. I had never met the major before, but nonetheless was very interested, primarily because his daughter was built like a real woman and was the high school "slut." I was still a virgin and dreamed of her often. As I was so frequently passive, at least initially, to most things, by the time lunch was over I had agreed to join the Air Force Reserves, which meant that within two weeks I would be leaving school and going to Texas for six months. My father and the Major seemed pleased that I had accepted their plan for my finally achieving manhood and responsibility. I felt more lost and frightened than ever.

My six months of active duty were basically a repetition of my behaviors in other places. It was clear I wasn't going to be a general, not even the mature and responsible young man my family was praying for. I had more fights than ever and was constantly on some kind of disciplinary routine. At one point, Major Jones personally intervened to prevent my early discharge. And I never did get to "screw" his daughter.

After basic training in Texas, we were shipped to a little air base in the cow and oil town of Casper, Wyoming. To that point, I had never had a drink of alcohol. My life was about to undergo a major change. On our first leave into town, I accompanied a group of older guys to a bar. I was small for my age and looked about 15 years old at that time. Casper wasn't a strict kind of town when it came to the law. Desperate to be manly, I ordered the most macho-sounding drink on the menu, a Salty Dog. My first drink was like magic. I quickly had another. The magic increased. All my fears and insecurities seemed to disappear. I felt like Mike Hammer in a Mickey Spillaine novel, my favorite reading at the time. I asked all the women to dance and insulted their companions. I couldn't drink enough. What a marvelous freedom, from self, this alcohol. No wonder my father said it was the devil's greatest tool. It was the greatest fun in the world! I wanted to call home to say I had found the solution to my problems; however, I knew intuitively that would not be the thing to do. Sometime during that night, I entered a blackout. I awoke the next day in my bunk, mouth and eye both cut and bloody. My head hurt like hell, and I was on disciplinary routine. None of that mattered because I'd found a freedom from my shyness, my fears, and my inhibitions. I couldn't wait to go drinking again.

After my six months of active duty expired, I returned to Albuquerque to finish high school. During my absence, my family had moved back to Idaho but had made arrangements for me to live with family friends from the church. I liked and respected this family. I lived with them for about a year and a half, an arrangement I was comfortable with, as my drinking would have been a major problem for my own family.

After completing high school, I was persuaded by my parents to attend university in Denver, Colorado. My father, by then was a member of the board of trustees of the university and would be able to get me admitted despite my dismal scholastic achievements. They chose to believe the military had succeeded with me. It took one semester to prove the error of that thinking. Because my sister was the senior class vice president as well as the homecoming queen, I initially enjoyed some popularity. My new ally, alcohol, was also helpful in some ways. I was elected freshman class president, which was good for an invite to almost any and all parties. By the end of the semester, I was asked to leave the school, having had one drunken brawl too many.

Young Adulthood

After my semester in college, I began the first of a series of geographical moves. I was continually restless and ill at ease and somehow thought that if I followed the example of writers such as Joseph Conrad and Jack London (my favorites), I would somehow, somewhere, find a place where I fit in. I traveled by hitchhiking and worked from time to time for temporary labor agencies. And I always fantasized about being someone or somewhere else. I hustled in the West Indies for six months until the authorities, during a session at the local police station in Kingston, told me that if I stayed longer, I would be a resident of Dunn Prison. I had been rolling gay men with regularity. You can only do those activities for so long in such a small place before you're noticed. I knew that the police everywhere were prejudiced against gays and that probably saved me from more drastic consequences.

After returning to the United States (via a cruise ship), I met a man who ran a home for orphaned boys and girls in the Appalachian Mountains of West Virginia. He offered me a place to live and a job, which I accepted. My two and one half years there were the happiest I had ever known and were to know for many years to come. I worked on the farm, which was part of the home, and came to love the farming life. Often, younger boys would be assigned to me for a work crew, and we would have great times working together. I had always associated hard work with manliness, and there were many opportunities to prove myself. "Tex" Jones, the man who took me to Zion Settlement, really seemed to believe in me. After one year, he insisted I begin school at the nearest community college, which was a six-hour drive away. He paid for me to live there through the winter so that I might attend both semesters. I was a better than average student, and no doubt he would have continued to pay for my education had I been able to keep my behavior in check. But away from the farm environment, I regressed to my former ways. While I hadn't drunk or even thought about alcohol for the past year at school, soon enough it became an issue again. I began to drink again, and it led to brawls. While I escaped accountability for so many of my actions, the sheer number dictated that I would eventually answer for some. Finally, the time came for me to leave West Virginia. I did so without ever saying goodbye to my friend "Tex" Jones. He was, to this day, the finest man I ever met. For a while, he believed in me so much that I even began to believe in myself. Eventually, my lack of character destroyed all that, and I resumed my self-destructive lifestyle.

From West Virginia I went to Washington State to work at the cattle feed lots. I lived at whatever ranch I was working at, and weekends were spent drinking in the cowboy bars. I went to jail several times for bar fights, which eventually led to my losing my final job. Although my employers liked me for my ability to work hard, they tired of my belligerent behavior. After about two years in Washington, I moved on to San Antonio, Texas. There I found work in a factory. In my off time, I found myself hanging around the local boxing gyms. I had a fantasy about becoming the middleweight champion of the world, and since I lost very few fights in the bars and on the street, I thought I'd try my hand in the ring. The day came when a local trainer put me in there with a professional fighter. I quickly learned the difference between a bar fighter and a boxer, but because I didn't quit, the trainer took me into his stable to see what I was willing to do. I was a hard worker and willing, but there were lots of hard guys in those Texas boxing gyms. After a year and a half and 21 amateur fights (of which I won 18), it became clear that my athletic abilities were limited. I was not to be the middleweight champ after all.

Up to this time, I had a long series of girlfriends. All of my relationships were chaotic. Often times they were volatile. I was, from time to time, physical with them, but to me it was always a case of "self-defense." However, my level of force certainly exceeded what was needed for my own self-defense. I never recall a time when I threatened physical force, and, in fact, I was always appalled at the idea of hitting a female. Those times when I did were the result of my experiencing a total loss of control. I often experienced "white rages," either drunk or sober. They usually happened when I actually thought I was totally in control. I would explode in a great burst of energy that would be over within about one minute. But during that momentary outburst, I was capable of doing great damage. Some of my female partners had children, but fortunately I had taken, from my own childhood, the determination to never lay a hand on a child. Since then, I have met other men who made that same vow but broke it repeatedly. I'm grateful that's one vow I was able to keep. Without exception, I was never one to brag about my abuse of women. On the contrary, I was deeply ashamed of that behavior. Never once was I involved with the law over my abuse of women because nobody ever made the call.

Since age 16, I had seen several therapists or psychologists. I never sought them out myself, but was referred to them by either my parents or some authority. My resistance was mountainous and nothing of significance was ever achieved. In retrospect, I know that ever since adolescence, I had huge fears concerning my sense of masculinity. My father, although a very large man, had many feminine ways and no interests of a masculine nature. I was always afraid people would associate me with him, and I felt that I had to prove my masculinity, especially to myself. If anyone ever made a remark that I interpreted as questioning my manliness, it was a sure fight. They'd only question that once. I went to constant extremes to reassure myself of it but, of course, it was never enough. My fears knew no bounds. I was very sexual and would literally wear my partners out. For me, sex was often a great deal of work. My need to prove my masculinity was, however, not all negative. As previously stated, my image of a man also involved someone who was a hard worker and was physically fit (up to a couple years ago, I was able to bench press nearly 350 pounds). I never had a problem finding work, and my ability to work hard was valued by my employers. I was always proud that I never drew unemployment or disability. "No public dole for me," I used to tell myself, "I am a man of principles."

At the age of 24, I began to think about marriage as a possible solution to my ongoing unhappiness (I was always looking for external solutions for my internal problems). I began looking for a suitable candidate in all the local bars. I shortly met a girl of 18 who was working with a false I.D. as a go-go dancer (the days before nude). During that courtship of 90 days, I met her father and mother. He was a daily-drinking alcoholic, and his wife was passive, subservient, and long suffering with his abuse. I felt right at home. Then I developed a venereal disease, which my, by now, "fiancée" had given me. She was so sorry. I was so understanding. In those days, we thought safe sex was a padded dashboard. I knew I was home, so to speak. Her family was everything I felt comfortable with. Oh, did I mention she had a 4 year-old son? She was pregnant at 13 (my kind of girl). We were ready to do the dance of married hell together. We were first married in a border town in Mexico and months later made it legal in the United States. I was drunk both times. My bride didn't drink at all, swearing to never be like her father. Ray Charles could have seen our future.

We decided we needed two incomes to live the kind of life we envisioned. It helped that Kim was also a hard worker. Since she was now a respectable married woman, bar dancing was out. She began a new career as a cocktail waitress in the kind of dives that would hire obviously underage girls. What a life. She worked nights and I worked days. Her mother took care of my new stepson. Kim would come home late from work and tell me about all the guys who had hit on her. I, of course, was still awake from all the amphetamines I had taken during the day. My mood was enhanced by the alcohol I was drinking to help induce sleep. My rage against "those guys" ensured her of my love. My insecurities and jealousies were towering. It was only a matter of time until I'd show up at her job and start a fight with one of her customers. She thought I was chivalrous. I kind of thought so, too. Never mind, she'd start looking for a new job. Lots of bars out there looking for pretty girls. The first time I failed to come home after work on her night off, she came looking for me with my stepson in tow. I was in a local dive being macho with my buddies. Having your wife demand your presence at home in front of your macho pals cannot be tolerated. To avoid a scene, I drank up and excused myself from my friends. My wife and I walked outside. I truly had no conscious idea of wanting to hurt her. Actually, I felt quite calm. Suddenly, I grabbed her by the throat and began to strangle her. My stepson, then, 5 years old, ran back to the bar for help, and several of my friends pulled me off of her. She regained consciousness, and we proceeded home as if nothing had happened. Except her neck carried bruise marks for some time. She complained to her mother, who thought we were settling into a normal marriage. I don't recall any "honeymoon days" of remorse. I do recall feeling that old feeling of deep shame and worthlessness that I always had after abusing a female.

I never felt being abusive with women was O.K. It just seemed to happen. On those occasions when I was violent with men, it was different. Then I was a winner, except on those infrequent occasions when I lost a fight. Then I was terrible to be around. I plotted dark revenges and once in a while carried them out. Kim and I separated perhaps six times over a period of four years. There were occasional additional acts of violence towards her. In 1968 we once again separated. She soon let me know she had a boyfriend.

Terrible Trouble

For several years, I had at times carried a gun with me. So did my friends. We were opportunists who would steal anything of value. We began to believe, I suppose, that we were some kind of gangsters. We loaned out small sums of money in those seedy little bars around San Antonio and collected with interest twice a month. We were would-be loan sharks. On the day my wife told me she had this boyfriend, I was armed. And I was stone sober. I remember thinking about my boss at work who, I felt, had been jerking me around for sometime. I was the foreman at a local factory. He came to work in the morning and left by 10:00 A.M. to go drink at a local bar. I did his work and mine. Years later I came to realize he was probably an alcoholic, just like I was. But at that time, he was just another one of those people who used and abused me.

When I finally lost it all, I recall sitting and listening to my wife talking and feeling like I was going to literally explode. I envisioned bits of myself on the ceiling and walls. Then I did explode. I pistol-whipped Kim until she couldn't fight anymore. Then I shot her five times. I walked outside and told a neighbor I encountered to call an ambulance, that my wife was injured. I got in my car and drove to the factory, where I was supposed to be working that morning. I then called one of my running partners outside and told him I had "lost it" and shot my wife. He asked how he could help me. I said, "Drive with me to where our boss is drinking and call him out back for me." Being my friend, he was anxious to help. When my boss met me out back of that bar, I pistol-whipped him, too. He pleaded with me not to shoot him. I made him beg me on his knees. Then I shot him twice.

A year before this horrible day, I had been in one of those altercations with my wife, and at the conclusion of it I held her against the wall and put a straight razor to her throat. Something wouldn't let me cut her, so I told her "watch this" and hit my own left wrist. Hard! I almost bled to death before the ambulance got there. It required a surgery to retie all the various things that had been severed. Then it was to Johnson State Hospital (a forensic facility for the mentally ill), locked ward. Attempted suicide, they said. They didn't understand either. Why had I done that? I was there for perhaps three weeks. Toward the end of my stay, during a session with a psychiatrist and my wife, he told her, in my presence, that she had better get far away from me, for my future was the gas chamber at San Quentin. I couldn't believe he said that to her. How could he say something like that about me? I could have killed him for such a comment! The shame involved in having been in a mental hospital was extreme. I felt terrible, more worthless then ever. I was inwardly enraged. My life was completely out of control. I made a decision at that point that if I ever really "lost it" again, I would use this experience to prove I was crazy.

After I shot my wife and boss, I had my partner drive me to Johnson State Hospital. I told him not to worry. He and I would stick to the story that I had kidnapped him. Forced him at gunpoint to do my bidding. To reinforce this scenario, after parking at Johnson's front door, I took him inside with a gun to his head. By this time, several law enforcement agencies were looking for me. After entering the hospital, I released my friend and promptly took three doctors hostage. Now the law had arrived. More guns than I'd ever seen. I'll never forget how cool those doctors were. My clothes and arms were bloody, I had a gun in their faces, and they were talking to each other like I wasn't there. Asking each other things like "Do you two know this guy?" "Is he a patient here?" So many guns were aimed at me, I knew at any minute I would be killed. I turned my gun around and told them, "Take it." One doctor reached out and took it from me. About a year later, I was to read in the paper that the governor awarded one doctor the state medal of valor. All three should have gotten one. He just happened to be the one with his hand out the farthest.

I was taken to Bexar County Jail in San Antonio and put in a cell with a group of other prisoners. My adrenaline and fear level were incredibly high. Mentally, I felt I had declared war, and now it was time to fight for my life. There were no more words to be spoken to anyone. I had learned from previous jail experiences the importance of quickly establishing ones "bona fides," or credibility. The first guy who made a tough-guy remark to me, I took on. My level of rage and power were seismic. He was taken to the hospital and I went to solitary, where I was to remain until I went "North."

I was told by a public defender that I had been charged with two counts of assault with intent to commit murder and one count of kidnapping. The fact that both shooting victims were alive didn't seem to register with me. I only recall feeling that

I was at war with "the world." I refused to speak to anyone. One day I was taken to Superior Court to be arraigned. I was seated in the box with a dozen other prisoners. I still refused to speak to anyone. For one to appear in court, they had to, by law, remove our chains. That day, the courtroom was full. I was seated in the top row of the box. All logic and reason had left me. In my "state of war," I saw this as an opportunity to escape. I jumped over the rail and attacked the first deputy to step in front of me. During this fight, his gun fell to the floor. We struggled for it. Of course, I lost that battle due to sheer numbers. I was beaten senseless.

Some days later, I was transported to Johnson State Hospital. I remained in chains. I was examined by a total of three doctors of psychiatry. One was the director of the hospital. I refused to speak to anyone. I later learned the director concluded I was faking it all. The other two said I was incompetent to stand trial. Weeks later, I was transported "North" to El Paso State Hospital for 90 days of observation. I was shackled to a known child molester and seated in the back of a station wagon, facing rearward. I remember being outraged by my company, thinking if I were seen with a child molester that I would be "socially ruined." Such was my erratic thinking. When I arrived at El Paso State, I began speaking again. I made myself useful on the ward in various ways. I was never medicated. I intervened between other men numerous times, preventing possible fights. This saved staff from having to write those hated "Special Incident Reports." They liked me. The ward charge talked to me toward the end of my 90 days. He stated that if I agreed to stay for a couple of years, he would do what he could to not have me sent back to court. It was my strong impression that the doctor (who you saw rarely and for only a few minutes) used the recommendations of the ward staff for his own recommendations. And so it was. I was home for the immediate future.

There may be those who would find this next bit of information rather unbelievable, but there are those, more informed, who will not be surprised. Before I left Bexar County Jail to go north, about two months after the shooting, my wife, in her wheelchair pushed by her mother, came to visit me in jail. We only had a minute before the deputies learned she was my victim and terminated the visit, but it was long enough for her to tell me how much she loved and missed me. I, of course, wasn't speaking, but I was touched enough to have a jailhouse tattoo of her name put on my arm. Ain't love grand?

About two years after arriving at El Paso State Hospital, I was processed to return to court for trial. My parents obtained a private attorney who was right out of the movies. Young, energetic, and bright, he managed to get me released on bail on the basis of the positive reports of my work at El Paso State. He then obtained continuance after continuance while I got a job and settled in with my now ambulatory wife. She had been visiting me at El Paso State and doing a little prostituting in Austin to get by. In the end, I was given three years of formal probation and was to report to my officer weekly. My male victim was outraged, as were the cops.

I knew my life with Kim was going to be a repeat of the past if we stayed together. At least I had gained that insight. I left her and went to Galveston, Texas, to live. Three months later, she came to see me. She was pregnant with my child. I recall feeling devastated. I had never wanted to father a child, because I knew I was incapable of being a parent. But here it was that I told her I would move back home to support her until the baby was born and she was on her feet again. Kim, her mother, and I settled in for the duration. After my son was born and Kim was back to work, I left again. I visited my son monthly for about a year until she disappeared with him. I was not to see or hear of him for another eight years.

Life Progresses

During this time I was driving truck. I injured my knee on the job and was unable to work until I recovered from the surgery. My probation officer suggested that I try going to school. I thought he was crazy, but he persisted, and I soon found myself enrolled at Galveston State University. I actually enjoyed the learning, although I felt out of place on campus. I stayed several quarters, finishing some classes and walking away from others. My drinking was again becoming a problem. I stayed away from bars out of fear of being violated from probation, but drank daily anyway. Soon I moved back to Galveston and resumed my studies at Galveston State University. At that time, I began frequenting the bars again. I soon took a job as a bouncer at a bar that really needed a bouncer. My three years of probation ended, and my restraints were off. I was soon living with a woman, going to school in the day, and working in the bars at night. On my off nights, I would frequently have my girlfriend dress in very provocative clothes and take her to different bars. I would walk away from her and wait for some guy to hit on her, at which time I would come up to confront him. Occasionally, this would result in a fight. This was our entertainment away from home. Bouncers seem to attract a certain kind of woman who likes to be fought over. I soon attracted one whom I married after a few nights out together. I paid for our chapel wedding with stolen credit cards.

Within a year of our wedding, two things happened that caused her to rethink her vows. First, I was involved in a bar fight in which my opponent, a federal officer of some kind, went to the hospital. I ran from that bar, but the law came to my house 10 days later and away I went. I pled guilty to battery and put in a little jail time. Soon I was out and on probation again for three years. Second, I had reconnected with some of my old San Antonio running partners and put together an idea for a big commercial burglary that would make us perhaps $30,000 each. My wife heard me discuss this with my friends and was present during the weeks of preparation. She really didn't think it would happen. When it did, she packed and left. The adventure of being with me became a little too much for her. She wasn't entirely stupid.

By now, I was 35 years old. Over the years, I'd blown out a knee, broken a leg, an arm, my collarbone, a hand, and foot. All required time in a cast. I was starting to worry about my future. Stealing is a high-risk, high-anxiety business. I saw the solution by becoming a businessman. But what kind of business should I try? I had some knowledge of construction and so decided to become a contractor. I did two more burglaries, enough to put together the tools required to start the business and then moved to the Sun City area near Austin. I contracted bootleg business for about a year, and then obtained a contractor's license. I opened an office near the town of Austin and soon married a respectable woman. My business grew and I prospered in a modest way.

Life Changes

One day I got this call from my wife. She said that I must come home immediately. A woman had dropped off a 9-year-old boy who said I was his father. To this day I don't know how Kim found me, but I'm grateful she did. I felt I might be ready to be a father, after all. Now I had the chance. My new wife was wonderful with my son, and he and I became friends. Although my drinking was ongoing, it didn't seem to interfere with my life. The two drunk-driving convictions I had accumulated were nothing, comparatively speaking.

Despite my many character faults, I strove to be a good father. I never hit or belittled my boy. We did numerous and frequent activities together. He was bright, enjoyed school, and soon became a straight A student. I asked him once how he had endured the trauma of being dumped off at a new home with people that were new to him. He replied that I didn't know what he had just come from and that he was relieved to be anywhere else. In later years, I would learn more about that situation.

My business continued to grow and soon, I was buying some property. But still, something was wrong. That old unhappiness was still with me. Despite all the diversions I would create for myself, sooner or later those old feelings of life's meaninglessness and an intense restlessness would reoccur. The one blessing was that the intense ferocity and rage that were a part of me for so long seemed to have dimmed significantly. That was a relief.

In an effort to stave off those unpleasant feelings, I sought another diversion. I thought I needed a new wife, one who was more sophisticated then the present one. And so I told my wife I wanted a divorce. I was unhappy and needed to grow. She, of course, didn't understand (who could?) but felt she had little choice. She took some money and left. My son missed her greatly. At times, I did, too, but soon filled that hole with a new wife, number four. We bought 13 acres of view property and put up a home. Now I was feeling O.K.

On Friday nights, I would have dinner with my accountant and the lawyer who did my legal business. Soon we were introduced to cocaine. It became the "in" party thing. For me, it quickly became the daily thing. As its use grew, so did my intake of alcohol. While I had at no time been physically abusive with my second and third wife, my fourth wife was not so lucky. She would confront my tendency to stay away from home by challenging me in a confronting way. When ignored, she would sometimes attack me physically. When she did, I would defend myself with, as before, more force than was required for mere defense. But neither of us would ever dream of calling the police. In that community, at that time, we were successful and respected people. That image seemed very important for us.

Serious Medical Problems and Alcoholics Anonymous

My drinking and drug use had taken a heavy toll. My business was neglected and in financial trouble. The IRS billed me for $78,000 in trust fund monies. All the employee withholding tax money had gone for cocaine. Physically, I was in serious trouble and ended up in the hospital. My body had given up. I was in a state of incomprehensible demoralization at the age of 46. I had no new plans to try, no more diversions to implement. Just about everything I had worked for was gone, or soon would be. I felt totally defeated, as if I had been at war with life and now had finally lost. There was some element of relief involved in this frame of mind.

I was discharged from the hospital with the instructions to never drink or use drugs again unless I wished to die. It was suggested I seek out Alcoholics Anonymous as a resource. I remember the few meetings my probation officer had me attend in the early 1970s, and the losers and idiots I remembered there. Was I now of that class myself? It was a crushing thought. However, I had nowhere else to turn. I began my journey into sobriety with AA as an angry, fearful, and resentful man. I did not immediately feel at home in AA as some do. I fought it as I had fought everything else in life for so long. But I didn't drink. It became clear to me over those first six months of sobriety that if I were to remain sober, it would require the greatest effort I had ever mustered for anything. I was desperate to remain sober, and believed, without reservation, that to drink again would be the end of me. Thoughts, serious thoughts of suicide came and went again. But my son was still with me and served as a real motivator to continue moving ahead. The trick was to learn to live life on life's terms, not my own.

When I was a boy of perhaps 10, I examined the notion of The God that ruled our home. I decided that if God was like my father, I wasn't interested. I described myself over the years as an agnostic. I didn't know if there was a God or not, and frankly, I didn't care. It made no difference in my life either way. I also had a great loathing for churches and what I called "church people." And now, here I was in a program that required me to acknowledge a higher power and adopt the notion of spirituality. What a bind to be in. The great thing was that I met others in the program that had felt as I did and they managed to make things work over time. I acknowledged AA as my higher power and it seemed to work, as I remained sober.

Six months after I entered the program of AA, I closed the doors of what was left of my business. My marriage had also ground to a halt. I took a modest note on our properties and drove away with my son, who was now a senior in high school. We rented a house together and began a new life, of sorts. I had been grateful for years that my son seemed to have escaped many of the worst elements of my character. He was intellectually very bright, literally a straight A student. Although a physically large man, he was totally nonviolent. There were times over his years with me that I was concerned about his passivity, but I never encouraged him to be otherwise. Whatever that rage was that I had carried for most of my life, wasn't present in him and I was just so grateful. He always found effective ways to solve his problems.

About eight months after I got sober, I found employment facilitating DUI classes. I would teach five to eight classes a week and found that I derived a great sense of reward from that activity. I actually enjoyed working with people. Who would have thought? I returned to school at the local community college and, like so many other recovering people, began taking courses in the chemical dependency program. When I had been sober approximately 12 months, I also began working part time at a nonprofit short-term residential program serving those with mental illness in crisis. I found I enjoyed working with the mentally ill more than with substance abusers. Then

I found that many of the mentally ill also had substance abuse problems. It was a wonderfully challenging population of people. After leaving my fourth wife, I had abstained from relationships for nearly a year. Then I met a woman who seemed to have all the "right stuff" and we were off and running together. But in a short period of time, our relationship was as turbulent and chaotic as any I'd had while I was drinking. Sobriety hadn't changed a thing in regards to my relating to women.

Therapy

After an incident in which I threw her physically out of my house, it occurred to me that though AA was keeping me sober and that my life was progressing in good directions, if I were to ever have any hope of having a healthy relationship with a female, I needed to try some professional help. I was referred to a female Ph.D. in Austin who agreed to work with me. And so began my journey in therapy. She seemed to know just how fast I could go and always kept me challenged. At times, she suggested I take a short break, and that was also helpful. She took considerable time to educate me on women's issues and how women think differently than men. I began to understand something about women's values and needs. To me, it was amazing stuff. Then came the day, after about six months, when my insurance ran out. I wanted desperately to continue but was unable to pay for the full cost alone. My therapist told me not to worry. She stated she had a strong belief in me and what I was doing and usually had one client she worked with without charge. She would keep going with me as long as it was productive. I have to say that of the many beneficial things that came from my almost two and a half years with her, her belief in me was the single most impacting event. I had always had so little belief in myself and been such a terrible disappointment to so many, that to have a person, especially a woman of her status, express belief in me was huge. When I reflect back over the years since then, that one thing still stands out.

I recall a time when, in an effort to express my gratitude for her caring and skills, I blurted out that I would, if needed, protect her, kill for her. She laughed and said, "If you want to do something for me, then please go love someone, and you might try starting with yourself." Obviously, I never forgot that either.

After about two and a half years at the crisis unit where I was employed, and having moved up through several positions, I became the associate director. We had, for some time, recognized that many of our clients were dually diagnosed. That is, they had both a major mental illness and a problem with substance abuse. I was sent to the few programs in the state that had a program to treat this diagnosis with the goal of creating our own program to address the issue. One of the places I visited was a program specifically designed to provide those services in a long-term, social model, residential setting. It was located on a beautiful plot of 60 acres in the Hill Country outside of Fredericksburg, Texas. I fell in love with the place and had soon changed places of employment. That was 10 years ago, and I'm still employed there today. I'm no longer in my original position but continue to greatly enjoy working with the mentally ill.

Epiphany

Soon after moving to the Fredericksburg area, I met a woman with whom I became friends over a period of about a year. I had been renting a room in her house. During this time, we would talk with each other every evening, about anything and everything. I finally stated that I would like to date her. She responded positively but told me that I would have to move because she didn't feel comfortable dating a man who was also living in her house. I was in shock. This was not the way I had envisioned things going. But move I did, and we began dating. After a few dates, I made my move to consummate our relationship physically. She explained to me that she didn't operate that way. She required things like a commitment, HIV testing, etc. I replied that I too felt that way. Sure I did. My respect for her continued to grow. This was a woman far different from any in my past. After dating for six months, we began to talk about marriage. At that point, we sought the counseling services of my therapist, whom I hadn't seen for a while. For another six months, sometimes singly, sometimes together, she worked with us on a weekly basis. It was time well spent. We were married and, yes, my therapist was there. Next month we will celebrate our sixth anniversary.

I have never abused my wife, either verbally or physically. Rather, I have learned from her how to love, to share, to care, and sometimes to stand back. Perhaps the single most important thing I have learned concerning being a man is that thing called "commitment." I've learned to keep my commitments and to not make them hastily. Although my life today is far different than it was years ago, I still have many of those old character defects waiting to rise again if the right sets of circumstance are operating. I do my best to stay out of those situations.

My values have reformed themselves over these past 11-plus years of sobriety. I have slowly developed a spiritual life, which has continued to deepen over time. My relationship with God, as I understand Him, is the single most important element in my life today. I have no complicated theology. I don't even understand how it works. All I know is that without God, my life was horrific. With God, my life is good. Some of the wreckage of my past I've been able to directly address. Much of it I haven't. My first wife, Kim, lives in the south, where she continues to be addicted to drugs. The father she was so determined not to be like, she has become. And to my great amusement, the father I was so determined not to be like, I have, in ways, also become. Unfortunately, he died of Alzheimer's before he could see my life really turn around. My wonderful mother, with whom I have a loving relationship, is around and clear minded at age 89. My son is now 28. After high school, from which he graduated with highest honors, he joined the Army. He was in the Desert Storm conflict, and after four years of service, again became a civilian. He graduated as a psychology major from college in San Antonio several years ago. While in the Army, he also began to drink and was by his account immediately out of control and in trouble. But before he had done any irreversible damage to his life, he, too, became a member of AA while he was stationed overseas. He has now been with us (my wife and me) in AA for the past eight years.

Today, I count myself as being among the most fortunate of men. How I survived myself is beyond my understanding. I was blessed with good parents, a stable home, and excellent values. There is no one to blame for the direction my life took for so many years. I don't have an explanation for my behavior that I'm comfortable with. Perhaps there was a biological element that would explain some things. I think perhaps there was. But the important thing for me today is to use my past experience to help others. I rarely disclose details of my past unless there is some clear way it will benefit someone. I am, to this day, deeply ashamed of my past behavior. But I'm one of the fortunate ones who are given a second chance to live life. And life on life's terms today is better than just good. It's better than anything I could have imagined for all those crazy years.

Comments about the Case

It would be too simple to diagnose Mr. R as having a *Personality Disorder, Antisocial Type*. Certainly, his behavior would suggest such a diagnosis. Several colleagues who read the case said that, unquestionably, he had an early onset *conduct disorder* that soon became a Personality Disorder, Antisocial Type. Like Mr. R, however, I'm inclined to think that there were other things at play here. Personality-disordered people sometimes make changes in their lives but usually not to this dramatic an extent. If something were the matter, organically, as he is inclined to believe, what might that have been? In the absence of any data, we're left in the dark, but we can speculate.

Clearly, his father's discipline suggests physical abuse. His childhood violent behavior is similar to that of many abused children. His description of his mother sounds as if she were trying her best to make up for the friction in the relationship between Mr. R. and his father. His hostility toward women, as witnessed by his treatment of many of the women in his life, sounds as if he had major concerns about his own masculinity, something he shares with us in his story.

Antisocial Personality Disorders of the very dysfunctional variety that Mr. R. appears to have had, rarely improve to the significant extent that his did. If anything, those with these disorders often tend to go into emotional decline in their midyears, marked by alcohol addiction and severe depression. Neither happened to Mr. R. Might there have been some transient psychotic features involved in his behavior? There is a type of personality disorder mentioned in the DSM-4 called *schizotypal personality disorder* (DSM-IV Code # 301.22), and a review of the criteria tend to confirm this diagnosis, to some degree. The DSM-IV defines this disorder as follows:

> A pervasive pattern of social and interpersonal deficits marked by acute discomfort with, and reduced capacity for, close relationships as well as by cognitive or perceptual distortions and eccentricities of behavior, beginning by early adulthood and present in a variety of contexts as indicated in five or more of the following: 1) Odd beliefs; 2) Unusual perceptual experiences; 3) Odd thinking; 4) Suspicious or paranoid ideations; 5) Inappropriate or constricted affect; 6) Lack of close friends; 7) Excessive social anxiety. (APA, 1994, p. 645)

Might he have suffered from bi-polar disorder exacerbated by use of alcohol? That may be a possibility, given his severe mood swings. But when all is said and done, a review of the case by four ex-alcoholics would suggest that Mr. R. was an alcoholic. Feeling odd and out of place as a child is how all four ex-alcoholics describe their feelings as children. All of the readers suggested that he was probably drinking heavily by elementary school, although he claims not to have begun drinking until adolescence. The epiphany he experienced upon getting clean and sober, they suggest, is typical of a number of ex-alcoholics who, once sober, make significant changes in their lives. The sense of love and redemption he describes after ending his alcohol abuse is common, and many ex-alcoholics find themselves attracted to the helping professions, as a result.

It may help in understanding this case to recognize Mr. R's considerable intelligence. Intelligence is a key aspect of resilience. He also had a very supportive mother and many social and work-related skills that helped him achieve success throughout his life. His family had very positive values, and while he questions many of the values, a fair number stayed with him throughout his life. And ultimately, he was able to use this combination of intelligence and values to build a new life. His strong relationship with his son and wife, and his commitment to working with others are all indicators that people change. We should always be positive and hopeful in our work because, with help, many people like Mr. R. make life changes that are miraculous.

Integrative Questions

1. Mr. R. appears to have had a well-developed conduct disorder by the time he entered grade school. If you were his therapist, what would you have done to help Mr. R. when his acting-out behavior became a problem in school?

2. As a pillar of the community, do you believe anything would have happened to Mr. R's father for his excessive use of force in punishing Mr. R.? Explain your answer.

3. There is a great deal of self-loathing in Mr. R's destructive behavior. Why do you believe Mr. R. had such low self-esteem, given the position of his family in the community and his loving mother?

4. Even before he stopped drinking and using drugs, Mr. R's behavior began to moderate itself. To what do you attribute this change in behavior?

5. Mr. R's son began to have an alcohol problem but was able to control it. What mechanisms do you think he used to control his drinking?

Reference

American Psychiatric Association. (1994). *Diagnostic and statistical manual* (4th Ed.). Washington, DC: American Psychiatric Association.

Eliminating Childhood Violence

This chapter was written after having conversations with parents who must deal with the violence their children endure at school, in the community, in shopping malls, and in almost every arena of American life. The chapter summarizes the tough feedback given by parents regarding their concerns about youth violence. Like the parents to whom I've spoken, violence in children frightens most of us. No child should have to be bullied or worry about violence at school, at a movie theater, as they shop, or at a party. We should assure our children that, as adults, we want them to live and grow up in a safe society. For many of us, however, the legacy of safety seems less and less assured. This chapter summarizes the parental feedback received and the research data to suggest ways of making America a safer place for everyone.

Have We Given Up on Controlling Violence?

More than just a few times in researching this book, I read articles by authors who have essentially given up on the issue of youth violence, which is to say that they have given up on children and, in a way, they've given up on America. Many of the authors writing about youth violence argue that we have a violent society and far too many dysfunctional parents to ever rid ourselves of violence. Others argue that a violent mass culture makes any attempt to reduce violence unlikely to succeed. And still others suggest that peer groups in America are so dysfunctional that even if children make it into their teenage years without being violent, somewhere along the way, maybe one time out of four, violence will rear its ugly head and children will be involved as victims or as perpetrators of violence. The experience will change them forever.

A few examples of the pessimism encountered by authors writing about youth violence are as follows: Rae-Grant, McConville, and Fleck (1999) write, "Because exclusive individual clinical interventions for violent conduct disorders do not work, the child and adolescent psychiatrist must seek opportunities to be a leader or team member in well-organized and well-funded community prevention efforts" (p. 239). Sprague and Hill (2000) complain about poorly matched treatment approaches that deny the severity of the problem. Elliott, Hamburg, and Williams (1998) report that counseling has no effect on the problems of antisocial and predelinquent youth. Steiner and Stone (1999) note widespread pessimism among clinicians regarding their willingness to work with violent youth. Fortunately others believe that treating violence requires the clinician to practice with flexibility and to maintain a positive stance on the likelihood of children to change, a position, seldom noted in the literature but summed up well by Saleebey (2000), who writes, "healing, transformation, regeneration, and resilience almost always occur within the confines of a personal, friendly, and dialogical relationship . . . the more the power of a caring relationship is actualized with those served, the better the individual's future" (p. 128).

While many authors call for communitywide efforts to combat youth violence, Robert Putnam (2000) writes that Americans have stopped joining organizations and have disassociated themselves from the political process. This lack of community and political involvement makes dealing with childhood violence almost impossible. In an interview with Stossel (2000), Putnam says that

> Americans today have retreated into isolation. So argues the political scientist Robert D. Putnam. . . . Evidence shows, Putnam says, that fewer and fewer contemporary Americans are unionizing, voting, rallying around shared causes, participating in religious services, inviting each other over, or doing much of anything collectively. In fact, when we do occasionally gather—for twelve-step support encounters and the like—it's most often only as an excuse to focus on ourselves in the presence of an audience. Supper eaten with friends or family has given way to supper gobbled in solitude, with only the glow of the television screen for companionship. (p. 1)

Almost all of the authors that were read for the preparation of this book call for increased effort on the part of America's schools to work cooperatively with the child welfare system and the police to identify abused children, school bullies, and children beginning to show the early signs of violent behavior. However, many of these same authors note that schools seldom report violent behavior to the police and that no-violence policies are often inconsistently handled. Schools are where youth crime frequently takes place, but the very center of youth crime activity, the school system, seems unwilling or unable to cooperate with law and child welfare enforcement to identify, report, and then work with community agencies. As examples of the lack of early identification and intervention in childhood violence, Craig and Pepler (1997) believe that bullying is often tolerated by teachers and estimate that teachers intervene in only 4 percent of all incidents involving bullying behavior. Murray and Myers (1998) report that only 9 percent of the juvenile violent crimes committed in schools are reported to criminal justice authorities, compared with a 37 percent report rate for similar juvenile street crimes. The authors believe that these data suggest that schools are avoiding involvement with the juvenile justice system.

One of the strongest complaints from parents is the violence children see in the popular culture. When a child sees 8,000 murders on television, videos, and video games by the time he or she finishes grade school, (Simons 2001), and we have a serious youth violence problem in America, we must begin to wonder if violent entertainment provokes and encourages violence in children. The American Psychological Association, on its national Web site (2002), notes a relationship between watching violence in the media and violent behavior when it reports,

> Children who watched many hours of TV violence when they were in elementary school tended to also show a higher level of aggressive behavior when they became teenagers. By observing these youngsters until they were 30 years old, researchers found that the ones who'd watched a lot of TV when they were eight years old were more likely to be arrested and prosecuted for criminal acts as adults.

Like most of us who read that violence is declining in America, what we see, feel, and experience every day in our lives suggests that violence data are incorrect. We have a great deal of information to suggest that Americans disagree with published reports by the FBI and the Justice Department that youth violence is decreasing. One indicator of the disparity between crime data and the underlying meaning of that data is provided in the Surgeon General's Report on Youth Violence (Satcher, 2001). In that report, youth were asked if they had been involved in violent juvenile crime, regardless of whether they had been arrested. The Surgeon General's Report (2001) noted,

> Since 1993, when the epidemic of juvenile violence peaked, youth violence has declined steadily nationwide as signaled by downward trends in arrest records, victimization data, and hospital emergency records. But the problem has not been resolved. Another key indicator of violence . . . youth's confidential reports about their own violent behavior . . . reveals no change since 1993 in the proportion of young people who have committed physically injurious and potentially lethal acts. Moreover, arrests for aggravated assaults have declined only slightly and in 1999 remained nearly 70% higher than the pre-epidemic years of 1982-1993.
> Arrest records give only a partial picture of youth violence. For every youth arrested in any given year in the late 1990s, at least 10 were engaged in some form of violent behavior that could have seriously injured or killed another person. (Satcher, 2001, p. 1)

Another indicator that published crime data paint a biased picture of youth crime is found in the Milton J. Eisenhower Foundation Commission on Violence Report (2002), which notes a 120 percent increase in the fear of crime since 1967. The Commission's report goes on to say in its 2002 Executive Summary,

> The short-run decline in fear and violence since 1993 has led politicians and the media to a new and misplaced "triumphalism." To some extent, the new triumphalism represents a state of denial—in which we exaggerate our recent successes against serious crime and ignore the implications of our high violence rates vis-à-vis other countries, not to mention our vast prison population. But there is also another prob-

lem. Although there have been significant reductions in violent crime since the early 1990s, the new triumphalism is misleading on the "why" of those declines. This interpretation is dangerous, in that it could lead us to adopt (or to continue) all the wrong anticrime policies while ignoring the things that could make an enduring difference.

When just murder is broken out in [the FBI reports on violence], the rate per 100,000 has gone down slightly from the late 1960s to the late 1990s. But this is so despite enormous increases in the prison population, and despite the very significant medical improvements in our ability to keep people from dying if they are badly hurt in an assault. The picture is considerably more troubling, moreover, if we look at murder trends among different age groups. For though murder deaths have fallen at all ages from the 1990s peak, they remain much higher for the young than they were in the era of the Violence Commission. Among 14–17 year olds, the risk of death by murder was almost half again as high in 1998 as in 1970, despite a sharp fall since 1993. For those aged 18–24, the situation is worse: their homicide death rate remained nearly twice as high in 1998 as it was in 1970. Long-term reductions in murder have come entirely among people over 25. In addition, in 1999, murder increased by about 10% in New York City, which has received so much attention over recent years of decline.

Eliminating Childhood Violence

What can we do? Childhood violence in America is a serious problem regardless of reports to the contrary. The following recommendations come from a number of parents, teachers, and professionals, all of whom are concerned about childhood violence and want to see it eliminated in this country.

A No-Tolerance Policy toward Child Abuse and Neglect

Herrenkohl and Russo (2001) note the relationship between abusive child-rearing practices and early-childhood violence:

> The significance of early childhood aggression for the child and for society is considerable. Aggressive young children have more difficulties relating positively to peers, have more school problems, tend to be more isolated, and have more emotional problems. Both child and society are affected by the demonstrated relationship between early childhood aggression and adolescent violent behavior . . . a relationship [exits] between abusive and neglectful child rearing and childhood aggression. (p. 3)

This book has repeatedly documented the finding that abused children are the most significant group of children to experience early-onset childhood violence. Clearly, early intervention on behalf of children is the most positive way to reduce childhood violence. If child abuse is the most significant cause of early-childhood violence, our child welfare system must do a much better job of investigating and intervening, when necessary, in child abuse and neglect. This is not to say that parents can't learn to modify their behavior or that children need to be taken from homes. There is ample evidence that when parents are offered help with child rearing practices and a number of other issues that negatively affect child-rearing, many improve their parenting styles and children do much better. Moore, Armsden, and Gogerty (1998), among others, report significant improvement in parenting with related improvement in the behavior of children when early intervention is offered. Commenting on their experience in helping abusive parents, the authors reinforce the need for early intervention:

> This study indicates that early intervention may mitigate some of [the] negative consequences in maltreated children. Researchers have called for early intervention programs to be included in crime prevention efforts. The results of this study champion that recommendation by documenting the far-reaching value of an ecological intervention model of parent education and support, and developmental and behavioral remediation of the very young maltreated child. (p. 14)

A Well-Trained Core of Professionals for the Criminal Justice Field

While the need for early intervention with abusive parents is obviously very important, the preparation of professionals to work with violent young children is equally important. One of the troubling findings discussed in this book is the lack of creative programs to limit violence. This suggests, for many people, a lack of creative professionals to work in the violence field who bring with them new and innovative ideas about violence prevention and intervention. This concern for well-trained professionals also relates to the level of scholarship in the criminal justice field. Many of the articles read for this book were full of praise for programs that, on close examination, were not doing well. Briscoe (1997), for example, found the juvenile justice system in Texas to be effective but neglected to mention the significant problem Texas has with crime. Texas, as you may recall from earlier chapters, has the highest incarceration rate of any state in the country, yet has half the population of California. In Texas, which incarcerates more people than any other state (one in five of the new prisoners in the United States are found in the Texas correctional system), the crime rate fell to only half that of the average of the United States and the least of any of the five largest states (Gamboa, 2000, p. 1A).

An astonishing 5 percent of the adult population in Texas (706,000 people) is in prison, on parole, or on probation. Of the 163,000 prisoners in Texas, 89,400 are incarcerated for nonviolent crimes. African Americans in Texas are incarcerated at seven times the rate of whites, while probation is given to black prisoners only 20 percent of the time, compared with the 45 percent of white prisoners. If the Texas Youth Commission is doing such a splendid job, then why the dismal overall crime statistics, unless, of course, none of the youth from youth commission programs commits adult crimes and all crime is done by adults new to the state.

It is this sense of disbelief in the reporting of crime data and the value of the current juvenile justice system that gives way to such pessimism among many Americans. They don't believe official reports, and they tend to think the public sector does little more than warehouse violent children who will, ultimately, move on to adult facilities as the seriousness of their crimes increases. An article by Lichblau (2001) is a good example of the discrepancies in crime reporting that leads many of us not to trust the reports or the people who prepare them. The U.S. Bureau of Justice reported that for the years 1999–2000, violent crime declined by 15 percent while property crime declined by 10 percent. The FBI, on the other hand, and for the same period of time, found that violent crime had increased by a tenth of a percent and that property crime was unchanged. "How can you trust crime data when you have this sort of major disagreement between two government agencies?" parents ask. How indeed? In fact, most of the parents with whom I spoke think of the criminal justice system as an inefficient revolving door where dangerous felons and not-dangerous felons are thrown together and where prisoners beat, rape, mutilate, and kill one another with impunity. "If they can't even count crime right, how do we expect them to know how to stop crime?" another parent asked. I don't know the answer, and unless we have a core of highly trained and creative professionals willing to work in the criminal justice field, this type of inconsistent data will continue to confuse us, and the troubled people who pass through the criminal justice system will do just that—pass through without any major change in their behavior. For very young children, that's criminal.

Control of Violence in the Media

It's time for us to take a serious stand against violence in the mass media. Children who watch violent behavior in the media are influenced by it. In time, they become so satiated with violent messages that they become desensitized to violence in its many forms. At some point, the violence they watch in their lives goes from fantasy to reality. A report by the Federal Trade Commission (FTC) addressed the question of violence in the media (Pitofsky, 2000). The FTC report reviewed self-regulation and industry practices in the motion picture, music recording, and electronic game industries with respect to their advertisement of products with violent content to youngsters (p. I). Two specific questions were raised in President Clinton's mandate to the FTC: (1) Do the industries promote products they themselves acknowledge warrant parental caution in venues where children make up a substantial percentage of the audience, and (2) are these advertisements intended to attract children and teenagers? The answers to both questions for all three segments of the entertainment industry were, plainly, "yes."

The Eisenhower Commission on Violence Report (2002) went a step further on the subject on a violent mass culture when it wrote,

> Local television news too often emphasizes violence and too seldom produces thoughtful stories on what works. This helps create a "mean world syndrome" in the minds of viewers, who then often conclude that nothing works. In terms of network television entertainment violence, not every child who watches a lot of violence or plays a lot of violent games will grow up to be violent. Other forces must converge, as they did recently in Colorado. But just as every cigarette increases the chance that someday you will get lung cancer, every exposure to violence increases the chances that some day a child will behave more violently than they would otherwise. (Summary of Findings)

While the urge to censor violent films, television programs, and video games is strong, another more democratic approach is suggested: parental vigilance and picketing of violent films and the organizations that make them. The best way to stop violence in the popular culture is to refuse to allow children to watch violent films, buy violent video games, or watch violence on television. Many parents do that now and it works. In a market-driven economy, once viewership is down, the belief that violence sells will no longer drive the mass culture, and we will have a great deal less media violence influencing young children.

Schools That Work to Limit Violence

Bullying in schools must be stopped. As Espelage, Bosworth, and Simon (2000) write, "Students who bully were themselves at an increased risk of being physically abusive and of having a criminal record as adults. The entire climate of a school can be affected by bullying behaviors if they go unchecked" (p. 326). Natvig, Albrektsen, and Qvarnstrom (2001) go a step further when they note,

> The main aims of health promoting schools are to provide a healthy environment and to encourage healthy lifestyles for the pupils. Bullying behavior is one aspect that is expected to have an adverse effect, and preventing such behavior is an important task. (p. 370)

Two questions many parents have of the schools is why such behavior is permitted, and why aren't immediate steps taken to prevent bullying with all of its negative impact on children and the school environment? Schools must do a better job of identifying children at risk of violent behavior. Bullying is one of the earliest signs of violence in children. Its existence is not difficult to identify for any trained teacher. If childhood violence is to be prevented, schools must do a better job of identifying children at risk for violence at an early point in their acting-out behavior. One trained mental health professional in a school can have an enormously positive impact on children through the suggestions provided to teachers in containing violence.

Funding for Research

Some negative things have been said about criminal justice writers who paint inaccurate pictures of violence in America, but many researchers in the field are doing very important work. Zolondek et al. (2001), for example, collected self-reports from youth waiting to be evaluated for sexual offenses and found that a very large number of them were molesting their younger siblings. This is significant research, and we can only applaud the researchers for a very tough and compelling piece of work. But there's just no way around it: We really are in our infancy in the treatment of childhood violence. Much more money needs to be spent on developing effective treatment approaches at the individual, family, institutional, and community levels to treat and then, ultimately, prevent childhood violence.

A Positive Attitude When It Comes to Children

We often like to think that we can predict behavior. In fact, a good deal of this book is about predicting the behavior of children who begin violent acting out early in life. However, research on developmental resilience has introduced ideas that challenge three prominent beliefs about the way children develop into adults, and these still dominate our thinking: (1) There are fixed stages of development, (2) childhood trauma usually leads to adult psychopathology (Benard, 1994), and (3) there are social conditions, interpersonal relationships, and institutional arrangements that are so toxic they inevitably lead to serious problems in the everyday functioning of children and adults, families, and communities (Rutter, 1994).

In previously cited research by Werner and Smith (1982), a third of the children evaluated by several measures who were thought to be at significant risk for adolescent problems actually developed into competent and confident young adults by age 18. In their follow-up study, Werner and Smith (1992) found that two of three of the remaining two-thirds of children at risk had turned into caring adults by age 32. One of their primary theories was that children have "self-righting" tendencies as they mature. This finding is supported by similar findings of serious antisocial behavior in children. The Surgeon General's report on Youth Violence (Satcher, 2001), in summarizing the research on youth violence, notes that "most highly aggressive children or children with behavioral disorders do not become violent offenders" (p. 9). The Surgeon General's report goes on to say that most youth violence begins in adolescence and ends with the transition to adulthood. If people didn't change, then these early-life behaviors would suggest that all violence in youth would continue into adulthood. The Surgeon General's report further suggests that the reasons for change in violent children often relates to treatment programs, maturation, and biosocial factors (self-righting tendencies, or what has more recently been termed *resilience*) that influences the life path of even the most violent youthful offenders. This and other research suggests that people *do* change, and that learning from prior experience appears to be an important reason for change. Continued research on resilience and self-righting abilities are absolutely essential if we are to understand how violent young children grow and change, and if creative treatment programs are to be developed.

More Treatment and Less Punishment

Unless we want to put more and more children in prison, where they learn to be really violent and where the probability is high that they will continue to commit violent acts, we should choose to build fewer prisons and place our emphasis on treatment. The Eisenhower Commission Report on Violence (2002) notes the political reality of sending increasing numbers of youth to prison:

> America's failure to reduce endemic fear and violence over the long run is paralleled by its failure to establish justice. Nearly 1 quarter of all young children live in poverty. America is the most unequal country in the industrialized world in terms of income,

wages, and wealth. As a result of the racial bias in our mandatory sentencing system, especially for drugs, 1 of every 3 young African-American males is in the prison-industrial complex, on probation or on parole in America at any one time. In big cities, it is about 1 of every 2. (Major Findings Section)

At a practical level, Glicken and Sechrest (2003) found little evidence that prisons reduce recidivism rates among violent children at a greater level than community outreach programs or group homes. If that's the case, why not channel the funding from juvenile prisons to treatment facilities where creative programming might help determine what works in treatment, and why? And if it works, we should be training more helping professionals to intervene in early-onset violent children. The illogic of building more and more prisons is found in California, a state that spends more on maintaining prisons than it spends on higher education. Putting children in jails seems utterly wrong. Ring-Kurtz, Sonnichen, and Hoover-Dempsey (1995) note the value of using a child's positive attributes (strengths) when mental health services are offered in a school setting. Oswald (2001) reports, "Individual child strengths may mitigate the impact of serious psychiatric symptoms and risk, allowing children to remain in homelike settings successfully" (p.9). There are surely other options to prisons for America's children who are beginning to exhibit violent behavior. And as Saleebey (2000) notes in discussing the strengths perspective,

> If healers are seen as non-judgmental, trustworthy, caring and expert, they have some influential tools at hand, whether they are addressing the depths of a serious depression or the disappointments and pains of unemployment. A relationship of this sort provides a milieu and context for confronting the difficult and considering the imaginable. (Saleebey, 2000, p. 131)

Parents Make Suggestions: A Case Study

Elliott is an 11-year-old fire setter. Thus far, his fire setting has been limited to abandoned sheds and old structures he carefully surveys to make certain that no one is inside. Elliott is fascinated with fire. He loves to watch the flames and reported how they change color and intensity in a notebook that, when found, was used to help convict him. Elliott knows that fire setting is dangerous and against the law, but seems unable to stop himself. He says that the sight of a fire is so beautiful that

> I feel like the world is peaceful when I watch a fire. I've always been that way. Whenever there's a fire in town, I can hardly wait to see it. One time an AMTRAK train went off the tracks and hit a gas line and the fire went on for a long time. I rode my bike to see it and I couldn't leave, it was so pretty. I don't hurt anybody. I make sure of that, and I'd like to be a fireman or a forest fire fighter when I grow up. Everybody I talk to says that they'd be too worried about me starting fires to let me have a job like that, but I know that I'd be fine. I'd never start a fire, and I'd know just how a fire thinks and acts, and I could put one out just like that. I hate arsonists. They burn for money and they hurt people. I start fires because it's beautiful. Just like some people paint pictures, I like to start fires.

Discussion

The parents who read this case had these comments to make:

1. This kid needs help, not jail.
2. This kid should be seen by someone who understands why people set fires, and he should be helped. I don't know if he should be in a juvenile facility, because he's not exactly like other violent kids, but he does need to be somewhere safe where he can't do any harm.
3. This 11-year-old kid is going to kill somebody at the rate he's going. He's got a serious problem, and he needs special help.

The DSM-IV notes the symptoms of *pyromania* (DSM-IV Code #312.33; APA, 1994, p. 615):

> Deliberate and purposeful fire setting on more than one occasion; tension or affect arousal before the act. Fascination with fire; pleasurable gratification watching fires; the fire is not done for profit or monetary gain; the episode is not better accounted for by a Conduct Disorder, a Manic Episode, or Ant-social Personality Disorder. (APA, 1994, p. 615)

Using the DSM-IV as a guide, Elliott doesn't seem to have a conduct disorder. There is something uniquely gratifying about fires for him. Some clinician's think that what's unique about fire setting is that it acts as a sexual gratifier, and they link early-onset fire setting with sexual issues. These facile ideas about fire setters seem completely off the mark. For a number of fire setters, fire has fascinated them ever since they can remember. Sakheim and Osborn (1999), in their study on serious versus nonserious juvenile fire setters, noted that firesetters often have a high incidents of family dysfunction, including drug and alcohol addiction, psychosis, and criminality. They also reported that research suggests that early-onset fire setters often have a high incidence of hyperactivity, psychosis, rage reactions, enuresis, and aggressive and antisocial behavior. When fire setters were compared with a comparable sample of nonfire setters, many of these differences did not hold up in studies attempting to find the individual characteristics of early-onset fire setters. In other words, it's difficult to develop a profile of fire setters, and it's difficult to know why children set fires, other than the stories they tell us and the reasons they provide. In suggesting the treatment for youthful fire setters, Sakheim and Osborn (1999) wrote,

> In our experience, the successful treatment and rehabilitation of the "severe" fire-setter requires early detection, accurate differential diagnosis, assessment of the degree of risk of recurrence, and appropriate intervention. "Minor" and "moderate" risk fire-setters are usually treated safely in the community with parent and child counseling, fire safety education, and social skills training. Only a program of long-term psychotherapy and behavior modification, however, augmented by case work with the parents to improve their understanding of the needs of their child, and their parenting skills, taking place within the confines of a structured residential treatment center, can help persistent (serious) fire-setting children to interrupt their attraction to fire [Lowenstein 1989]. (p. 431)

(continued)

Continued

When this quote was read to parents, they all thought it was a worthwhile approach to helping Elliott, whom they categorized as a moderately serious fire setter. As one parent said, "It's helpful when you know what people say who have studied the problem. If the juvenile court knew about this research, they could probably be a lot more helpful than if somebody made a recommendation who knew nothing about fire setting." Most of the parents agreed. The use of what is called "evidence-based practice" to help children like Elliott makes good sense. Evidence-based practice comes from the medical field and indicates that professionals should know which treatments might best help a condition before a treatment is begun. If there are no treatments that are solidly linked to successful treatment, then we should be cautious because the treatment selected might cause more harm than good. In the violence field, many interventions are used with poor research validation, which may explain the pessimism in the field for work with violent offenders.

This is not to say that nothing should be done when we're uncertain about the best choice of interventions. It is, however to note that clinicians should have a very good understanding of the relevant literature before a treatment intervention is used. And once it is used, the clinician should evaluate the effectiveness of the intervention and share it with other clinicians. This sharing of small pieces of data is one important way for the helping professions to build a body of knowledge about the most efficacious treatment interventions with violent children.

Summary

This chapter describes the feelings of some parents on the subject of childhood violence. Many feel that violence is out of control and that the authorities are dealing with it badly. There is also a feeling that far too much abuse and neglect of children exists. Parents wonder about the competence of our social agencies to help lower the rate of violence to children. The popular culture is criticized for its obsessive selling of violence to children and its unwillingness to take responsibility for the negative impact violence has on children. School systems are criticized for not dealing with violence in the classroom and for permitting far too much bullying. More research into understanding the developmental paths of early violence is called for, and much effective treatment approaches for violent children are encouraged.

Integrative Questions _____

1. Can you think of some positive rewards we can give parents for controlling the amount of violence their children are permitted to view in the media?

2. Why do you think schools do such a minimal job of controlling bullying in and out of the classroom?

3. The child welfare system has been criticized for not responding well to child abuse and neglect. What would you do to improve the work of child welfare agencies in America so that they intervene quickly and effectively in child maltreatment cases?

4. The lack of effective treatment approaches for early violence suggests the need for better-trained professionals and more money for research. Why do you think we provide so little money for research and training when youth violence is such a serious problem?

5. In this chapter, much was made of the lack of credibility of reports on the amounts of violence in America. Why do you think people are so cynical about reports showing that violence and crime are down in any given year?

References

American Psychiatric Association. (1994). *Diagnostic and statistical manual* (4th Ed.). Washington, DC: American Psychiatric Association.

American Psychological Association National Website.(June 2002). Is youth violence just another fact of life? Available online at www.apa.org/ppo/issues/pbviolence.html

Benard, B. (December 1994). Applications of resilience. Paper presented at a conference on the Role of Resilience in Drug Abuse, Alcohol Abuse, and Mental Illness, Washington, DC.

Briscoe, J. (September 1997). Breaking the cycle of violence: A rational approach to at-risk youth. *Federal Probation*, 61, 3–13.

Craig, W.M., and Pepler, D.J. (1997). Observations of bullying and victimization in the schoolyard. *Canadian Journal of School Psychology*, 13, 41–60.

Elliott, D.S., Hamburg, B., and Williams, K.R. (1998). *Violence in American schools: A new perspective*. Boulder, CO: Center for the Study and Prevention of Violence.

Espelage, D.L., Bosworth, K., and Simon, T.R. (Summer 2000). Examining the social context of bullying behavior in early adolescence. *Journal of Counseling and Development*, 78, 326–333.

Gamboa, S. (August 28, 2000). Texas incarcerates most, fastest in U.S. *San Antonio Express News*, p. 1A.

Glicken, M.D., and Sechrest, D. (2003). *The role of the helping professions in treating and preventing violence*. Boston: Allyn & Bacon.

Herrenkohl, R.C., and Russo, M.J. (2001). Abusive early child rearing and early childhood aggression. *Child Maltreatment*, 6, 3–16.

Lichblau, E. (February 1, 2001). Survey reports 15% drop in crime. *Austin American-Statesman*, pp. A-1, A-11.

Lowenstein, L.E. (1989). The etiology, diagnosis and treatment of the fire setting behavior of children. *Child Psychiatry and Human Development*, 19, 186–194.

Milton J. Eisenhower Foundation Commission on Violence Report. (2002). *To establish justice, to insure domestic tranquility: A thirty year update of the national commission on the causes and prevention of violence*. Washington, DC: The Milton S. Eisenhower Foundation (www.eisenhowerfoundation.org/aboutus/publications/fr_justice.html)

Moore, E., Armsden, G., and Gogerty, P.L. (1998). A twelve-year follow-up study of maltreated and at-risk children who received early therapeutic childcare. *Child Maltreatment*, 3, 3–16.

Murray, B.A., and Myers, M.A. (April 1998). Conduct disorders and the special-education trap. *Education Digest*, 63, 48–53.

Natvig, G.K., Albrektsen, G., and Qvarnstrom, U. (2001). School-related stress experience as a risk factor for bullying behavior. *Journal of Youth and Adolescence*, 30, 561–575.

Oswald, D.P. (Fall 2001). Child strengths and the level of care for children with emotional and behavioral disorders. *Journal of Emotional and Behavioral Disorders*.

Pitofsky, R. (September 2000). Marketing violent entertainment to children: A review of self-regulation and industry practices in the motion picture, music recording and electronic game industries. *Report to the Federal Trade Commission*.

Putnam, R.D. (2000). *Bowling alone*. New York: Touchstone Books.

Rae-Grant, N., McConville, B.J., and Fleck, S. (March 1999). Violent behavior in children and youth: Preventive intervention from a psychiatric perspective. *Journal of the American Academy of Child and Adolescent Psychiatry*, 38, 235–241.

Ring-Kurtz, S.E., Sonnichsen, S., and Hoover-Dempsey, K.V. (1995). School-based mental health services for children. In L. Bickman and D. Rogs (Eds.), *Children's mental health services: Research, policy, and evaluation* (vol. 1, 16.117–144). Thousand Oaks, CA: Sage.

Rutter, M. (1994). Stress research: Accomplishments and tasks ahead. In R. J. Haggerty, L.R. Sherrod, N. Garmezy, and M. Rutter (Eds.), *Stress, risk, and resilience in children and adolescents: Processes, mechanisms, and interventions* (pp. 354–385). Cambridge, England: Cambridge University Press.

Sakheim, G.A., and Osborn, E. (July 1999). Severe vs. non-severe fire-setters revisited. *Child Welfare*, 78, 411–434.

Saleebey, D. (2000). Power in the people; strength and hope. *Advances in Social Work*, 1, 127–136.

Satcher, D. (2001). Youth violence: A report of the surgeon general. U.S. Department of Health and Human Services, Office of the Surgeon General. Washington, DC. Available online at: http://surgeongeneral.cog/libraray/youthviolence/report.html

Simons, L. (2001). Media violence. *Offsprings*, 1, 12–16.

Sprague, J.R., and Hill W.M. (Spring 2000). Early identification and intervention for youth with antisocial and violent behavior. *Exceptional Children*, 66, 367–379.

Stacher, D. (2001). Surgeon General's Reports on Youth Violence (2001). Available online at: http://www.surgeongeneral.gov/library/youthviolence/

Steiner, H., and Stone, L.A. (March 1999). Introduction: violence and related psychopathology. *Journal of the American Academy of Child and Adolescent Psychiatry*, 38, 232–234.

Stossel, S. (September 21, 2000). Bowling alone. *Atlantic Unbound*.

Werner, E., and Smith, R.S. (1982). *Vulnerable but invincible*. New York: McGraw-Hill.

Werner, E., and Smith, R.S. (1992). *Overcoming the odds: High-risk children from birth to adulthood*. Ithaca, NY: Cornell University Press.

Zolondek, S.C., Abel, G.F., Northey, W.F. Jr., and Jordan, A.D. (January 2001). The self-reported behaviors of juvenile sexual offenders. *Journal of Interpersonal Violence*, 16, 73–85.

Index